HPBooks

Fast Fords

Alex Gabbard

Published by HPBooks
A division of Price Stern Sloan, Inc.
360 North La Cienega Boulevard
Los Angeles, California 90048
©1988 Price Stern Sloan, Inc.   Printed in U.S.A.
1st Printing

NOTICE: The information contained herein is true and complete to the best of our knowledge. All recommendations on parts and procedures are made without guarantees on the part of the author or HPBooks. Because the quality of parts, materials and methods are beyond our control, the author and the publisher disclaim all liability incurred in connection with the use of this information.

Library of Congress Cataloging-in-Publication Data

Gabbard, Alex.
  Fast Fords.

  Includes index.
  1. Automobile racing—History—Pictorial works.
2. Ford Motor Company—History—Pictorial works.
I. Title.
GV1029.15.G33   1988   796-7'209   87-23615
ISBN 0-89586-498-3

Dedication

This book is dedicated to the memory of those who tinkered with, raced and otherwise built Ford and Mercury cars into legends and those who continue to make history with Fords and Mercurys. It is also dedicated to those who find Ford and Mercury cars fascinating, interesting and fun, whether old or new.

To Shel, John, Bill, Cale, Scott, Johnny, Wally, Willy, Bob, Tom, Rickie, Fred, Klaus, Lyn, Kenny, Michael, Jack and Ford fans everywhere, this book is for you.

CONTENTS

1
FOUR BANGERS
The Beginning

Left: Henry Ford, the first Ford hotrodder. Courtesy Edison Institute of the Henry Ford Museum.

Below: Henry Ford and his first car: 1896 quadracycle, *with chain drive and bicycle wheels. Courtesy Edison Institute of the Henry Ford Museum.*

THE MAN/THE COMPANY

Ford is a great American success story. This applies to Ford the man and Ford the company—both are marvels of success. Henry Ford, the man, stands alone as the last multi-millionaire industrialist who forged a manufacturing giant owned by himself, his wife and son, but controlled entirely by himself. Ford, the company, grew from humble beginnings into a worldwide industrial complex with vast holdings in the billions of dollars.

During its humble beginnings, Ford Motor Company was simply Henry Ford, the man, with no holdings and nothing more than ideas and a commitment to bring them to reality.

Today, it is virtually impossible to appreciate the struggle, the long hours, the sacrifices it took for Henry Ford and the handful of dedicated men who worked with him to bring his ideas to fruition. This is the great American success story: the struggle against all odds, intense competition and the ever-present doubt that other people heaped on inventors like him who carved out success by shear determination. That's what made the Ford name, out of the many early pioneers in the automotive industry, a worldwide, household name.

The rise of Henry Ford from a Michigan farmer to the greatest industrialist of his time is a personal success story that will likely never be repeated. This tinkerer, this mechanic, this believer in the future of machines, was so convinced that machinery would relieve the drudgery of mankind that he once remarked:

"MACHINERY IS THE NEW MESSIAH"

In our modern world of assembly-line products, everywhere we look, it is virtually impossible to imagine a time when industry in America was made up of craftsmen building their products by hand the "old world" way. Craftsmen had to be skilled in all facets of their trade, and production of their products was both time consuming and expensive.

Henry Ford changed all that. His quest for an inexpensive "everyman's" car came about with the advent of assembly lines where thousands of machines were manned by armies of unskilled workers who turned out each reliable, durable and inexpensive Ford car in as little as 20 minutes.

From the front, note small size of Ford's quadracycle, the best of 1896. Imagine this as the car leading to Bill Elliott's 200-mph Thunderbird. Courtesy Edison Institute of the Henry Ford Museum.

Retouched composite photo by Van Leyen & Hensler of Detroit, of Henry Ford and Spider Huff racing in 1901. Courtesy Edison Institute of the Henry Ford Museum.

Inexpensive cars changed the world as the lure of individual travel came within the reach of every family. Prices of Ford cars fell as production increased. As a result, into the early '20s, more than half the cars on the road were Fords. Hard-surface highways spread across America while auto service stations sprang up everywhere, and Americans took to the road in ever-increasing numbers. The age of the car was born with Henry Ford's Model T—his everyman's car.

His modern manufacturing methods were copied by the entire automotive industry, and his high wages, $5 a day— then later $7—led the industry. Combined with a short work week—five days versus six—Ford workers had time off the job to enjoy their wages and their cars. Thus, Henry Ford, more than any other individual, can be credited with introducing the consumer age in America.

From an estimated 300 automotive pioneers, he made no significant contributions to the *technical development* of the automobile. Ford's effect was simply to overwhelm the emerging automotive industry with manufacturing methods that produced a product so good and so inexpensive that he was bound to succeed. Henry Ford put America on wheels with the Model T. And because his cars were so plentiful and so easy to hotrod, he also put America behind the wheel of racing cars.

Ford Is Spelled R-A-C-I-N-G—In the earliest days of the automobile, many people worked on motor carriages, and a variety of trials, tests and races were held that attracted widespread attention. Ford noted the acclaim and enthusiasm automobiles brought, so he built his first cars to race to establish his name. He also noted the prize money, sometimes as large as $10,000.

Oliver Barthel and Ford built a racer for the October 10, 1901, races sponsored by the Detroit Driving Club. $1000 was offered the winner of a 25-lap feature at the 1-mile course of Grosse Pointe, a beautiful track bordering the Detroit River. The entire city was in a frenzy over the event. Even the city courts adjourned so officials could witness the races, a true spectacle. When it came time for the feature, preliminary races had taken so much time that the main 25-lap race was shortened to 10 laps. To the starting line came three entrants: Henry Ford aboard his racer, the famed Alexander Winton on his, and another driver who discovered a mechanical problem and withdrew.

Thus, it was a showcase for Henry Ford against the top driver in the country. Ford had never raced before, but fortune was in his favor as Winton's machine began leaving a trail of smoke after three laps. Ford and his 28-horsepower car passed his 70-horsepower adversary on the eighth lap. Being both a local and the underdog, Ford's victory resulted in thunderous cheers from the partisan crowd. The win also aroused local pride in motorcars to the extent that it made Ford a hero. Racing had indeed brought what he wanted— acclaim. But the experience was such that Ford retired as a driver saying, "Once is enough."

5

Barney Oldfield, Henry Ford (standing) and 999 car named for the New York Central locomotive that held the world land speed record in 1903. Henry Ford set a new land speed record of 91.37 mph on the ice of Lake St. Clair on January 12, 1904, the first automobile to exceed 90 mph. Car weighed 1,600 pounds and produced 70 HP from 1,080 cubic inches! Courtesy Edison Institute of the Henry Ford Museum.

Henry Ford built several racing cars early in his career and won fame with his exploits. Note T-handle for steering. Courtesy Edison Institute of the Henry Ford Museum.

That success led to the formation of the Henry Ford Co. on November 30, 1901. This company didn't go in the direction Ford wanted, so he left to join forces with Tom Cooper, the foremost cyclist of the time, in building much more aggressive racers, the famed Arrow and 999.

The 999 was the first actually raced. And, because of its potential speed, Ford became concerned about his driver's safety. Barney Oldfield had never raced a car before, but was daredevil enough to put his cycle-racing experience on the line. He practiced at Grosse Pointe the week before the occasion of the next race, the Manufacturers' Challenge Cup held October 25, 1902.

Four drivers started, the main opposition being Winton again. Oldfield led from the start, as he opened up 999 and didn't let off. His lead grew to the point of lapping the two lagging cars and, soundly beat Winton, who dropped out on the fourth lap. With victory won, pandemonium resulted: The crowd broke over the fence and lifted Oldfield from the car amid thunderous cheers.

Oldfield's time of 1 minute, 6 seconds set a new American speed record for the closed mile. Ford himself had turned 1:08 times in practice and, thus, proved he did indeed have a better idea. Ford's 999 with its 70, perhaps 80 horsepower (HP), was described as "low, rakish and makes more noise than a freight train." It was in that machine that two things happened: Oldfield made Ford famous and Ford made Oldfield famous. Both went on to become the most recognized figures in early motoring—Ford as a builder, Oldfield as a driver.

Having accomplished his objectives with racing, Henry Ford returned to his earlier idea of an "everyman's" car. The automobile market had expanded considerably and the times were better. Ford found backing once again for his third attempt at manufacturing. In November 1902, the Ford & Malcomson Company, Ltd. was formed.

This firm was successful and experienced sufficient growth that the Ford Motor Company was established on June 16, 1903. Two days later, the Ford & Malcomson Co. transferred holdings to the Ford Motor Co. for 510 shares of stock that were divided equally between Ford and Malcomson. Their 255 shares each gave the two men principle holdings. With a total of $28,000 invested, the Ford Motor Co. became solvent. Ford himself had put up no money—just his ideas, dedication and determination. Each of the 12 original investors soon became millionaires—and Ford cars became America's favorite.

In the following chapters, the story of "Fast Fords," from the earliest to latest, will be told in some detail. This book makes no attempt to cover all types and models of fast Ford cars, but will attempt to provide highlights of some of the most famous Ford performance production cars and racing machines.

FORD MOTOR COMPANY, THE EARLY DAYS

Henry Ford was correct in his assessment of the contributions machinery would make to America. By 1904, this country was enjoying a radiant prosperity brought by increasing production that produced rising incomes and an improving standard of living in all segments of the population. A vigorous program of domestic reform proved healthy for the economy. Never before had technology and invention made such advances toward increased comfort and convenience.

The electric light, bicycle, phonograph, gas-cooking range, modern plumbing, telephones, typewriters, cash registers and automobiles, in particular, were becoming widely popular and purchased in increasing quantities. In 1902, there was about one car for every 1,500,000 people in America. By 1907, largely because of Ford's efforts to produce a low-priced car for the masses, the ratio was increased to about one car for every 600 people! As factories produced

Sensational growth of Henry Ford's empire is shown in these three photos. Upper left is converted coal bin at 58 Bagley Avenue, where he built his quadracycle in 1896. Upper right is first true Ford Motor Co. factory. At bottom, is the vast Rouge plant that was first in the world to put into practice efficient production. Courtesy Edison Institute of the Henry Ford Museum.

more, prices went down, salaries went up, consumer buying power increased and America moved into an era of plenty.

Three manufacturing factors were mainly responsible for such growth: standardization, simplification and interchangeability. These keys to modern, efficient manufacturing had been around since Eli Whitney, but putting them into practice took a gestation period of some decades. That time was spent developing machines that removed the need for skilled labor and greatly reduced the time required for hand assembly. Mass production became the temper of the time, as unskilled operators at lower salaries could produce more in less time than skilled labor had ever done.

Henry Ford described time as the enemy, and the idea of efficiency became the driver for his company. The battle was on for a cheap car; he had fierce competition. The 57 automobile manufacturers in America who employed 2,241 wage-earners with a product value of $4,750,000 in 1899, grew to 178 manufacturers in 1904, with more than 12,000

workers and a product value over $30 million. Supporting them were some 60 companies specializing in bodies and parts, with 1,800 workers and a product value of about $4 million. In just five years, the automobile industry doubled twice, and Michigan was its center.

The public was now in automobile frenzy. Builders were swamped with orders and dealer networks grew throughout the nation. Production in 1905 was 11,180 cars, and Detroit was the site of six major works. Ford was among them, but not yet the industry leader the company would become.

The impact of more and more cars had another side effect that changed the face of America. Roads were miserable. As voters became car owners, protests abounded for improving the surfaces the cars rode on. There had been a growing movement for improved roads for decades, but it took the automobile to firm up demand that something be done to pull America from the mud and keep it from choking on the

Ford Model T (No. 8) and other cars line up for Munsey Tour in 1908—11 period. This was racing for the enthusiast of the time. Courtesy Edison Institute of the Henry Ford Museum.

dust. But rather than complain about miserable roads, Henry Ford met the challenge of producing cars that could negotiate existing roads and, thus, provided buyers another incentive for buying Ford cars.

In 1905, the Ford Motor Co. offered three models: Model C ($800), Model F ($1000) and Model B ($2000). The C and F models were powered by his 2-cylinder opposed (horizontal) engine; the B received a 4-cylinder. It was clear that the price of Ford cars was moving away rather than toward the $500 car Ford wanted to produce. That disturbed him.

Once again, to promote his cars, Henry Ford turned to racing. He did this by announcing he would break the world speed record. On January 9, 1904, he had the snow scraped from the ice covering Lake St. Clair, just northeast of Detroit. The icy surface was covered with cinders over a four-mile-long strip, then he and "Spider" Huff set out to become the fastest team in the world. They recorded an unofficial time of 36 seconds for the measured mile (100 mph). This was encouraging, so they returned on January 12th with official American Automobile Association (AAA) timers to post a time of 39.4 seconds (91.37 mph)—a new world record!

That performance heaped acclaim on Ford and his cars. First-year sales (1903—04 season) totaled just over 1,700 cars and a gross return of $1,162,836. Second-year sales (1904-05 season) surpassed all expectations. With 450 dealers, the firm had no difficulty selling every car it made, grossing $1.2 million in the spring months alone, $1,914,903 for the year, and showed a gain of $752,067 over the previous season.

Ford and company expanded their works. Moving toward becoming the industry leader was taking shape. Profits were up, but Ford Motor Co. was still just an assembler of parts. The company received engines, frames, gears and other equipment on contract from the Dodge brothers. Ford wanted to manufacture all components within the firm, thus keeping profits paid to Dodge and other outsiders to a minimum. Ford's partner, Malcomson, differed from Henry's view. He wanted to build more expensive cars. Thus, Ford and James Couzens, the company's office manager, contrived to decrease the importance of Malcomson's position in the company. They did so by setting up another company, the Ford Manufacturing Company, which would keep manufacturing profits internal and, at the same time, reduce Malcomson's holdings in the enterprise by not allowing him to purchase stock in the new company. Malcomson was incensed.

On November 22, 1905, the Ford Manufacturing Company was incorporated with a capital of $100,000. Its purpose was to manufacture engines, drive-train hardware, parts and all kinds of machinery necessary to manufacture Ford cars. Its role was to supply components for the proposed low-cost car, but Dodge was kept on as supplier of equipment for other models as usual.

A crisis in the growth of the Ford Motor Co. had developed, but a vigorous statement of policy had been forged that would make the firm preeminent in its field. Malcomson responded by forming another company of his own in competition with Ford, the Aerocar Company, and set himself up as president. This weakened his legal position because it was a clear conflict of interest to also be treasurer of Ford.

To add to the drama, the suit filed by George B. Selden against the Ford Motor Co. for patent infringement was reaching the stage of requiring attention in 1904. Selden had received a patent on gasoline-powered vehicles on November 5, 1895 (patent number 549,160). It covered such vehicles in broad terms and its interpretation was sweeping: Any gasoline-powered motorcar manufactured for sale was subject to payment of royalties to Selden.

Selden was a lawyer by profession and sensed that huge profits were to be made once the automobile industry got moving. So, he held back his patent request while making "improvements" to his invention. Patents lasted for 17 years. His aim was not to waste time in the early years of low productivity, but to receive greater returns when the industry was booming. He claimed that until 1912, the automotive industry was legally subject to him.

In support of his patent, the Association of Licensed Automobile Manufacturers was formed by those firms accepting the patent as legally binding. As an organization, the ALAM attempted to protect its position by warning independent manufacturers of legal entanglement and encouraged buyers not to buy unlicensed cars. Also, the ALAM assumed the role of watchdog of the industry and claimed the right to deny licenses to manufacture cars. Thus, if the suit was won, Ford and all other independent manufacturers could be out of business instantly. However, public support was on Ford's side. ALAM membership of 26 firms came across menacingly with the shadow of monopoly, a word that was hotly debated at the time as the worst form of business practice, one that conspired against the consumer for the financial gain of the monopoly holders.

The U.S. government promoted growth of industry and established the Sherman Antitrust Act in 1890 to protect the rights of small companies. But, the Selden patent and his Electric Vehicle Company had repeatedly won important settlements. As of October 1903, the Ford Motor Co. stood alone against Selden. Public interest was keen because the Selden suit on March 20, 1903, had gone in favor of the patent and the ALAM formed afterwards looked to be a strong legal force.

Although staunchly independent by nature, Ford had looked into licensing in the summer of 1903, but was told by the president of the ALAM that his company was not considered an automobile manufacturer, just an "assemblage plant," and an application for license would not be taken favorably. But Ford never accepted the notion that his firm was in any way inferior to other manufacturers. He had always been a winner and a pioneer in the industry.

When the case came to trial, a mountain of evidence had been accumulated over some years, totaling 14,000 pages and 5 million words. Ford's attorney took the stance that no invention was shown in the Selden patent, that the idea of the motor-powered carriage had been shown in "prior art," and that Selden held no rightful claim to any patent of such broad, sweeping character. Hundreds of patents preceded Selden's and showed that "prior art" had indeed been established. As the case drew to a close, suspense gripped the automotive world, for the verdict would be fateful.

Selden won, but Ford didn't give in and vowed to fight to the end of his company's assets. Detroiters and many of their countrymen rallied around Ford's appeal. A decision was returned in 1911 that Selden's patent was valid as far as his modification of the Brayton engine was concerned, but not to gasoline-powered vehicles in general. Henry Ford was vindicated and emerged a hero, a fighter for the cause of the people, and the most famous automotive manufacturer in the world.

By then, the Ford Motor Co. was big. It had built a solid reputation with the Model N, a 15-HP 4-cylinder runabout weighing 1,050 pounds that could reach 45 mph and got 200 miles on 10 gallons of gasoline—by Ford's estimate. At first selling for only $500 in quantities of 10,000—15,000, later increased to $600 with larger tires, this car led directly to the Model T that proved Ford's ideas of a popular car for the masses was exactly what the public wanted.

Sales of the N greatly exceeded other models and, since its profits easily could be siphoned off by the Ford Manufacturing Company, Malcomson recognized he was defeated and sold his 255 shares in the firm—about one-fourth of the interests in the company—to Ford for $175,000. The three stockholders that had stood by Malcomson sold their interests the following year and another investor died. By the fall of 1907, Henry Ford was in firm control of his company with 585 shares; Couzens was next with 110 shares, and the roster of stock holders totaled only eight people. Ford was voted in as president and, at that point, he thought he was in supreme control to carry forth his ideas. He would be tested again—and he would win again.

It had been years of struggle through all sorts of convulsions in both the industry at large and in his own company. But the times were good and now flush with profits. Henry Ford turned an eye toward a new plant at Highland Park that exceeded anything yet achieved in the industry. And the Model T was born.

"We're Building Race Cars, Not Trucks!"—Before the Model T had come a set of first-generation Fords, all in the quest for an inexpensive, but reliable and easy-to-work-on car. The first was the Model A of 1903—04, costing $850 in cheapest form—the Runabout. Models B, C, F, N, R and S followed

FORD SCRIPT LOGO

At the time when the Ford Motor Company began its first dazzling rise toward success, two men had become intimately involved with Henry Ford. The first was James Couzens, Malcomson's office manager and business advisor, who was assigned the task of managing the firm financially while Henry concentrated on developing his automotive ideas as designer and engineer. Couzens was a cautious bean counter with a suspicious turn of mind. They were, after all, trying to make money, not fame as Henry seemed to be after with his 999 racer designs.

The second man was C. Harold Wills, who was chosen by Henry as his principle shop assistant. Wills was a skilled draftsman, machinist, toolmaker and metallurgist with a passion for mechanical design. He was also a congenial working partner for Ford, who contributed significantly to the development of both the cars Henry wanted to sell and those he wanted to race. The two were largely in an adversarial role, pursuing their ideas in opposition to Malcomson and Couzens.

When 999 won, everyone basked in the publicity and glory that followed. Henry found his associates more willing to conform to his ideas. As other successes followed, the company's assets grew rapidly. For the next 12 years, the work of Wills and Ford is impossible to disentangle. Afterwards, Wills went on to become head of his own Wills-St. Claire automobile company.

It was during the period of publicity and early rapid growth that dissatisfaction was expressed with the appearance of the company logo. Wills took it upon himself to design a new logo and rummaged through the attic at home for the calling-card printing outfit he had used in his mid-teens. He had become accomplished with script printing back then, and produced the flowing Ford Motor Company logo seen for decades.

The oval surrounding the FORD script was a later addition when the company's logo was shortened to just FORD. Thus simplified, the Ford logo became an add-on item rather than a stamping in metal radiator shells as was done on the Model T and other Ford vehicles. Today, the oval has come to imply Ford Motor Company's attention to aerodynamics.

---

through 1907. Those cars totaled 19,865 units sold, and grossed $15,173,176.37.

The first Model T appeared in October 1908. The 15,000,000th Model T rolled off the assembly line on May 26, 1927, among the last of the "Tin Lizzies" built. By then, Henry Ford had built a vast empire valued in the billions of dollars. With his strategy of vertical integration, he left nothing beyond his control. This ranged from iron-ore mining to seat-cushion stuffing. In 1925, he employed over 155,000 people and offered buyers his cars in cheapest form for just $295, all accomplished in 20 years!

The social impact the Model T had on America and the world cannot be overstated. The cars were so inexpensive, so reliable and so common that as late as 1949, over 200,000 were still licensed. They outsold all other makes combined. They were the cars that got America out of the mud and put the average man on wheels. They saw extensive duty during WWI and became well known for being tough. They were known as the "do anything, go anywhere" automobile, yet were the brunt of all sorts of jokes. You could drive your family to church on Sunday, then hook up your Model T to power a sawmill on Monday. If it broke down, pliers, a screwdriver and a piece of wire were usually all that was needed to get it going again. That was how Henry planned his people's car to be. But as time passed, buyers became impatient with his refusal to modernize his cars.

Although joked about by people who could afford more, the availability and low cost of Fords did more than put

America on wheels; it put drivers behind the wheels of racing cars. Backyard mechanics, mostly kids who wanted to go racing, could buy a discarded Ford for $10 or less, then concentrate on fixing it up to race in local dust bowls. That meant hotting up the engine, removing as much weight as possible and, if there was enough money for exotic equipment, a rapidly growing aftermarket industry for the Model T offered a vast array of speed equipment.

The American Automobile Association (AAA) sanctioned racing at the time. Where the Model T was concerned, AAA officials mostly turned their backs. "Stock car" Class A rules were set up according to the cost of the vehicle. These ranged from Class 1 ($4,001 and up) to Class 6 ($850 and below). The Model T fit in Class 6. Class B rules applied to "stock car" chassis with special bodies that were classified according to engine capacity and minimum vehicle weight. B-Class 1 cars with 451—600-cubic inch engines had a minimum weight requirement of 2,400 pounds; B-Class 4 cars using 161—230-cubic inch engines, in which the Model T fit, had to weigh more than 1,500 pounds.

These rules provided Henry Ford with one of his many attacks on racing regulations. It was easy for enthusiasts to build a competitive racer from a Model T, the sort that could put the needle to all sorts of more exotic machinery. But AAA rules prohibited them from running in sanctioned events without carrying additional weight, thus making them uncompetitive. As usually brought to the track, the stripped-down, hotted-up Model T was ruled too light.

It seemed that AAA rules were drawn up expressly to keep Fords from front-line racing, the sort that Frank Kulick had shown Ford cars capable of. This was one reason why, in 1913, Henry Ford retired from factory racing. He considered the sport dangerous and no longer needed the publicity to sell his cars. They sold themselves. His cars were capable of challenging far more expensive machines, but the rules didn't allow it. And there was nothing to gain by competing with cars in the price range of the Model T. Fords had very little competition.

Since the AAA wasn't interested in "open competition," Ford got out. In an official statement, he said, "If the Ford car were too light, open competition with heavy cars would quickly prove it." He expressed his position by saying, "We're building race cars, not trucks."

Lightweight Ford racers that ran the dirt tracks of America, the sort that AAA looked down upon as "outlaw" racing, were leading the way toward the sort of car that would, in time, become known as the *sports car*. The battle between the two types of machines—big versus little—was a contest that eventually saw the demise of the big cars in favor of the virtue of lightweight racing cars. It took some time, though, and some convincing of stalwarts of the old view who held that "sophisticated" racing cars were not built from Fords. It was, in fact, the Model T that did more racing than all other marques put together and introduced more big names. Most drivers of the time cut their first laps in Model T homebuilts.

By the 'teens, racing was a way of life where large purses allowed some drivers to turn pro. Barney Oldfield, Spencer Wishart, Eddie Rickenbacker, Eddie Pullen, Bob Burman and many others became famous in their faster, more powerful machines like Rickenbacker's Maxwell Specials and Burman's Blitzen Benz. From the dust of "outlaw" racing came a lot of unknown drivers who reached for fame driving modified Fords. One of these was Wilber Shaw, who went on to win the Indy 500 three times. Others—the Chevrolet Brothers, for instance—became famous for manufacturing speed equipment for Fords.

EARLY FACTORY RACING

Soon after Henry stepped down from driving his own cars, other drivers stepped into the limelight of winning in Ford cars. One of the first five Ford Motor Co. employees was a man who was to become Ford's top factory driver for a decade. Frank Kulick drove Ford T racers in all sorts of races, set all types of records and challenged the traditional racing cars with spindly flyweights that continually beat them. In his class, Kulick rarely lost a race and, in what would be classified as "open competition" where it's "run what you brung," he provided many upsets that brought Ford cars a lot of publicity.

During the 1904—13 period, Ford Motor Co. became the largest auto manufacturer. There was little need for publicity. However, Henry used the acclaim generated by racing to further his cause, increase sales, and kept an experimental shop busy with all sorts ideas that turned up in racing and record cars.

Ford entries for Transcontinental Race of 1909; No. 2 won New York to Seattle race. Courtesy Edison Institute of the Henry Ford Museum.

"Transcontinental Fords" outside Cleveland, Ohio, pick up an escort. Endurance racing was really enduring in those days. Courtesy Edison Institute of the Henry Ford Museum.

In the early years, he was always ready for a challenge that would test his cars against other makes. No challenge was too bold. Perhaps his boldest undertaking was answering the challenge posted by Robert Guggenheim. The Alaska-Yukon-Pacific Exposition was to open on June 1, 1909. Since no automobile had even made it cross-country from New York to the far northwest, Guggenheim seized upon the opportunity to promote the Exposition with a coast-to-coast contest. Ford jumped at the opportunity to promote his cars.

Two Fords were entered: stripped down 20-HP Model Ts, completely open with only the two front seats provided for the drivers. They weighed under 950 pounds, down from the normal 1200. Much fanfare accompanied the promotion and start of the Ocean-to-Ocean race, but at the flag, only three other cars were there. One was a 3500-pound, 48-HP Acme; another was a 4500-pound, 45-HP Shawmut; and the only foreign car was a 4000-pound, 50-HP Itala.

At the time, roads in the east were fairly well developed and usually passable. But as the trek made its way through the plains states of Wyoming, and beyond dirt roads became mud bogs during rain storms. Crossing the snow-covered Rockies in Idaho and down the other side into Washington State proved difficult in the extreme where uncharted logging and railway access roads were about all there was for passage through the wilderness.

The race was followed very closely every step of the way to ensure that no rules infractions occurred. Newspapers car-

ried progress reports, and each town along the way received the contestants with considerable fanfare. By the time the first car checked in at Seattle to win—Bert Scott and Jimmy Smith in the ε2 Ford—it had taken 22 days and 55 minutes to cover 4,106 miles. The Shawmut was 2nd, 17 hours behind. Some 15,000 spectators cheered the Ford in, and Henry Ford was there to receive the weary heros.

Thus proven for endurance, the lightweight, low-horsepower Model T Ford became recognized for its potential as a racer because of its favorable power-to-weight ratio. Kulick and other drivers raced them against top cars of the day—Palmer-Singer, National, Fiat, Renault and, in a memorable bout with the famed Blitzen Benz, the world's fastest car in a straight line, Kulick came away victor and attained front-rank status as a driver. With a special car from Henry's experimental shop, Kulick went up against the Benz at the Detroit Fairgrounds on September 26, 1911, where he turned a flying lap in 50 seconds. The best of the Benz was 51.4 seconds, giving a clear Ford win.

With that racer, dubbed 999 II, Kulick was later said in a "Ford Times" to have set a "new world record" of 107.8 mph for the flying mile, a sensational speed for the time. Unfortunately, this was not a record: Burman had gone 141 mph at Daytona Beach the year before.

Regardless of what was really a record, it was good enough for the locals. Ford cars were seen to be well proven at speed, and Henry probably unwittingly set the stage for

Well-outfitted endurance racer of 1909: How would you like to travel cross country in such a rig? Courtesy Edison Institute of the Henry Ford Museum.

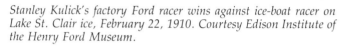

Stanley Kulick's factory Ford racer wins against ice-boat racer on Lake St. Clair ice, February 22, 1910. Courtesy Edison Institute of the Henry Ford Museum.

what would later become a sweeping movement. The excitement his cars generated became the source of explosive growth in racing after WWI when costs were low and hotrod kids could put together a competitive racer in the barn out back, then rip around roads in preparation for races at local dirt tracks.

All 177 cubic inches of a Model T engine blasting through four stubby exhaust pipes gives a raspy sound that was no doubt heard through many of America's back doors in preparation for storming around fairground race tracks. In making his Model T simple and reliable, Henry also made them easy to work on. And that gave early-day hotrodders the material to go fast.

All sorts of hotted up Fords were built. Those with fenders were known as *Speedsters*; those without copied the look of Indianapolis 500 cars of the day. In either form, the vast majority of early racing cars and hotrods were Fords. Not only had Ford become the car of the people, it also became the speed machine from which the hotrod spirit could build almost anything.

The Equipment—Because the Model T engine had a large reserve of potential power and reliability, it received considerable attention by racers. So much so that the Chevrolet brothers—Arthur, Louis and Gaston—became famous for their racing conversions of Fords. They won the Indianapolis 500 in more sophisticated cars of their design. Such acclaim helped sell more speed equipment for Fords.

The Chevrolet Motor Company was organized in 1911, but was unable to stay independent as did the Ford Motor Co. It was absorbed into General Motors in 1918 as the low-priced competitor to Ford cars. With that, the brothers returned to racing and supported their best efforts financially with complete *Fronty*—for Frontenac—Fords and racing hardware sold separately for Fords.

It is ironic that the names Ford and Chevrolet, which began independently, were later linked closely in some of the best racing machines of the time, and then became arch-rivals. GM sold Chevrolet cars, and the Chevrolet brothers built speed equipment for Fords! Their products were marketed nationwide, so if you were looking for more power from your Ford, you were likely to get it using equipment from the Chevrolet brothers' shop.

Ford in racing was nothing new. Having more or less founded his company on the acclaim received from winning races, Henry Ford was well aware of the publicity and sales potential that racing brought. On the streets and highways of America, modified Fords were among the most exciting cars to be seen; they received widespread attention.

As mentioned earlier, one Ford was the Speedster. These "kits" were little more than alternate bodies that came in a variety of forms to give a Model T racy lines similar to the far more expensive Mercer Raceabout and Stutz Bearcat. All sorts of modifications for Model T Fords were marketed. And if you had the money, the ultimate was the Morton and

Dust and the glory in a Model T: Kulick at speed in his factory Ford entry during Elgin Road Races. Courtesy Edison Institute of the Henry Ford Museum.

1912 Model T at 1951 Indianapolis 500 with Henry Ford II at the wheel, and starter, singer James Melton, wearing 1912-vintage motoring garb. Courtesy Edison Institute of the Henry Ford Museum.

Gaston Chevrolet in his 1920 Indy 500-winning Monroe powered by 183-cid 4-cylinder Frontenac engine. Gaston and his brothers were among the leading Ford racers and engine builders of their time. Gaston's green and white William Small Co. entry started 6th and won at a 88.16-mph average. He qualified at 91.55 mph. Courtesy Indianapolis Motor Speedway Museum.

Brett boat-tail body and a Frontenac cylinder head from the Chevrolet brothers of Indianapolis, or a Rajo conversion from Joe Jagersberger, the racing driver from Racine, Wisconsin.

The Rajo, a contraction of Racine Joe, was a highly re-garded conversion for the Model T. But the most famous by far was the Frontenac. More than 10,000 Fronty-Ford heads were manufactured over the years. When WWI was over, one of the roars of the roaring '20s came from Fronty-Fords. They were everywhere races were run. Fitted with a Bosch

14

Louis Chevrolet and riding mechanic with Frontenac at Indy in 1919 qualified second fastest at 103.10 mph and finished 7th, averaging 81.03 mph. Courtesy Indianapolis Motor Speedway Museum.

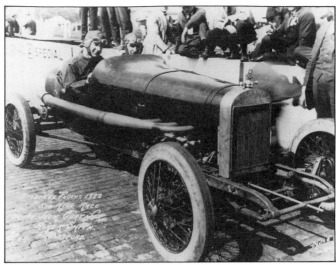

Indy racers of 1922, Jack Curtner and mechanic Homer Smith, on Brick Yard ready to go in their Fronty-Ford. Curtner's red entry did not qualify, but started 21st and finished 14th. Courtesy Indianapolis Motor Speedway Museum.

L. L. Corum in lightweight Fronty-Ford. Car was built on Model T chassis. It was the best Ford finish at Indianapolis until the '60s. Corum's car was entered by Barber-Warnock, painted orange and ran a 122-cid 4-cylinder Model T engine with a Chevrolet brothers Frontenac head. Engine produced 80 HP at 3,600 rpm and propelled car to a top speed of almost 100 mph. Corum qualified at 86.65 mph, started 7th and finished 5th overall in 1923 Indy 500, averaging 82.58 mph. He completed all 200 laps of the race. Courtesy Indianapolis Motor Speedway Museum.

Frontenac conversion to Model T with two updraft carbs was among the most desired hotrod Ford item of the '10s and '20s. Author photo courtesy of IMS.

or Mallory distributor, even a dual point, a Winfield manifold and twin carburetors, perhaps Zenith carbs, and an assortment of some of the other 5,000 or so accessories available for Model T Fords, a homebuilt runabout was a handsome and fast car.

The ultimate was a Frontenac with 16-valves, 4 per cylinder, and double overhead chain-driven cams. But most Frontys had single overhead cam heads. These Fronty-Ford conversions of the Model T were capable of turning 5000 rpm and reaching more than 100 mph. One of them, the Barber-

Exhaust side of the Fronty-Ford: Notice (in order from right to left), oil pump, water pump and magneto mounted under exhaust manifold. Basic drive setup is similar to that used on today's Formula 1 and Indy Car engines. Author photo courtesy of IMS.

Warnock special driven by L. L. Corum, finished fifth overall at the 1923 Indy 500, the best finish of a Ford powered car until the Lotus-Fords of the '60s dominated the 500.

These were the cars that ripped up the 1/2-mile dirt tracks of America. They were practically unbeatable on the dirt, and for the price, nothing could compete with them. A full-tilt 16-valve Fronty-Ford would set you back around $2300; cheap for an Indy class racer. A Fronty-Ford with the S-R head cost $2000; $1850 with the R head.

If you wanted the ultimate in racing machinery, it was a Miller, a 7500-rpm jewel of an engine with a price tag of $15,000, well beyond the typical home builder. Millers and Duesenbergs were the top cars on the top tracks of the time, most of which were *board tracks*, those built of heavy timbers with high banks and long straights. Most of these tracks were financial failures.

One that didn't fail was Indianapolis. Made of brick, it lasted and became known as the *Brickyard*, with the famous Gasoline Alley where all the great builders and racers came to compete. The Indy 500 became the top race in America—"the greatest spectacle in racing"—and was recognized throughout the world.

It was on the bricks at *Indy* that the Chevrolet brothers developed their more sophisticated Frontenac 4-cylinder car that won in 1920, and the 8-cylinder that won in '21. In the 1923 race, one of the Fronty drivers was the English driver Alfred Moss who had come to Indianapolis to study dentistry and to race. The latter legacy was carried on by his son, Stirling Moss, who became Great Britain's greatest driver in the '50s.

It was also at Indy that Arthur Chevrolet was seriously injured while practicing for the 1920 race and, unfortunately,

Gaston was killed on the board track at Beverly Hills, California.

As the roaring '20s dropped into depression, the high cost of maintaining board speedways speeded their demise as hard times set in. The main fare of the '30s returned to dirt tracks.

Although Indy remained the most famous, hometown dirt was where most drivers got their start; and most spectators saw the spectacle of speed brought by stripped down, hotrod Fords.

THE NEW MODEL A

By the late '20s, Henry Ford was in complete control of a vast industrial complex that reached from the depths of iron and coal mines to expansive forests to ships and trains, all leading to and from the most modern and largest manufacturing site the world had ever known—the River Rouge plant. His company had made immense fortunes by bold and enlightened management techniques such as the famous $5 day, double the wage of the time. He saw to it that working conditions were good, safe working practices were observed and he made production the most efficient it could be.

Thus, working for Ford Motor Co. was tough, all in accordance with Henry Ford's expectations. He paid the best and went a long way toward promoting good relations and prosperity among his employees. But he showed a ruthless side as well when he wanted something done. He was a folk hero for his battles against higher prices and won the loyalty of many Americans. He was also a dictator who got what he demanded . . . or else.

His was a one-man management plan. He alone made the important decisions. No industrialist had ever had so much power, but the failing of his single-handed control was having too much faith in the sales potential of low prices. Buyers were gradually shifting from old-fashioned Fords to more modern cars of other makes.

Vehicle registration in 1910 had been 468,000. By 1920 vehicle registration was nearly 10 million. And in 1926 the number doubled to almost 20 million vehicles. Americans spent and were traveling like never before. And the low cost of Fords allowed commuting to jobs; thus, suburban living became possible. Vacations to Florida beaches were possible for more and more people, and the Chicago speak-easy style of night life flourished.

Still, most cars on the road in 1926 were Fords, but newer 4- and 6-cylinder cars from competitors were making inroads into Ford sales, as buyers became willing to spend more. Although GM was pushing the more modern Chevrolet as its low-priced alternative, it still cost $190 more than a Model T. Overland was the closest competitor at $50 more, but these higher prices were somewhat negated by the growing use of installment buying. Buyers could afford more on the time-payment plan and wanted more speed, more colors and more convenience in the cars they bought. Ford was being outclassed and Chevrolet sales steadily climbed.

Sales of Model Ts were showing a steady decline. Women now had more influence in buying, and they wanted closed

Henry (left) and Edsel Ford compare first Ford with 15-millionth, a Model T. Between the two cars came the $265 Ford and concept of the disposable car. Photo is posed in front of what is now Ford's Engine Engineering building. Courtesy Edison Institute of the Henry Ford Museum.

cars. Ford responded with Model Ts in closed Tudor and Fordor sedans. Sales picked up for a time, but a new car was needed; one that responded to the times. The Model T, built virtually unchanged for 20 years, had "frozen to death."

There's no doubt that Ford knew his Model T couldn't last forever, but he stubbornly hung onto the ancient car in the face of mounting evidence that even diehard Ford buyers were slipping away. Even his dealers were beginning to go over to GM, and his top executives were powerless to change what they clearly saw as the problem: Henry Ford's commanding power was strangling the company.

In 1920, he had begun experiments on a radical "Model X" engine—four cylinders up and four down in an "X" pattern—but it proved to be a dismal failure. Then, some time in late 1926, he finally came around to the need for a new car, although he believed the Model T still had a lot of potential.

The public did not know of the "X," and at the time, Ford had only an idea of what the new car would be. But once rumors of development of a new Ford was out, it spread across the nation, generating high expectations and speculations of just how great it would be. After all, Henry was the master car builder. He knew what the public wanted: more speed, more style and more convenience. He also knew the car had to be perfect; no engineering defects or the public wouldn't accept it. His reputation was at stake.

Approaching the new car from an engineering point of view, rather than marketing or sales or styling, he and a dedicated staff conceived new manufacturing methods, new materials, new everything for the 5,580 or so parts it would take to build each car so it could be as rugged and reliable as the T had been. It would do the 50-60 mph the public wanted; it would come in different colors; in enclosed models, and be every bit the Ford the public had come to admire.

He and his son Edsel immediately decided on wheelbase and size. And Edsel's influence on body design made the new Model A lower and much more stylish. Once the details began unfolding, the new car took shape. However, research and testing of parts remained the old Ford way, cut and try rather than real scientific methods as were being used more and more by competitors such as GM's highly regarded engineering and testing facilities.

Ford and his men had complete confidence that they could produce a better car than a Chevrolet, Dodge or Overland. And with almost $250 million on hand and the resources of an industrial complex now worth over $900 million, they did just that.

Edsel announced the design of the new car was complete on August 10, 1927, and the immense job of retooling 34 assembly plants in the U.S. and Canada—along with 14 foreign sites—was well underway. On October 20th of that year, Henry Ford stamped the serial number in the first

Model A engine that went into the first car the next day, a Tudor sedan. The Rouge assembly line slowly cranked up, 20 cars a day at first, but they were used for extensive testing rather than for sale.

On the first day of December, full-page newspaper ads all across America announced the arrival of the new Fords. The public was so excited about the Model A that over 100,000 people jammed into Detroit showrooms. Other cities experienced the same situation. It was estimated that 10,000,000 Americans went to see the cars in their first 36 hours of showing. The New York Stock Exchange registered a huge jump as 400,000 orders, many submitted before the public had seen the Model A, meant Ford Motor Co. was back on line and would be a big buyer of raw materials.

Buyers loved the cars and were astonished to learn they were still cheaper than a Chevrolet. At only $10 more than a Model T, the Model A coupe cost $495, $125 less than its GM counterpart. Many admired the Model A body, calling it the "baby Lincoln." Now in seven body styles, Fords came with a variety of colors. And their prices and reliability showed that Henry Ford was still building quality cars for the masses. It had cost him $250,000,000 to do so.

The Model A was another 4-cylinder Ford at a time when other makes were switching over to 6-cylinder engines. It was an all-new engine producing 40 HP at 2,200 rpm and was capable of accelerating from 5 to 25 mph in about 8-1/2 seconds. That was equal to or better most 6s or 8s. With a top speed of about 65 mph, the Model A was better in every way than a Model T at virtually the same price.

Even though public enthusiasm remained high, there was a problem: Few cars were being delivered. The summer of '28 dragged by as production delays held them back. Most dealers didn't even have an example of each type, and the void produced by the lack of Fords pushed Chevrolet sales into the lead, over 1,000,000 in 1928 to Ford's less than 800,000, mostly in the last half of the year. But the new year showed Ford was again on top in the sales race, with production of 1,870,257 cars in the U.S. alone.

Ironically, most of Chevrolet's success was due to the ability of William S. Knudsen, once a top Ford executive who had been discharged in one of Ford's many management shake-ups. And even more ironically, his son, Semon (Bunkie) Knudsen, was to play a similar role between Ford and GM a half century later. Knudsen's strategy was not to produce the cheapest car, but one that could be updated each year with new offerings to bring back loyal Chevrolet buyers. Part of their loyalty was because the Chevys were roomier and their engine was a smoother, more powerful 6-cylinder that gave slightly higher top speeds. Thus, Ford versus Chevrolet loyalties had clearly developed in the late '20s—it hasn't changed much since.

When the stock market crashed on "Black Tuesday," October 29, 1929, the world was plunged into the worst depression ever. Ford Motor Co., General Motors and third-place Chrysler remained profitable in the first two years, 1930—31, but many smaller firms closed their doors.

Then, in 1931, Ford Motor Co. was not profitable. The Model A was falling into disfavor for the same reasons that killed the Model T. But, unlike the T's long life-span, the A had lasted only four years.

It was clear that with sales well down and millions of people out of work, competition in the low price field was fierce. To win buyers, Ford needed a new car, but instead he updated his car with a new engine.

2
FLATHEADS
The New V8

New-for-1932, V8 Ford engine was a sensation, another bold and innovative step by Henry Ford. First V8-powered Ford production car was a Victoria, assembled on March 10, 1932. In Model 18 Fords, the 221-cid engine developed 65 HP at 3,400 rpm with a compression ratio of 5.5:1. Block and heads were cast iron initially, but heads were changed to aluminum the next year in the Model 40. With 6.3:1 compression, peak power increased to 75 HP at 3,800 rpm. Courtesy Ford Motor Co.

By the late '20s, hotrod Fords had become the most widely recognized form of spirited transport in America. On both road and track, fast Fords were the cars the public most easily identified with. They were such that a farm boy from Iowa could dream about doing big things with them at Indianapolis.

The Fronty-Fords were legendary by then, but when the rules for Indy cars changed to 1.5-liters (91.5 cubic inches) in 1926, real race cars pushed the Fords aside. But on the local scene, Fords were still by far the winningest cars of any make. And with the new Model A to tinker with, Ford enthusiasts were on their way to building the next generation of hotrods and race cars. Model T conversions were becoming outdated because more power was available from the Model A. However, because the T was around for so many years before, there wasn't nearly so much aftermarket equipment for the A.

Thus, a lull in Ford performance set in. The factory had not been racing for years, so it was the loyal diehard that kept Ford performance alive. The pattern of inconsistent factory commitment to performance was repeated in the '40s, '50s and '70s. The glorious '60s and Ford's return in the '80s are notable exceptions; the '60s was the era of Ford dominance, the stuff of often-told legends.

Unfortunately, economic conditions in America and around the world were changing in the early '30s when the Model A should have been at its peak. The exciting times on America's dirt tracks were fast fading. Even the thrill of

Model 18 V8 roadster was a hot number in 1932. Styling by Edsel Ford was along lines of the Lincoln—very fashionable. Courtesy Ford Motor Co.

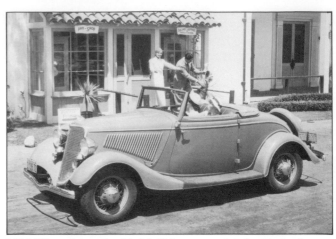

1934 V8 roadster, the Model 40A, was up-dated with the famous Stromberg 48 2-barrel carburetor on a new manifold. Horsepower increased to 85 at 3800 rpm. Courtesy Ford Motor Co.

whisking along a leaf-swept two-lane road in an open hotrod became out of reach for a lot of would-be enthusiasts as "hard times" swept over the nation and lasted longer than anyone predicted.

The Depression was a time when new car sales from all makers slumped and all lost money, particularly in 1932. However, some excitement was generated in the Ford camp when word got out that Henry was working on another new car. Chevrolet had increasingly attracted would-be Ford buyers with their smooth and classy 6-cylinder-powered cars. And Chrysler's popular Plymouth was making inroads into the low-price field, the arena that Henry's cars had dominated for more than 20 years.

Ford's were still powered by 4 cylinders, and Henry was shrewd enough to realize that what he needed was a new engine. His cars were handsome enough with proven reliability and features comparable to the competition, but at a much lower price. He reasoned that a sensational V8 would be the ticket to draw buyers back. But a V8 in the low-price field was unheard of. With undaunted enthusiasm for a man well into his 60s, he tackled the task and brought out the first Ford V8 in the 1932 Model B. And it was sensational.

However, it was not the first V8 engine in production. Henry Leland had introduced an excellent V8 in the 1915 Cadillac, but Ford's was by far the most successful. Instantly, hotrodders had a new power plant to develop into racing engines. For the next 21 years, the flathead V8 powered millions of Ford cars and trucks. It was the choice of the enthusiast for going fast in stripped-down rods. It also found a home on the dirt tracks the Frontys had run on. And the new V8 was soon to be raced at Indianapolis. Aftermarket equipment poured out of shops across the country, as the Depression eased toward the late '30s.

Another name that later became a Ford arch-rival, Zora Arkus-Duntov of Corvette fame, was at one time in the business of manufacturing speed equipment for the flat-

head. His hemi-chambered *Ardun* heads (for *Arkus Dun*tov), converted Ford flatheads to overhead-valve engines and are highly sought-after items for collectors today.

Multiple carburetors and, eventually, supercharging, became available for the flathead. Hotted up flatheads with carbs went racing at Indianapolis. The return of Ford Motor Co. to racing was at the instigation of a colorful man, Preston Tucker, who seemed able to promote ideas where others had failed.

"Ford at Indianapolis," America's foremost automobile race, was the theme. Tucker presented the idea to Edsel Ford instead of Henry because he was sure Henry would turn it down. Edsel was a highly skilled and well-educated manager. He had a keen sense of what he thought the company needed: a positive public image, planning for the future and improved sales. Tucker pressed these ideas with the image and prestige of a Ford 1-2-3 victory and its effects on Ford Motor Co. new-car sales. Edsel liked the idea, but his father didn't.

While Edsel saw the benefits of planning and delegation, his father did not. Additionally, Edsel wanted to generate excitement through Tucker's Indy effort; Henry was content not to. The elder Ford saw little need of engineering research and development for long-term product planning, there was little record keeping useful for planning anyway, and he was certainly not prone to delegate authority for directing company policy.

It was, after all, Henry Ford's company. He had directed it from a tiny workshop into an industrial giant, America's largest industry. And success had followed success because of his insistence on quality and efficiency in an inexpensive car.

However, Henry Ford's method for developing new products was largely by *crisis management* rather than following trends and planning for smooth transitions of models. The Model A was the answer to the crisis of sagging Model T sales and resulted from the entire Ford complex essentially

V8 Fords were by far the fastest in the low-priced field and were instant favorites among racers. Large V8 emblems on the sides and on top of hood made this "official car" for the 1933 Harmsworth Trophy Race unmistakable. Courtesy Ford Motor Co.

shutting down while Henry invented a new car. The V8 Model B was the answer to lost Model A sales, and again Henry stopped production while he invented a new engine.

Although a huge success that revitalized his company throughout the Depression years, the V8 was another example of crisis management. Neither of these crises need have arisen if Henry had instituted the use of modern management methods (the sort GM was known for) along with his modern manufacturing techniques (the sort that GM copied). He could have saved millions of dollars, lots of time and kept more loyal buyers with an effective research and development organization that responded to changing buyer interests with new products. Again, GM had the model of a modern R&D facility; Ford did not.

Most of all, what Henry Ford could have done with thorough planning and delegation of policy responsibilities was retain the leadership role he had built in the automotive industry. That role was also lost to GM, as his arch-competitor surpassed his company in both size and number of cars built.

It was this sort of difference of opinion that increased the growing rift between the two Fords—Henry and Edsel. When Tucker came along with the Indianapolis 500 idea and Edsel chose to go for it against his father's wishes, it was to become a major point of dissension in the steady decline of their previously close association.

The wholesome father-son relationship they once shared was never restored. It was replaced by Henry's harsh contempt of his son's educated lifestyle and artistic interests. Edsel died in 1943 from ulcers that turned into stomach cancer, and fever contracted from drinking unpasteurized milk from the Ford farm. Even then, Henry passed off what others saw as a tragic loss by saying his son had not lived right.

Henry Ford settled for nothing but success as measured in his own terms, and had no patience with anything less. Tucker's idea wasn't a bad one; it just wasn't given enough time for proper development. Henry seemed to regard it as a significant failure on Edsel's part. In any event, the return of Ford to racing at Indianapolis in 1935 became a fiasco taken as an embarrassment for the elder Ford. It was sufficient to keep his company out of racing for almost 20 more years.

FORD GOES RACING

Buyers liked the fashionable lines Edsel gave the '32 model, an adaptation of his highly regarded Lincoln design, but sales were at an all-time low: 212,757 Fords in 14 models were built. Money to buy any car was hard to come by but, although the inexpensive 4-cylinder engine was still available, it was the V8 that captured the public's interest. Its 65 HP pushed Ford cars along at maximum speeds of 80 mph, by far the fastest low-price mass-produced car.

Chet Miller raced Fronty-Ford in the 1930 Indy 500 to 13th overall. He qualified at 97.35 mph and started 15th. The next year, Gene Haustin qualified his Fronty-Ford at 108.393 mph, started 34th and finished 23rd. His qualifying speed was close to Miller's 1934 V8 Ford entry. Gold and black Bohnalite Ford shown qualified at 109.784 mph. Both Miller and Charles Crawford qualified their V8s, Crawford turning 108.784 mph. Unfortunately, Miller went over southwest wall on 11th lap. Courtesy Ford Motor Co.

When the '33s came out showing more rakish lines and a more powerful engine, Ford won a lot more buyers. Sales increased to 326,664 in 14 models, more than 50% greater than the year before. An improved engine developed 75 HP and again gave more than 80 mph top speed. Known as the *Model 40*, Ford cars were the only V8s under $2000 and certainly the fastest cars on the road for the money. For as little as $515, a V8 Ford was a lot of car. Gangsters used fast Fords for quick getaways, only to be pursued by cops in other fast Fords.

It was during 1933 that Ford Motor Co. set up a racing department to race modified stock cars. Fred Frame had won the Indy 500 in 1932 and is said to have established 21 international speed records on other occasions. His association with Ford reached high acclaim on August 26, 1933, when he won the Stock Car Race at Elgin, Illinois, in a fenderless V8 Ford. Rules limited engine displacement to 231 cubic inches and the race was over an 8.25-mile course. The 1933 Elgin race was the first major road race in America since its last running in August 1920, and Frame led a parade of seven Fords across the finish line. He averaged 80.22 mph for 203 miles, and the dominant performance of the Fords showed that Henry's cars were still winners.

The 1934 models were a continuation of the '33 line, with a number of improvements that brought increased sales to 517,047 cars in 12 models. A new option installed by dealers was a Columbia two-speed rear axle that acted as overdrive.

Noticeable improvement in economy and quieter traveling was its feature. Although the V8 engine was too new for the average hotrodder, racing men quickly saw its potential under Indy's *Stock Car* formula for production engines up to 366 cubic inches. Preston Tucker was one of them.

Tucker had been around the Indy 500 for years and witnessed the domination of Harry Miller's great racing cars and engines. Miller was the foremost designer/builder of the time, but the economic hard times had taken a toll on his works.

With smaller turnouts of both cars and paying spectators, Indy organizers had their problems, too. Thus, the Stock Car rules helped both racers and the Indy 500. Home-builts and factory teams running production-based engines had been doing fairly well, and Tucker recognized the combination of Miller's expertise with Ford's new V8 in a well-developed and sophisticated car to have high prospects for winning.

That idea had been shown by Chet Miller, who raced the Bohnalite special in 1934. The Bohn Aluminum Corporation entered the car to publicize its new aluminum heads for Ford V8s. Thus modified for Indy, the car developed 140 HP at 4,400 rpm from 221 cid, good for the time in a lightweight speedster. The car retained its Ford grill, and ran in an open-wheel configuration characteristic of Indy cars of the time. Unfortunately, Miller crashed the car on the 11th lap after a not-so-grand showing.

Tucker's ideas took shape following the race. When he

One of 1935 factory Ford Indy cars illustrates result of Indy's adoption of the stock-car formula. Preston Tucker sold to Edsel Ford idea of racing Ford V8s on the basis that Ford would win 1-2-3.

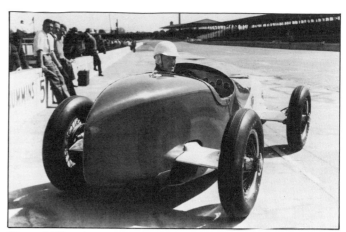

Harry Miller, famous Indy Car builder, designed and built these Fords. They were highly advanced Indy cars of their day, but suffered from lack of proper development. Steering boxes were too close to the left-side exhaust manifold and seized after heat boiled out grease. Courtesy Ford Motor Co.

approached Harry Miller about building a first-class Ford powered car, Miller jumped at the chance. In his state of financial decline, it appeared to be a good opportunity. They set up Tucker-Miller, Inc., and went about lining things up. Miller quickly laid out the basics of the car, the first front-wheel drive, four-wheel independent suspension racer to be seen at Indy. His reputation was sufficient to sign top drivers. While Tucker worked on Ford officials, time dragged on.

It wasn't until January 1935 that the program really got moving. By then, even the best of efforts were likely to fall short because of so little time. To build, test and fully develop cars for top-level racing in May, just four months later, looked more hopeless as each day rolled by.

Tucker proposed to Ford that, for a cost of $25,000, Tucker-Miller, Inc. would provide 10 race cars, an impossibly low price even in Depression-ridden times. Ford Motor Co. declined involvement for legal reasons and turned the project over to N.W. Ayer, its advertising agency at the time. The money was to come from dealer and advertising funds, which meant that Ford Motor Company's role would be financing only.

As word of the effort got around, great excitement was generated about Ford's return to Indianapolis. But as time went by, it became increasingly clear that Ford Motor Co. would have to save the effort. It took a crash program at the River Rouge plant to keep Ford from the embarrassment of not showing at the Speedway.

When the first car arrived on May 12, testing had been going on for two weeks; qualifying began a week later. The cars were beautiful, "way ahead of anything that had been seen at the Speedway," as driver Bob Sall remarked. Their streamlined, all-enclosed bodies promised high speeds. But with so little time to work out any problems that arose, the team could only race what they had with no hope of making improvements.

The cars ran basically stock engines turned around for

front wheel drive. With a compression ratio of 9.5:1 and four single-throat carbs or two twin-throats, a racing cam, light alloy heads and lots of attention to internals, they produced around 150 HP and looked to be capable of the 160 mph shown on their speedometers—the cars had no tachs. One questionable item was the steering box mounted close to the left-side exhaust manifold. Everything else seemed very well done, but this design flaw alone doomed the effort to failure.

The competition Ford faced among the stock-block category included the rather well-developed and handsomely built factory Studebaker team of 366-cid, 196-HP straight-8 powered cars. Cliff Bergere qualified at 111.5 mph and finished 3rd in his number-22 Studebaker in 1932. Red Shafer's in-line-Buicks had done well with a 5th place finish in 1933. Hudson, Stutz, Chrysler and other modified stock engines were seen from time to time and, although their larger displacements always looked good against the 150—200 cubic-inch Millers and Duesenbergs, the stockers were never quite up to an overall win in the 500.

Against the pure racing cars Ford would have to beat to win were the proven Miller marine specials like Bill Cummings' winner of 1934. In 1931, Miller's engine man, Leo Goossen, had designed an all-new 16-valve, double overhead-cam 4-cylinder engine but, unfortunately, Harry Miller filed for bankruptcy in 1933 before it became significant financially. His loss became an opportunity for his engineer, Fred Offenhauser, who purchased the new engine, its design and inventory of parts.

In 1934, the Offenhauser Engineering Co. was established. After hiring Goossen and former Miller machinists, the team set to building 200-HP, 220-cid engines for more and more racers. An enlarged 255-cid Offy that cranked out 255 HP at 5,500 rpm soon became the legendary engine that dominated the Indy 500 for the next 30 years.

There were 11 of the new 16-valve Offy engines entered in the 500 of 1934, but an older Miller 8-valve marine won. Kelly

Qualifying at Indy: Fords proved to be not as fast as expected, and failed to finish. The Indy 500 embarrassment widened the rift between Henry Ford and his son Edsel, which was never mended. Courtesy Ford Motor Co.

Close proximity of steering gear to exhaust manifold caused grease to boil and freeze gear, dooming '35 Ford Indy effort. Courtesy Indianapolis Motor Speedway.

Ted Horn and his mechanic Bo Huckman in the last factory-backed Ford to run at Indianapolis until the mid-60s. Courtesy Ford Motor Co.

Cockpit of '35 Indy Fords was well equipped and functional. Author photo courtesy of IMS.

Petillo qualified fastest at 119.2 mph in a 16-valve car, and he won the next year with a 255 Offy.

The fastest qualifier that year was Rex Mays with 120.74 mph, and rookie Ted Horn was the first Ford driver to make the field at 113.21 mph. Thus, the Fords were off the pace a bit and things were suddenly not so promising. Three more Ford drivers qualified, and some hope was held out for the Miller-Fords to win based on the tighter fuel rules. Only 42.5 gallons were allowed for the 500 miles. Then, after only 22 laps, the first Ford was out with a frozen steering gear. Ted Horn was the last to go out with the same problem after 145 laps.

An easily correctable design flaw in the cars had stopped the Miller-Fords embarrassingly short of anything noteworthy. Henry Ford was so mad over the failure that he cornered all the cars and hid them away in a warehouse. A few years later, they began to show up again in various forms, but Ford Motor Co. was out of racing again. This time for 17 years.

FORDS BEFORE THE WAR

By the spring of '35, the V8 Ford was well established and the public was hoping for better times. In the four years following the collapse of the nation's economy, average hourly wages had dropped by more than 50% and over 25% of the labor force was unemployed.

Sales were picking up as the worst of the Great Depression had passed, and sales of new Fords showed another healthy increase to 815,289 in 13 models. The 1934 models, regarded by many Ford buffs as the classic pre-war design, received many updates to become a new series designated the *48*. Major engineering changes centered around moving the engine forward 8-1/2 inches. The new Fords were more fashionable, more rounded and more flowing as opposed to the crisp lines of the '32/33s, but still retained the classic touch.

Franklin D. Roosevelt had put millions of workers back to work with his WPA and CCC government-sponsored work programs. Many roads, parks and other public sites were built or improved, and millions of Americans have enjoyed the results ever since. One example is the 469-mile Blue Ridge Parkway through the mountains of Virginia and North Carolina that traverses some of the most spectacular scenery in America. More people were working and traveling, and with more income they were taking in more movies where fashionable cars, dashing gents and elegant gals had become features of the silver screen.

The following year, 1936, brought many subtle changes. The new cars featured a redesigned grill for a more aerodynamic look. Sixteen models were featured that year, and sales increased again—to 923,734 this time. Over one-million Ford cars and trucks were sold, making 1936 the biggest year of the V8.

Sales were off a little in 1937. With 15 models, Ford built 915,188 cars. The Depression was showing signs of being over, and Ford Motor Co. set goals of 1,300,000 V8 sales, but fell short by a sizable margin. Regardless, America was almost back to normal, and the radio had become the commonplace home entertainer. They carried President Roosevelt's Fireside Chats, the World Series final as the New York Yankees beat the New York Giants, and news from overseas that ominous events were taking place. Hitler and Mussolini became allied, and Japan invaded China. Another new grill was the most noticeable change in Ford's styling.

The '38s brought a considerable setback in Ford sales. Eleven models in the car lineup totalled only 408,220 sales, the poorest since 1933. The beautiful Phaeton was gone, so was the 3-window coupe and sporty Roadster. Ford cars had become sedate in range, style and name. The classic Cabriolet was now called simply the Convertible Coupe. This year was the beginning of the turtle-back Ford sedans seen in the '39 and later models until the dramatically different and all new 1949 Ford. Ford styling had foundered and the company itself was experiencing all sorts of problems from labor to management.

Henry Ford, now 76 years old, was still leading the company, and it was clear to anyone looking closely that the Ford Motor Co. was headed for disaster. WWII intervened, per-

Home-builts and dealer-sponsored cars like Lau Motors Special were tough cars to beat in the dust bowls of local dirt-track racing in the '30s. Courtesy Ford Motor Co.

haps a "fortunate intervention" that provided clear direction of Ford products because of huge war orders. The war years also allowed time for Henry Ford II, his grandson, to reach 25, an age that allowed him to become a viable candidate to head the company, rather than one of the top Ford officials who were vying for power.

Returning from the Navy in 1945, Edsel's son Henry II and family members faced a turbulent and uncertain period in Ford Motor Company's future. Management problems were rife and the transition of power from the elder Henry to Henry II had to be forced. This was an interesting episode in the history of the people who controlled a multi-billion dollar industrial giant.

HOTTED UP V8s

Two aspects of European cars that attracted American enthusiasts was their handling—better than American cars— and their exciting performance. But when an engine gave up or its driver wanted more power, the easiest fix was swapping out the engine for a Ford. The Model A 4-banger provided a sizable increase in power over most low-buck foreign engines—and far more aftermarket equipment was available for Ford engines. That made them much easier to maintain.

For the racer, it was foolish to sink lots of money into building a European engine for racing when it was likely to be out-run by a home-built Ford. Thus, the legacy of the fast Ford was continued in sports-car racing through engine swaps. Ford Motor Co. was into racing and the Indianapolis 500 fiasco, if nothing else, resulted in the factory getting the experience and parts necessary to build hot engines for any high-speed event, be it auto, boat or airplane racing.

Drivers became famous with their V8 Fords. Here, Shorty Cantlon pilots Stark Hickey Ford. Cantlon and Fred Frame raced their fenderless '33 Fords in a number of races and were the '30s' counterpart of Fred Lorenzen, A. J. Foyt, Bill Elliott and other modern Ford racers. Courtesy Ford Motor Co.

Henry Ford still liked racing, and being an old hand at the sport, he seemed to be receptive to independents who wanted to race and win with a Ford. Certain people at Ford could be tapped for acquiring a hot V8. Fred Frame's engine, the one that won the Elgin Road Race in '33, was thought to have been a Ford internal job, but such things were not public knowledge. However, racers with the right contacts could get inside Ford for a factory-prepared engine or two.

One was Joel Thorne, who raced an Automobile Racing Club of America road race in a fast Ford roadster in 1935. Off-road excursions dropped him to 2nd overall, but the Ford-built flathead proved to be the fastest car of the day.

Like the Indianapolis 500 engines, Thorne's and Frame's stock-car V8s were tough. Although not front runners at Indy, the power plant soon become legendary in its exploits elsewhere and quickly became the hotrodder's engine. Flatheads powered all sorts of specials and won a vast number of club races.

It wasn't until the coming of the overhead-valve Cadillac V8 stuffed into Allards that flathead Ford powered sports/racers began finishing 2nd. Then the sophisticated Ferrari V12s of the late '40s and Jaguar double overhead-cam sixes of the early '50s showed the oldtime flatheads that the modern age had arrived.

A page from September, 1933 issue of Ford News. Featured was Ford victory in 203-mile Elgin Road Race, taking the top seven positions. Courtesy Ford Motor Co.

1936 Fords were very stylish. Rumble seat roadster is sample of first production Ford that didn't use wire wheels—3862 were built.

About mid-year, Ford's V8 for 1936 got steel pistons in place of aluminum. No change in horsepower was reflected.

Many of the names-to-be in racing rose through the ranks from beginner to master in Ford powered home-builts. One was Juan Manuel Fangio of Argentina, who built single-seat V8 cars. He drove them to victory in South American races years before he became five-time world driving champion in Alfa-Romeo, Mercedes-Benz, Lancia and Maserati Grand Prix cars of the 1950s.

While Ford V8 hotrods trained drivers and flourished as home-builts with high-performance potential, another sort of racing was beginning on the beach near Daytona, Florida. Along this strip of packed sand, the age of speed had matured in America. It was here in 1935 that Sir Malcolm Campbell took his 2,300-HP supercharged V12 Rolls-Royce powered Napier-Railton Bluebird up to 276 mph. It was also here that stock-car racing as we know it today was born.

Later that year, on a flat stretch of dried lake bed called the *Bonneville Salt Flats* in Utah, Campbell reached 301 mph, and the world land-speed-record cars would never be back to Daytona. In an effort to retain the city's racing reputation, Daytona city officials staged a stock-car race in 1936. One entrant was a young family man who had run out of money on his way south and settled in Daytona. Bill France had built and raced hot Fords for years, and at this point in his life, stock-car racing was a natural.

The race was sanctioned by the American Automobile Association (AAA) and run on the beach and an adjacent road in an oval pattern covering 3.2 miles. It attracted all sorts of big names in racing, including Bob Sall, the AAA's champion of 1933. It also featured a variety of cars, from Wild Bill Cummings' supercharged Auburn Speedster, to Henry McLemore's Lincoln and Sam Collier's Willys, that covered the field top to bottom. In this handicap race, Collier, being the slowest, got a 30 minute head start in the 250-mile race.

But before it could be finished, the race was actually

Bill France, shown here in the late '30s in his Ford stocker, had no idea how far stock-car racing would go. Courtesy NASCAR.

washed out as the tide came in before the planned 78 laps could be completed. Milt Marion and his Permatex special Ford was declared winner after 75 laps, and that gave Permatex an extra bit of promotion. The engine in Marion's Ford had been put together without gaskets and used only Permatex sealer.

An estimated crowd of perhaps 30,000 saw the race, but many of those were non-paying spectators who sneaked in. The city lost money, and the next year was no different. A local restaurant owner and France teamed up for the 1938 race, and they split a profit of $200. It was clear that public

Stylish fenderwork and hoodline of the '36 Roadster incorporated smoothed grillework and much shorter louvering along side panels of hood than prior years' models.

interest in stock-car racing was strong and the promoter side of France saw even more profits to be made.

For the '39 race, he proposed doubling the ticket price to $1 and received wisecracks that he was crazy. When the same size crowd turned out to see another good race, France and his partner split $2,000. There was nothing crazy about that.

Thus, stock-car racing was on its way up, and France became its principal advocate. He held beach races through 1941, all as unsanctioned events where drivers simply raced. No points were awarded, so there could be no championship. After the war, France sponsored several races, but still could not get national sanctioning.

In 1947, a group of independents including France got together and solved the sanctioning problem; they formed the National Association for Stock Car Racing (NASCAR). In June 1949, NASCAR held its first official Grand National race on a 3/4-mile dirt track near Charlotte, North Carolina. Glen Dunaway won in a Ford, but was disqualified for illegal modifications. The 2nd-place finisher driving a Lincoln was declared the winner.

Since then, NASCAR has become the dominant sanctioning body for stock-car racing, largely due to the efforts of Bill France. The crowning jewel in his racing career was the opening of the Daytona International Speedway in 1959, with the first annual running of the Daytona 500, a superspeedway built on the beach near where it all started.

Last flathead Ford to run at Indy was Pete Romcevich in 1947 entry built by Andy Granatelli. Pete qualified at 117.218 mph, started 17th and finished 12th after being sidelined on lap 168. Courtesy Indianapolis Motor Speedway Museum.

INDIANAPOLIS MOTOR SPEEDWAY, 1947
PETE ROMCEVICH

A total of 23,704 Convertible Coupe Fords were built in 1940. Several improvements were featured in the driveline, suspension and interior comfort. Output of the flathead V8 reached 85 HP. Style—Comfort—Convenience was Ford's advertising motto. Courtesy Ford Motor Co.

In 1946, Henry Ford II introduced the Sportsman, Model 71, in an effort to boost Ford's return to car manufacturing after WWII. Courtesy Ford Motor Co.

THE NEW FORD MOTOR COMPANY

Henry Ford II described himself as "a young man reaching for answers." Whether or not his company could survive the paralyzing management upheavals of recent years was yet to be demonstrated, and the young president estimated worker efficiency at one-third of what it should be.

The transition from war goods to peacetime manufacturing had left the firm with substantial cash on hand: $685,034,982 as of June, 1945. Yet, to survive in a competitive world, Ford cars would have to be brilliantly successful. They were, but it took time, and Ford was losing $10,000,000 a month because of all sorts of inefficiencies.

Not only did Henry II establish an organized financial-management plan, he brought in a group of young managers from the Army Air Corp, who were charged with the responsibility of discerning what was wrong with the company and to propose fixes.

Charles "Tex" Thornton was the head of the Army's Office of Statistical Control. He was made a full colonel at the age of 32 by implementing revolutionary management measures that made every facet of the Air Corp's aircraft available on demand. His thorough techniques of clear record keeping, planning purchases and charting future needs made his branch of the military far more effective and efficient that it had ever been. He had also arranged for the Harvard University Business School to train selected Air Corp members whom he brought into his organization.

As peacetime drew near, Thornton and two of his highest ranking officers recognized that their abilities would be in demand in the private sector. They selected seven of the more promising members of their staffs and proposed to Ford Motor Co. management that their group of 10 could work just as brilliantly in manufacturing cars as it had in aircraft. Their timing was perfect, and once in Dearborn,

Thornton's group became known as Henry II's *whiz kids*. Among them were Robert S. McNamara, who later became president of the Ford Motor Co.

Thorton's group searched out every facet of the company and put together wide-ranging plans for improvements. Henry II came to realize they were indeed a valuable source of talent, and also realized that his own inexperience was a problem. To fill that void, he sought a skilled vice-president to perform the duties of daily operations and to model a new Ford organization along the lines of GM. Ernest "Ernie" R. Breech, President of the Bendix Aviation Corporation, was brought into the Ford fold. With considerable talent displayed in acquiring the right people, Henry II showed he was an astute young man in his measure of people. More high-level staff members were added, and the new Ford Motor Co. began.

Because of heavy post-war demand for cars, hopes for a turn-around were bright and prospects steadily improved from the chaos that had nearly ruined the life work of its founder. From his home, Fair Lane, a short distance away from today's huge Ford World Headquarters building in Dearborn, the elder Henry Ford traveled and occasionally visited factories of the industrial giant he created.

He and Clara stopped in at the design studios where the 1949 Ford was being developed and both liked the new car. After a visit to the Rouge plant and Greenfield Village on April 7, 1947, the Fords retired to bed early. Spring rains had swollen the Rouge River, and its 30 feet above normal partially flooded the powerhouse of Fair Lane, leaving the Ford residence without electricity, heat or telephone.

At 11:15, Henry complained to Clara that he had a headache and a dry throat. She sent the chauffeur for a doctor, but before their return the legendary Henry Ford passed away of a brain hemorrhage.

Cars that saved the Ford Motor Co.: Henry II made the bold move to all-new styling in '49. They were immensely popular.

As America's last billionaire industrialist, he had promoted machinery to relieve man of drudgery. Ironically, Henry Ford's last moments were accompanied by wood heat, flickering candles and an oil lamp, little more than he had known as a farm boy before the machine age that he, more than any other person, helped create.

THE NEW FORD

When Henry Ford II was released early from the Navy in 1943 for the purpose of gaining control and reorganizing the Ford Motor Co., many people speculated he could neither wrest control from Charles Sorensen and Harry Bennett, nor could he save the company from its decline into collapse. Henry Ford, feeble and senile by now, had allowed Bennett to rise to power because of his ability to get things done, however brash. He seemed to distrust Sorensen, although the man had been with the company for years and proved his management ability continually.

Bennett was no manager and wielded power because of his close association with the boss, Henry Ford. He did so by instilling fear. Sorensen was the real backbone of the operation, compared to Bennett, and the two were bitter rivals. The entire management structure of Ford Motor Co. was rife with discontent. Anyone with automotive design and engineering talent had left. There was a noticeable lack of middle staff personnel, and many observers of the automotive industry predicted that the company would fail once the elder Ford relinquished power. The Ford Motor Co. was in dire need of a new man with the will to succeed in the manner that Henry Ford had shown in the early days. That man was Henry Ford II.

In a power play that used the elder Ford's feeble state, Bennett squeezed out Sorensen by encouraging the old man to believe Sorensen sought control of the company. Meanwhile, Henry II had been elected Vice-President, and he alone could challenge the absolute power of Bennett. Early in 1944, he was elected Executive Vice-President and, with the backing of his mother and grandmother, both large shareholders in the company, his power began to rise.

Then, in an element of intrigue and suspense, it was learned that Bennett had arranged a secret but legal document connected with Henry Ford's will that would place control of the company in the hands of trustees for 10 years after Ford's death. That meant power would be in Bennett's hands for he held sway with the trustees.

Facing such potentially strong opposition and possible loss of the Ford empire, Clara Ford insisted that her husband relinquish presidency of the company to their grandson. Henry declined. Then, in a master stroke of force play, Mrs. Edsel Ford told the old man that, if he did not, she would sell her stock. Old Henry had never wanted his company to go public and this act would end everything he had worked for. He relented, and transfer of power papers were drawn up. Henry II became President of Ford Motor Co. on September 21, 1945, and his first official act in that post was to fire Harry Bennett.

Thus, a new age of Ford began, and 28 year-old Henry II proved to be as able as his grandfather. But one difference in his management method was his willingness to place bright young men in positions of authority. Still another was establishing an official chain of command, something that had never been done at the top of Ford Motor Co. Another was

Custom Deluxe Convertible Coupe found 50,299 buyers in 1950, a high-style Ford that was very popular. Courtesy Ford Motor Co.

The "new Ford" of 1949 boosted Ford Motor Co. into a million seller. This '50 model shows the Ford emblem that replaced the word FORD *spelled out on the hood.*

establishing records for purposes of long-term planning. A smooth and orderly transition from manufacturing war goods to cars, and the beginning of a new, more modern car were also planned.

With the war over, Ford Motor Co. began retooling for the post-war boom that was generated largely by five years without civilian autos. Additionally, returning soldiers and sailors brought home immense talent and ability. They went off to college, they went to work and they ordered new cars—lots of them—so many that production lagged well behind demand.

The famous flathead engine was now up to 100 HP. Although the new cars for '46 were little more than restyled pre-war models, 372,917 Fords in nine models were produced. The '47 and '48 models—601,665 and 549,072 each year in several models—were also restyled pre-war models. But for 1949, Henry II called up an entirely new and modern car, redesigned from front to rear.

By then, over 6,000,000 V8 Fords had been built. The only thing the all-new Ford gave up to any competitor was a new overhead-valve V8 in Cadillac and Oldsmobile cars.

Henry II set his team to work on the new car. Fourteen months and $37 million later, the new Ford captured the imagination of the public, which was more enamored by cars than ever before. The project began as the "X-2900," "X" for experimental and 2900 for the projected weight of the car in pounds. Although that mark was missed by some 250 pounds, the final product was about 200 pounds lighter than earlier models.

Compared to the '48s, the engine was moved forward 5 inches; both the front and rear seats were moved into a

A three-speed shifter on the column and a V8 up front produced a fast Ford in 1950.

"mid-ship" location for the first time; the cars were wider for more interior room; the frame was redesigned; and the rear axle was improved. Gone was the transverse leaf spring, solid-axle front suspension, in favor of a double-wishbone, coil-spring suspension. At the rear, paralleled leaf springs were used sans the torque tube. The car's lower silhouette was a great improvement over the earlier turtle shape, and gone forever were running boards and balloon fenders.

1950 Crestliner was Ford's styling leader. Courtesy Ford Motor Co.

Fords of the '30s have always made favorite hotrods. Coupes such as this are the basis for most street rods.

Almost everything was new except the basic engine design. The flathead was retained.

The 1949 models appeared first on June 8 at the Waldorf Astoria Hotel in New York with great fanfare. First shown to the press, they found the cars both different and exciting. The following six days were devoted to public viewing. Tremendous enthusiasm generated thousands of orders and showed that the new Ford, Mercury and Lincoln cars hit the mark. After retooling industry wide, the $37 million invested in design, engineering and initial manufacturing had grown to $118,000,000.

Thus, the investment was a major step for Henry II's rebuilding program. And, it proved that his team had the right idea. This was the fourth time Ford Motor Co. had launched a notably different car. The first was the Model T, then the Model A, then the V8. But unlike those earlier cars, the new Fords were brought about in an orderly fashion . . . and in a far smoother transition.

The public loved the new Ford cars. To illustrate, production picked up to 841,170 in 1949, a huge increase of almost 300,000 over the year before. Many of the minor defects in the '49s were corrected in the '50 models, although the overall design changed little. Production again increased almost 350,000 more than in 1949, reaching a total of 1,187,122, the highest since 1930.

1950 was the company's most profitable year in two decades. It showed that Henry II had effectively revitalized his company. Ford Motor Co. soared into 2nd place, leaving Chrysler well behind. And Ford car production closed on Chevrolet, still the low-price leader. Market shares that year were Chevrolet 20.5%, Ford 17.6% and Plymouth at 10.4%.

New models for 1951 brought some styling changes along with the re-introduction of the Victoria to the Ford line. These high-style Fords sold 110,286, showing that buyers wanted style even in a low-priced car. But with the outbreak of the Korean war, government quotas were placed on manufacturing of vehicles for civilian use. Passenger-car production dropped to 900,770.

Another new Ford design was introduced with the 1952 models. They were modernized and considerable attention was given to fit, finish and functional refinements. The new Fords were stylish and very appealing. Production of 777,531 that year jumped to 1,184,187 Ford passenger cars in '53 and to 1,394,762 in 1954 when wartime quotas were lifted.

The same basic design was carried over to 1953, and Ford received the distinction of being selected as the official Indy 500 pace car. The ivory and gold trimmed convertible was a beauty with immense appeal. Its wire wheels, fender skirts, Continental kit and official detailing were seen by thousands of people at Indy in 1953. This car can be seen on display in the Henry Ford Museum in Dearborn.

Ford's flathead V8 had been in production since 1932, but the 1953 model car was the last to use it. Although becoming obsolete by then, the flathead was a good engine that delivered more performance and reliability than any of the low-price competitors. Beginning with 65 HP from 221 cubic inches in 1932, the engine grew to 337 cid and 152 unmodified HP in the 1951 Lincoln. It was well proven, but old-fashioned among a growing number of performance buyers who looked on overhead valves as the modern engine.

Ford Motor Co. produced its 40,000,000th vehicle in 1953 at a time when a new OHV engine was being readied for production. Fresh new styling was in the works for Ford cars, and a sleek two-seater was in design. Ford Motor Co. soon found itself going racing again.

3

OVERHEAD VALVES

Good Ol' Boys & Purple Hogs

"Fireball" Roberts on Daytona Beach course in convertible race of February 25, 1956 was backed by Heintzelman Ford of Daytona Beach, whose motto is displayed on the front fender. This was "win on Sunday, sell on Monday" at its best. Teammate Curtis Turner won to begin a roll of 22 wins out of Ford's 27 Convertible Division victories. Chevrolet and Buick tied for 2nd with 10 wins each. Courtesy NASCAR.

Ford Motor Company celebrated its 50th anniversary in 1953 with nationwide fanfare. Behind the celebrations, Ford employees were quietly working on expansion, lower production costs, increased output and both a new engine and two new lines of cars. These were major ingredients in Henry II's revitalization plan.

The national appetite for new cars was still unsatisfied, and there were more buyers in the higher-priced fields. With recognition of that market, Ford officials announced the return of the Continental to the Lincoln line. The second line of new cars was a sensational two-seater, the Thunderbird, which was designed to counter Chevrolet's Corvette.

As for its engines, Ford Motor Co. had always been able to boast that its V8 was the most powerful engine in the low-price field. Even OHV Cadillac and Oldsmobile V8s had little effect on Ford sales. Then, Chevrolet introduced a more powerful 6-cylinder and announced that it would produce an overhead-valve V8 for its 1955 lineup. Suddenly, Ford's dominant role as the V8 leader was threatened. Ford

High-style Crestline Victoria of 1954 was Ford's top Y-block V8-powered car. This was the third and last year of this styling. In 1955, Ford introduced the beautiful Crown Victoria. Courtesy Ford Motor Co.

Ford's famous flathead V8 was replaced in 1954 by the Y-Block. It was Ford's first overhead-valve engine and bested Chevrolet in the "horsepower race" of the mid-50s. It was both larger in displacement—272 cubic inches versus 265—and more powerful—162 HP with a 2-barrel carb and 182 with a 4 bbl. The still larger 292 previously reserved for Mercury was made available in 1955. It produced a very fast Ford in 198-HP form; the 205-HP Interceptor was even faster. Courtesy Ford Motor Co.

engineering countered the top Chevy rating of 180 HP with a flathead rival upped to 182 *rated* HP. However, overhead valving was competition that couldn't be contended with on paper. A completely new engine was required.

Ford engineering set to work on a new overhead-valve engine. Called the *Y-block*, it was introduced in the 1954 models. First advertised as a 256-cubic inch overhead-valve engine producing only 160 HP, the new V8 was not regarded as being able to compete in the developing horsepower war with Chevrolet. Therefore, by the time the all-steel Thunderbird was introduced on September 23, 1954, the Y-block had been enlarged in two versions, both larger than Chevy's small-block V8 introduced in '55. The basic engine displaced 272 cubic inches delivering 162 HP in 2-bbl carburetor form and 182 horses with a 4-bbl carb. The larger was the 292-cid Mercury engine that became the Thunderbird and top Ford powerplant. Its 8.1:1 compression ratio produced 190 HP with a manual transmission and 198 with automatics. Topping the line was a 205-HP police-interceptor mill offered late in the '55 model year.

Against Corvette's 265 cid and 195 horses, Ford was still on top—at least on paper. Road tests showed the Y-block Thunderbird capable of 0-60 mph in 10.75 seconds and a top speed of 118 mph. Overall, the cars were similar in performance. But while the T-Bird was clearly a higher-quality car with far broader appeal, handling was sacrificed in favor of a smoother ride. T-Birds were America's top personal luxury car while Corvette became America's leading production sports car. In 1958, the two-seat 'Bird became a 4-place luxury car; the Corvette has remained Detroit's version of a sports car to this day.

The Thunderbird was Ford's showcase car, but in the low-income Southeast, 'Birds remained little more than dreams. It was in that part of the country that Ford and Chevrolet, along with all other manufacturers, found that full-size, fast cars were the ticket. The reason was such a car did two things: haul moonshine during the week and race on Sunday.

It was in the hills of Georgia, South Carolina, North Carolina, Tennessee and the Virginias that the good ol' boys brewed up their white lightnin' and carried it to market in souped-up flathead Fords. Rarely were anything but Fords considered for the job simply because they were available, cheap and lots of hotrod equipment was available for them.

Hotrodding in California had already become the basis of drag racing, a sport that would soon spread across the country. But in the South it had a different purpose. Running moonshine might have been against the law, but it was a common way of earning sizable amounts of extra dollars. And the faster a driver's car, the better his chances of outrunning the "revenooers."

The Feds couldn't always find where the booze was made or where it was sold, but it was transported on the public roads. So, the logical place to work at stopping the moonshine traffic was to catch a driver with a load in his car. To prevent that, a driver had to drive fast at times, and because he was carrying a heavier load than the Feds, his car had to be sturdier and more powerful to outrun them.

Thus, the moonshine trade trained drivers and mechanics very well. And, since driving fast with souped-up Fords was such a big part of stock-car racing, these moonshiners and their cars became part of the growing sport.

Although mostly fun in the beginning, in time, stock-car racing became a bigger business than anybody imagined. Huge crowds jammed into dusty ovals to see the races and, suddenly, drivers and their cars were becoming famous. This was too much action for Ford and Chevrolet to ignore. By 1956, they were deep into racing as arch-rivals. Stock-car racing spread throughout the Southland, and factory-backed cars became a big part of the show.

Where they raced was changing, too, from dirt to asphalt. During a poker game one night, racing was under discussion and Harold Brasington proposed that a real paved race track be built right there in the middle of nowhere. The place? A slow South Carolina cotton and tobacco town called Darlington.

Looking back from today, it seems incredible that in 1950 the 1-1/4 mile Darlington oval was built (increased to 1-3/8 miles in 1953). Even though the businessmen who built it had some difficulty getting a sanctioning body to race there at first—stock-car racing had always been done on dirt—it wasn't long until Darlington became the mecca of stock-car racing. Bill France and NASCAR were in the middle of it all. And it didn't matter that Darlington had no accommodations for the thousands of people who poured in for the race; they came anyway—30,000 strong right from the beginning! And they nearly tore the gates down to get in.

Stock-car racing was an itch that drove drivers, mechanics and spectators to endure whatever it took to be at Darling-

Poodle skirts and Elvis, teddy bears and saddle oxfords were features of 1956 remembered with nostalgia with the gorgeous Sunliner. On the stock-car circuits, Ford ragtops won 27 NASCAR Convertible Division races to Chevy's 10. In Grand National, Ford took 14; Chevy three.

ton. Soon-to-be big names, Red Byron, Johnny Mantz and Curtis Turner, the first full-time stock-car drivers and first kings of stock-car racing, were among the 75 drivers who started the first Southern 500. Mantz drove a lowly Plymouth to win because his car was light and he had connections with tire people in Dayton, Ohio. Other cars ran standard highway tires and had blowouts, as many as 22. Mantz changed only three tires, keeping him on the track where he averaged 76.26 mph for the 6-1/2 hours it took to run the 500.

All this was exciting stuff. As the local press picked up on the racing, the people and their cars, interest in stock-car racing grew like mad. Atlanta, Charlotte and Daytona were soon to have their own giant ovals, and other small towns like Rockingham in North Carolina and Talladega, Alabama "grew" their own, too. Most southern towns of any size had a stock-car track, and if racers couldn't afford to run on asphalt, they ran on dirt.

During the flathead days, Sunday stock-car races had become a haven for fast Fords, but they were no match for the new overhead-valve engines. Oldsmobile "Rocket" V8s were the fastest cars at the turn of the '50s decade. They showed this by winning 36 of NASCAR's 69 races staged during 1949-50-51. Through '55, Ford could win only three races; Chevrolet captured just two. Olds and Hudson winnings accounted for 148 of NASCAR's 221 races during the period of '49-to-'56. Then things changed.

At Chevrolet, Zora Arkus Duntov was developing all sorts of high-performance equipment for the make's new small-block engine. From that time on, over-the-counter heavy-duty parts were available to the public. Ad men were quick

The 292 was enlarged to 312 cid and over 200 advertised horsepower in 1956. The Thunderbird engine gave a lot of go to Fords. Stock-car racers got upwards of 325 HP out of their Y-blocks.

to pick up on any Chevrolet high speed achievement for sales promotion. Jack Tapscott of Deland, Florida, going 112.113 mph at Daytona in a '55 Chevy was big news. Then Herb Thomas won the first NASCAR short-track race of the '55 season at Fayetteville, North Carolina. All of a sudden the staid old Chevrolet make was a racing make. Its 6-cylinder of 1937 design was eclipsed by the new V8.

Ford and Mercury won a total of 19 NASCAR Grand National Division races in '56, well ahead of arch-rival Chevrolet's paltry three wins. Curtis Turner, shown here on the beach in his Schwam Motors "Purple Hog," won at Darlington, the biggest race of the season. Courtesy NASCAR.

Chief engineer Ed Cole liked what he saw and money began to be funneled into racing and advertising. Engines and complete cars were made available to the "right" people. And even though Chevrolet won only two rather obscure races that year, the ad men gave Chevy wide circulation. Although advertising racing was a shocking pitch to most people in 1955, southern dealers loved it because it brought in more people who wanted to see what sort of car won races. All of a sudden, Chevrolet built exciting cars that were now described as "the Hot One."

Ford had to do something. Robert McNamara, Ford general manager, began asking questions. There were few if any racing buffs in the Ford organization, so the decision was made to get outside help. Ford had to look good against the upstart V8 Chevys, and Darlington was the showcase. Ford management wanted to go racing, but didn't know how. So the corporate decision to do so came from Bill Benton, Ford's field service manager over the Charlotte, North Carolina district, who had racing connections. It was probably the last time a corporate decision was made at that level, but it was the right one.

Two cars built in Ford's experimental garage were accompanied by Ford engineers when sent to Charlotte. Racer Buddy Shuman then took charge because he knew what it took to run a 500-mile race. The Ford men were skeptical, though. Things just were not done like that back in Dearborn, but if old Henry Ford had been around, he would have recognized race preparations. He had been there over a half

century earlier. Like Henry, Shuman was obsessed with victory. It wasn't long until he had everyone working long hours.

Schwam Motors of Charlotte was the entrant for Ford, and Charlie Schwam had the cars painted purple. Ferocious snorting hogs were depicted on each side along with the Schwam motto: "What we say it is, it is." Over the driver's door of one car went the name, *Curtis Turner*. The other was handled by his buddy, *Joe Weatherly*. Both were the best drivers around, giving Ford big names to go with the showmanship Schwam displayed in how the cars were painted.

Weatherly qualified his *Purple Hog* at 109.006 mph, but Turner could get only 106. Shuman was not impressed, so he jumped into the Ford. He promptly ran 109.054 mph, to which Turner received guffaws about being out-driven by a mechanic. Ford fans were delighted with the show, even though neither Ford qualified in front. The soon-to-be-legendary "Fireball" Roberts was on the pole with a Buick at 110.682 mph; Tim Flock qualified the second day and set a speed record of 112.041 mph in one of Carl Kiekhaefer's Chryslers.

Kiekhaefer was the Mercury outboard marine engine tycoon who raced as a private team on a scale that only the emerging factory teams could match. His cars won the NASCAR Grand National championship in 1955 and '56, but because no one at Chrysler seemed to care, there was little if any mention of his victories in advertising. When a Chevy won even a little thing, corporate ad men beat it to death.

Ralph Moody, later to become half of the famed Holman-Moody shop located in Charlotte, raced a Southeastern Ford Dealers entry, shown here being urged on by a Ford Industrial official. Courtesy NASCAR.

Joe Weatherly, known as the clown prince of NASCAR, and his buddy Curtis Turner, combined to win 23 of the last 29 races of the '56 season. Turner's 18 wins were backed up by Weatherley, giving Ford a 1-2 finish in 14 races during the season. Weatherley bagged five wins himself. Courtesy NASCAR.

And Ford soon learned that "winning on Sunday meant sales on Monday."

Factory racing was heating up. Some of the good ol' boys were having loads of fun in top-quality factory cars supported with lots more money than what they were accustomed to. In fact, they put Keikhaefer out of business. He quit after the '56 season, but others went into business because of factory interest in stock-car racing. One pair that became famous was John Holman and Ralph Moody in Charlotte. Their firm of Holman & Moody was to become Ford's main racing arm in the South. As Grand National racing grew, they became another great legend in Ford racing.

Fans who had come to Darlington to see a Chevy show were treated to a Ford show as Turner charged out front at the start. No doubt the embarrassment of Shuman out-qualifying him riled Turner a bit, and perhaps not. It was his hard-charging style to put on such a show, and Weatherly wasn't far behind.

Then, about midway through the 364 lap race, the front suspension let go and Turner crashed. On the 180th lap, Weatherly took the lead, then pitted on the 278th lap. That let Herb Thomas' Chevrolet take the lead but, once back out with fresh tires and a load of fuel, Weatherly's Ford showed a considerable level of superiority over the Chevy. He regained the lead on the 304th lap and raced through the Chevys to stretch his lead to a full lap on Thomas.

The race was the most exciting seen at Darlington. Here was Ford and Chevrolet going at it hot and heavy. But fortune was on the side of Thomas when the suspension of Weatherly's Hog collapsed and he crashed, too. Ironically,

Thomas won his third Southern 500 in 1955 with a Chevy that averaged less than his winning Hudson of 1954, at 93.28 mph compared to 94.93 mph.

The crowds saw a great race, one that said Ford was back even though a Chevy won. Although a disappointment to Shuman, Benton, Turner, Weatherly and all the Ford fans, the level of excitement was astounding. It was, in fact, the first race of a new age, the age of Ford's corporate commitment to race and win with stock cars. For the next 12 years, Ford won more NASCAR Grand National races than any other make. Through 1967, Fords won 202 races, Plymouth took 113 wins and Chevrolet was victorious in 106. And it all began in the middle of nowhere at Darlington, with a pair of Purple Hogs.

THE RACE IS ON

Ford advertising men dealt with promoting cars on a national level—and it was working. Production soared to 1,394,762 passenger cars in the U.S. alone in 1954, and the new V8 accounted for a goodly portion. Over 210,000 more Fords were sold than in '53. The following year, 1955, was spectacular, with Ford car production reaching 1,764,524.

The Crestline was replaced by the new higher-styled Fairlane, named for the Ford estate in Dearborn. And tops in the Ford lineup were the beautiful Crown Victoria and Sunliner convertible. A total of 35,164 buyers drove home in new '55 Crown Vics—1,999 of those had the optional green-tinted Plexiglas top in the section over the front seat. In 1956, the 58,147 Sunliners produced proved to be far more popular than Chevy's 41,268 BelAir convertibles. And Thunderbird trounced the 674 Corvettes sold, with eager 16,144 buyers.

As Ford Motor Co. surged out of its postwar doldrums with the new V8 and beautifully styled cars, the image of the typical Ford buyer was steadily upgraded. By 1955, the pitch was to own a Thunderbird or Crown Victoria. But among the steady upgrading of Ford cars, the promotion people had some difficulty with stock-car racing, a phenomenon local to the Southeast. Clearly, stock-car racing involved a very different type of Ford car and a very different sort of person. This was a different world altogether, and it took some time before the sales benefits of race wins were recognized to be useful at all. It was driven by the desire to scrub Chevrolet and reassert Ford's supremacy.

Ford engineers also had a problem accepting the ability of shade-tree mechanics. Bootleggers knew how to soup up Fords…they did so for a purpose that was proven regularly on the public highways. Racers took this ability a step further to perfect cars to endure the punishment of flat-out racing. Both had a practical knowledge of race-car preparation that far exceeded that of any Ford engineer despite their college degrees. They distrusted each other, and it took some time before they began working together.

When they finally got together and combined their talents—seat of the pants and theory—the cars went faster and faster. Unfortunately, racing was not fully appreciated by Ford management, but Chevrolet engineers, led by Duntov, had a great deal of racing experience and full support of management. In an effort to get some racing organization, Pete DePaolo, a well known racer, was tabbed to organize and manage Ford's racing arm. He set up headquarters in Long Beach, California, a long way from Darlington.

DePaolo was apparently interested in Bill Stroppe's American Automobile Association Mercury experience rather than NASCAR racing. Stroppe's factory Mercs were doing well on a number of AAA tracks, but never approached the level of NASCAR racing. Managing a racing effort from that distance with a sport unfamiliar to him served up many problems. Thus, Ford's re-entry into stock-car racing was not smooth.

Four cars were built by Ford and four drivers were lined up for the 1956 season opener at Daytona, still run on the beach. Turner and Weatherly were joined by "Fireball" Roberts, and eventually by Ralph Moody who was a driver looking for a job. This one offered $1,000 a month, big money at the time! With this foursome handling two hardtops and two convertibles, Ford should've had a top team, but things were a mess as friction remained between Ford engineers and the racers. Somehow, the work got done as Daytona approached. Moody was the highest Ford finisher, 3rd behind Tim Flock's winning Chrysler 300 and Billy Myers in one of Stroppe's Mercurys.

Things looked good at times, but dissension led to Ford man, Joe MacKay, being assigned the job of getting factory racing on track. One of his first moves was to bring John Holman on board. Holman, an ex-Stroppe man, was experienced with race cars and engines. He was a tool and die maker with extensive machining ability. He had also been a long-haul trucker. Mostly, Holman got things done. His natural ability to manage combined with such broad knowledge was the ingredient in his pitch to run Ford's eastern stock-car operation.

It took some time, but Holman got results. Moody won a race in West Memphis, Arkansas, although officials showed him 2nd behind a Mercury. Holman protested the lap count. After checking, they found him to be right. Moody got the win and the Lincoln-Mercury guys were furious. Holman wasn't concerned; he was supposed to get wins for Ford and he did. "Fireball" Roberts followed this up with a win at Raleigh, North Carolina, beating a Kiekhaefer Dodge. The crusty millionaire immediately filed a protest, one of many. But when the Ford was torn down, it checked out OK. Holman was heading up a tough Ford program that was sinking Kiekhaefer's back-to-back NASCAR championship team.

During this period, Fords and Mercs took eight Grand National races in a row. Fords won seven out of 10 convertible races. Both the eastern and western Ford organizations were becoming more effective. One astounding feat they accomplished was setting record after record in speed trials at Bonneville, most notably setting an average of 108.16 mph for 50,000 miles!

All the racing and winning proved that Ford had a lot of better ideas in 1956. The cars were fast and reliable, and they racked up 14 wins, 11 in the last 25 Grand Nationals following Moody's win at West Memphis. Chrysler still led in the win column with 22 victories, but Ford was second. Dodge was third with 11 wins; Chevrolet was an also-ran with 3.

In the Convertible Division, Turner and Weatherly simply walked away with the victories. They were 1-2 in race after race. Turner accounted for 22 of Ford's 27 wins. Weatherly got the other five. Chevrolet took only 10 wins.

All this meant that Ford factory racing was indeed on track and rose to glory at Darlington, the big one. Unfortunately, Buddy Shuman wasn't with the good ol' boys and the Purple Hogs this time. Months earlier, he had fallen asleep while smoking in bed and was asphyxiated. Turner and Weatherly promised themselves that they would return to Darlington with the Hogs and win it for Buddy. Perhaps it was a melodramatic touch, but it was real life just the same.

Horsepower figures of the competing cars were batted around a good deal and mixed with a lot of speculation. Fords were said to run 260 HP from 312 cubic inches; Chevy advertised a lowly 225 HP from their 265, but everyone knew they were more powerful. But both Ford and Chevy engines had less power than the 340-HP Chrysler 300s with their 354-cid *Hemi* engines—cylinder heads with hemispherical-shaped combustion chambers with angled valves for improved airflow and combustion. Buck Baker's 300 set a qualifying record of over 119 mph; Speedy Thompson took the pole with 118.68 mph in another 300. Turner pushed his Hog to just under that figure, and out of the top 15 qualifiers, eight were Fords and Mercurys. Where were the Chevys? In this race and for most of the '56 season, they were backmarkers with only 3 wins.

When the flag dropped on the 75 starters, the heavy Chryslers took off. But in less than an hour, it was an all Ford show. Fords led for most of the race and, with 162 laps to go,

Turner roared into the lead. He held this lead to the finish, setting a new record in the Southern 500 with a 95.067 mph average, even though he backed off for the last 50 miles. Thompson's Chrysler was 2nd more than a minute behind, then another Ford. Finishing 4th was the first Chevy.

It had been a great day for Ford, and Turner had the satisfaction of winning it for Buddy.

UPS & DOWNS

With the first full season of factory-backed racing behind them, 1957 looked to be the year Ford would flatten Chevrolet. ,Duntov didn't see it that way. His Corvette performance options, along with the small-block enlarged to 283 cubic inches, were Chevrolet's response to the few stock-car racing wins in 1956.

The big news was fuel injection. It gave a rated 283 horses to the 283 engine in showroom form; two 4-bbl carbs resulted in 270 HP. All sorts of heavy-duty Chevrolet parts were made available over the counter. All that resulted in the Corvette emerging as America's hottest sports car with a succession of victories and championships.

Ford found itself without the range of performance parts to compete with Chevrolet, but Ford's engines remained larger. There's no easier way to make power than with more cubic inches, the theme of the muscle car outrage a decade later. Although the 312 had proven itself well, the new season was tougher. To get around the problem, Ford engineers took the quickest route to more power—supercharging.

In stock-car racing tune, the injected Chevy cranked out around 310 HP. Pontiac made its entrance with a 325 horse, 347-cid engine. Olds showed up with a 371-inch V8 at over 325 horses. Dodge and Plymouth, with their 318s, were out of it because of too little power—and Kiekhaefer pulled out. The legendary Chrysler 300s were too big and too heavy despite the 354-inch Hemi enlargement to 392 cubes and 390 horses, the most powerful in the industry. All makes were racing overhead valve V8s and the competition was fierce, but mostly in the low-price field of Ford versus Chevy. Pontiac and Olds shared in 7 wins; Ford and Chevy won 46 between them. Ford led in the win column with 27 Grand National victories to Chevy's 19. "Fireball" Roberts was the leading Ford driver with 8 wins, but Buck Baker was Grand National champion by virtue of 10 major wins, all in Chevrolets.

Ford racing was rolling in early 1957. With the fastest cars, best drivers and top mechanics—Smokey Yunick had been enticed over to Ford—the fast Fords were unstoppable. In the inaugural Rebel 300 at Darlington, "Fireball" Roberts won by averaging 107.94 mph. The Ford team was clever, too. John Holman had found a loophole in the rules and put hard compound tires on the outside of his cars and softer tires on the inside. It worked and Roberts was the only driver to go the distance on one set of tires.

Convertible Division? Turner and Weatherly totaled 17 of Ford's 26 wins against 12 wins for Chevrolet. But, in the end, it was Chevrolet on top again with Bob Welborn becoming the Division champion after winning 8 times in Chevys.

Ford was the official pace car in 1953; Mercury was so honored in 1957. With 368 cid and 335 HP without the supercharger available on Fords, Mercurys in the hands of Tim Flock and other stockers made a good showing. Courtesy Ford Motor Co.

Winged in 1957, the new Fairlane 500 was named for Henry Ford's estate in Dearborn. Curtis Turner won 11 of Ford's 26 NASCAR Convertible Division wins against Chevrolet's 12. Glenn "Fireball" Roberts was the Ford hot-shoe in Grand National with eight of Ford's 27 victories against 19 for Chevrolet.

How did that happen?

By 1957, there were lots of races held all over the country that counted in NASCAR championship points. Bigger races carried more weight. As the season opened with one Ford win after another, GM President Harlow (Red) Curtice pulled out a deft bit of corporate maneuvering that sent Ford to the showers.

It was clear to people watching closely enough that stock-car racing was highly partisan and sold cars. Spectators who saw their favorite make winning did more enthusiastic promotion by word-of-mouth than anything Dearborn came up with. Yet, it was not so clear to the bean-counters that the cost of racing really brought improved sales. Thus, it was

Marvin Panch—car 98—kicks up sand at '57 Daytona. The giant tri-oval was built two years later. Panch won five of Ford's 27 Grand National Division victories in 1957, second to "Fireball's" eight wins. Chevrolet's total wins came to 19. In the Convertible Division, Ford had 26 wins to 12 for Chevrolet. Courtesy NASCAR.

Joe Weatherley leads Billy Myers' Mercury and another Ford on the beach at Daytona in 1957. Weatherley finished 2nd behind Tim Flock's Mercury and ahead of Myers, another 1-2-3 Ford sweep—a year that Fords dominated stock-car racing. Courtesy NASCAR.

easy for desk-ridden pencil jocks to conclude that racing was an unnecessary expense. Well-built and nicely styled cars sold themselves, or so they said.

Lulled into a mood of such doubt, Robert McNamara allowed himself to be hustled into an agreement that his Chevrolet counterpart had no intentions of honoring. More careful probing of the matter would likely have produced a different perspective, and saved Ford Motor Co. a lot of embarrassment in future years when they had nothing to race with. As it turned out, Ford ended its factory-backed

Cruisin' was big in the '60s. Owners from Classic Ford Association relive the good ol' days.

Supercharged Fords were the hottest from Dearborn in '57, although Ford's factory involvement in drag racing was almost nil. Courtesy Ford Motor Co.

racing in mid-season, and the bean counters claimed victory when Ford production soared to 1,889,705 by year's end, 220,539 more than the year before.

Supercharged 312-cid Fords with 325 HP and Mercurys with the 368-inch normally aspirated Lincoln engines that cranked out 335 HP were forces Chevrolet couldn't stop on the race track. NASCAR officials eyed the McCulloch superchargers with a bit of suspicion, but it was "Red" Curtice's proposed ban on factory-sponsored racing that stopped Ford. Curtice suggested that factory teams were really competing with customers, so they should be banned. That was offered up in the February 1957 meeting of the Automobile Manufacturers Association (AMA). When all members agreed to it, including McNamara, Ford racing successes were doomed.

There were 21 Grand National races before the ban went into effect in June of that year. Ford won 15; Chevrolet five. Out of the 32 races after the ban, Ford won 12 and Chevrolet 14. Among those were several major wins.

The AMA ban supposedly was an agreement to end factory-sponsored racing and delete all high-performance hardware from parts catalogs. Horsepower ratings were not to be advertised nor anything associated with speed or acceleration. McNamara went for it hook, line and sinker. All such items, except police pursuit equipment, were eliminated and funding for racing dropped to nothing. But not at Chevrolet.

Henry Ford, who did things his way and rarely gave competitors little more than a cold shoulder, must have turned over in his grave. He had been keen to such competitive trickery, and after building an industrial empire ruled by the ideal of being better than Chevrolets and Plymouths, here was GM dictating Ford policy. One can imagine old Henry's ghost raging up and down the halls of corporate Ford kicking rumps for letting it happen. Ford factory racing was history.

GM used the AMA ban to strengthen its position in the marketplace. Its engine was well developed, and lots of high-performance equipment such as a 4-spd transmission was available both over the counter and in production cars. Sports-car racing with Corvettes and specials using Chevy engines and transmissions continued to improve the potential of Chevrolet equipment and furthered the reputation that Chevrolet was the hotrodder's store. Then there were the Pontiac and Oldsmobile divisions working on performance equipment for their cars.

Ford shut down, but racing went on anyway. Since earliest times, Ford was the hotrodder's make, but there was no development of the stuff that made Fords go as fast as Chevys, except for blowers. Ford told customers about how safe and stylish their cars were while discouraged racing enthusiasts who didn't know of the ban wondered where the fast Fords went. Chevrolet racing flourished while Ford engineering slid into doldrums that would come back to haunt the company. As an example, 1957 Chevys won the Southern 500 the next three years, doing it each year with progressively higher average speeds.

Ford sales plummeted in 1958. It was a year of economic recession nationwide. Ford production dropped to 1,219,422 cars, 670,283 less than the year before. The company lost millions of dollars and came close to financial failure. No doubt the bean-counters concluded that cutting off racing saved a lot of money. For sure, buyers were not coming into showrooms to see fast Fords that won races.

By this time, Jacque Passino was in charge of Ford racing, and he knew that, sooner or later, his company would have to get back in it to recapture that growing segment of the market who were performance minded. There was little he could do but encourage Ford racing on a private level. But at the same time, he was developing the knowledge and contacts that he would use in the next decade when Ford finally got back into racing.

Holman & Moody teamed up in Charlotte with Passino's encouragement, and got Ford's racing-parts inventory for a

Thunderbirds old and new, 1956 and '86: The "classic" 'Bird of '56 was a two-seater that came with 12-volt electrics for the first time, and lots of charisma. Modern 'Birds are best known for record stock-car wins and have become favorites for customizing, like this '86 example.

nominal investment. It was fortunate that they did because in the following lean years of Ford racing and performance, it was Holman & Moody that kept Ford alive.

Although Yunick was paid off to satisfy his two-year contract, he wanted to live up to his end of the bargain, so he tried the best he could. Paul Goldsmith was still his driver, and Turner joined them for another round at Darlington. Their two black and gold Fords and the lone Holman & Moody car driven by Roberts were the top Fords. Goldsmith was involved in a crash that put him out on the 28th lap; Roberts spun into the wall on the 101st lap while leading. That left Turner to carry the Ford banner. He and Lee Petty in an Olds battled for the lead, but when Petty put Turner into the wall on the 281st lap, Ford's best chance was through. At the finish, it was Speedy Thompson's Chevy. Yunick was out of business with crashed Fords and so was Holman & Moody.

On GM's side was the knowledge that Holman & Moody had all that inventory of racing parts. It was hard to believe that two old racers had the finances to mount such an extensive racing campaign without factory support. It was easy for GM racers to conclude that Ford was cheating by putting all that stuff in the middle of stock-car-racing country at Charlotte.

Semon "Bunkie" Knudsen, whose father had left Ford 30 years earlier and built Chevrolet into the industry leader, was building Pontiac into a force. Olds was building, too, and rumors of infractions on both sides flew like mad. Nobody was sure just what was going on. Lee Iaccoca, Ford Division marketing whiz, saw that GM still had performance

parts offered and suggested that Ford do likewise. McNamara reiterated his non-racing directive that was no help, and a letter was sent to GM in February 1958, reporting the infraction. A reply came back after Daytona that promised to remedy the problem, but a year later they were still there and everybody at Ford knew why. GM was racing.

"Red" Curtice may not have thought out the entire plot, but his coup over Ford was complete, at least for a time. Simply put, GM was cheating, but that's all part of the game. Complete cars built specially by GM, and lots of performance hardware and financing was suspected in the garages of several GM racers. All Holman & Moody could do was race what they had on a shoestring budget that amounted to sponsorship on a race-to-race basis.

The Rebel 300 at Darlington looked to be in serious doubt when both the Turner and Weatherly Holman & Moody cars were heavily battered in a minor race that Turner won. Somehow, a miracle was achieved when the mechanics managed to get the cars together for Darlington. Then, Turner and Weatherly put on an all-Ford show to win 1-2 and they were followed across the line by two more Fords. Nobody in the GM camp believed Ford was out of it after that.

In at 5th was a past Ford favorite, "Fireball" Roberts in a Chevrolet. Ford didn't have a seat for him and soon the loss showed. Roberts took his '57 Chevy to victory in the Southern 500 at the highest average speed yet achieved, 102.59 mph. Chevrolet won 22 Grand National races that year, and Lee Petty was Grand National champion with nine wins in Oldsmobiles. Ford was victorious 16 times, mostly in smaller

The 312-cid Y-block was new for '56. It was rated at 215 HP with a manual and 225 with an autoshifter. The Thunderbird name came from southwest American Indian lore. Its outstretched wings emblem was a symbol of power, swiftness and prosperity, and was regarded by the Indians as a good-luck omen. From an early news release, a Ford pensman wrote: "No man, say the Indians, could see the Thunderbird except in flashes as it flew swiftly through the clouds."

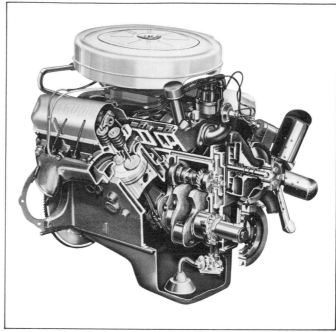

Most popular big-block Ford was the 390. Production was delayed until '63 model year because of AMA ban. Courtesy Ford Motor Co.

races, and six of those were by newcomer Junior Johnson, who saved a little glory for Ford. Otherwise, it was a miserable year. What's more, Bob Welborn won the Convertible Division again in Chevrolets, with 10 of Chevy's 13 wins to Ford's six.

The AMA ban worked to GM's great advantage. And Ford management found itself with another major problem to overcome. How were they to get buyers back into Ford showrooms? By 1959, the answer was clear: racing. But with sales way down in 1958, the company was hard pressed for capital to stay alive, much less afford a crash program to develop high-performance parts and finance a racing program to boot. Thus, Ford was in a vicious circle: no money to promote racing to increase sales to get the money to go racing.

Things had to get better.

DOLDRUM & REBIRTH

The best thing that happened to Ford was Chevrolet's miserably styled winged wonders of 1959. Ford passenger-car sales jumped 525,987 over the 1958 sales year to 1,745,409. It was a welcomed surprise that gave Ford some financial breathing room.

The stock car scene was changing a little as it became clearer that GM was heavy into performance. Evidence of all sorts was collected by Ford's only man allowed to have involvement with racing, which showed that Ford should get back into the fray. The opening of the giant Daytona International Speedway and the fanfare GM gave the inaugural running of the Daytona 500 was all it took for Ford to

let go of some bucks for racing.

To most observers at Daytona, Ford was behind the six Holman & Moody Thunderbirds that started. Corporate Ford actually had nothing to do with the racing. The cars were put together from Ford scrap parts Holman was able to buy at junk rate like anyone else buying reject parts. For his purpose, they worked fine, considering that his mechanics had to build race cars anyway. The only catch was their engines, 430-cid Lincolns that were optional in T-Birds, but were not strictly legal under NASCAR rules. France allowed them to add some spice to the 500. To the delight of Ford fans, four of the 'Birds finished, and unknown Johnny Beauchamp of Harlan, Iowa, drove one to a photo finish with Lee Petty's Olds. It took over 60 hours for officials to declare Petty the winner. The excitement of the race and suspense following it went a long way in rebuilding Ford's performance image among spectators.

Ford introduced a new series of engines in 1958. The FE series, or *big-block* Ford, first came in 332 and 352 cubic inches, although it was expandable to much larger displacements. The 300-horse 352 was the top Ford engine, although it wasn't any more powerful than the top 312. The soon-to-be legendary FE was in its infancy. In fact, the 390 planned for release in 1958, with an eye toward stock-car racing, was held back because of the AMA ban.

A fledgling performance-parts development crew of three men was allowed to operate within a framework of "limited re-entry" to racing, but with little funding and no priority. What they did was produce a 4-bbl oval-track intake and a three 2-bbl drag-racing induction system for the FE series as

Following Darlington's lead, stock-car racing at Daytona moved in 1959 from the beach inland to this giant tri-oval. Fans pack the facility for the Daytona 500. Courtesy NASCAR.

a new beginning. Power reached 360 HP, the highest in the industry. Chevrolet introduced its 348 that year, the engine that was to become the highly touted 409. Both were big-blocks, signaling the beginning of the cubic-inch wars that made for great excitement in a few years.

Holman & Moody carried the Ford banner well, and advertised "T-Bird Power Products" for going 150 mph in a complete race-ready stocker for $4,995. It was the only place you could get a Ford like that, and they continually showed their stuff in "Competition Proven" products.

Along with Daytona, Darlington was joined by two more super-speedways: Charlotte and Atlanta in 1960. Now there were four major showcases for stock-car racing, and Ford saw the increased exposure of eight major races a season as more reason to go racing again. The sport received growing radio coverage. And television audiences were treated to the spectacle of speed on the high banks. Stock-car racing had matured as a high-dollar sport with wide popularity. A new era of stock-car racing began, and Ford was interested.

A new name, Fred Lorenzen, had carried the Ford banner in USAC races and he had just come South to racing on the big ovals. Another name that was to have a drastic effect on Ford racing—indirectly, of course—was John F. Kennedy,

who was President of the United States. What he did was to tap McNamara for his Secretary of Defense. That left a job open for performance-minded Iacocca to move into.

The first thing Iacocca did was to institute a change in Ford's image. Called *Total Performance*, it spelled the beginning of the great age of Ford racing.

A few Ford diehards had kept the marque alive in drag racing but, like stock-car racing, Ford was finding it tough going on the 1320-ft asphalt strips. In the first NHRA Summer Nationals, a driver by the name of King won with a 143.95 mph run in 10.30 seconds. The next win was Rod Singer, who took the 1959 NHRA Summer Nats with a 9.76 blast in a rail dragster powered by a blown Lincoln. A number of Fords found drag-racing duty on local levels, but they rarely emerged in the nationals. One example was the A/Fuel Dragster run by Bill Kenz and Roy Leslie of Denver, Colorado. Their GMC 6-71 supercharged 390 Ford powered short-wheelbase rail cranked out 9.58s at over 142 mph in 1962. Those stats were certainly national caliber, but the likelihood of winning a national meet was small because there were so few Fords running.

With Iacocca running things at Ford, racing wins of all sorts were in the making.

4
TOTAL PERFORMANCE

. . . the most ambitious racing program
in the history of the automobile industry . . .
Leo Levine's *The Dust and the Glory*

Mercury fastback Marauder at speed in hands of racing star Parnelli Jones. Courtesy Ford Motor Co.

Just past his 36th birthday, Lee Iacocca became the youngest general manager of the Ford Division, the largest of the Ford Motor Company. He knew that Ford cars were not highly regarded among the soon-to-be largest segment of the population, the *baby-boomers* of World War II who were approaching driving age. Racing would get their attention, and that was the origin of the company's *Total Performance* image. The new Ford motto was not so much an ad theme as it was a statement of policy. Ford was going racing in a big way.

At the time, the company was working toward introducing a new type car, the Cardinal. An American "Volkswagon," it was a front-wheel-drive, low-bucks, no-frills basic transportation car. Iacocca killed it and thought doing so was the greatest thing he did for Ford. As an alternative, he proposed a different idea that was targeted at the emerging youth market, which came from Donald Frey, Ford Product Planning manager, who presented the item in April 1961, it became the Mustang, a car for the kids. Built of basic Ford

components already on hand, it was just put in a package with youth appeal. This was done for $50 million, a modest investment for what came of it. Styled along the lines of a scaled-down Continental with a short rear deck, Mustang was an instant favorite.

During that time, Ford racing was extremely thin. Even Holman & Moody was having trouble staying afloat. If it hadn't been for Autolite sponsorship—not yet a Ford subsidiary—H&M might have folded. As it was, they were down to racing Studebaker Larks in small car classes. Autolite was talking of running a Dodge in 1961. Lorenzen, eager to race in the big time, was on tap, but things were bleak.

Passino managed to keep Holman & Moody in the wings with a promise of near future Ford help, but any Ford racer had little chance. This was the year of Pontiac. Knudsen had honed his Indians into fine shape, the most powerful and best developed cars in stock-car racing. Their 440-horse, 389-cid engines cranked out 30 more HP than Ford's largest, the 390 at 410 HP in Grand National tune. Pontiacs domi-

Introduced in 1963, the soon-to-be-legendary 427 side-oiler came with single or dual 4-bbl, or three 2-bbl carbs as shown. Engines were derived from the high-performance 390s and 406s in Ford's FE family of big blocks. Top rating was 425 HP with two fours. Courtesy Ford Motor Co.

Old-style NASCAR decal of the '60s. Squire Gabbard Photo.

nated, and Roberts, Weatherly and Marvin Panch, all ex-Ford drivers, won big ones in them.

There were two bright spots for Ford: Nelson Stacy's surprising win in the Southern 500 at Darlington, and Lorenzen's victory in the Rebel 300, also at Darlington. Stacy's battered Ford held together long enough to set a blistering new average speed record of 117.787 mph in a duel with Panch's Pontiac in the 500, almost 12 mph faster than the year before when Buck Baker won in a Pontiac. Freddie was even faster in the 300, averaging 119.520 mph—over 17 mph faster than Weatherly's Ford win the year before. In spite of little financial support, the few Ford diehards still racing gave Dearborn encouraging results.

All totaled, Ford won seven Grand National races in '61, and got some much needed exposure with Stacy and Lorenzen at Darlington. Production had been up in 1960, reaching 1,892,003 passenger cars. This made the company more solid financially and, along with Iacocca's pro-racing stance, Ford was beginning to move. Passino regularly reported useful and interesting race-related and production information that went a long way to promote Ford performance internally.

Still rebuilding in 1962, Ford was able to win just six Grand Nationals that year. Again, Ford ruled at Darlington. Stacy won the Rebel 300 and newcomer Len Frank took the Southern 500. Stacy really excited Ford fans with his victory in the World 600 at Charlotte, where he set a blazing new average speed mark that exceeded the Pontiac win the year before by almost 14 mph. His 125.552-mph average showed that Ford had the endurance and speed to win the longest Grand National race on the circuit. Lorenzen won the Dixie 300 at

Atlanta, and Stacy won again in the Old Dominion 500 at Martinsville, Va.—and that was about it.

All told, 1962 wasn't all that bad. The foundation had been laid for Ford's big push that began in '63. Production soared to 1,935,203 cars that year, and Ford was flush with money. Investing in Total Performance was paying off, but no one could have predicted the vast success that lay before them.

FASTBACKS & SIDE-OILERS

Ford's Engine and Foundry (E&F) engineers knew they had a problem. Ford management had set a course toward racing in all forms, but the "race on Sunday, sell on Monday" philosophy wasn't working as well as hoped because Ford wasn't winning very often. Something had to be done.

Ford engines were down on power. The 1957 AMA ban on factory racing had slowed Ford's engine development to a snail's pace, and its effect was still being felt. The *horsepower war* was soon joined by the *cubic-inch war*, but Ford engines were coming up short except for the big Lincoln and T-Bird V8s.

The FE engine series progressed from the 332 of 1958 through the 352 and 390 versions, later to include the 406 in 1962. But even though engine displacement had increased, power lagged behind the big Pontiacs that won both NASCAR and USAC championships that year. The Indian's 421 cubic inches was turning out upwards of 465 HP; the 406 could just manage 430 at the beginning of the '62 season. Dodge and Plymouth were in there with their 413s, and Chevy's 409 proved to be rather unsuited to stock-car racing. The competition was tough, and Fords just weren't performing as hoped.

Fred Lorenzen, one of Ford's top drivers in the mid-60s, was among the most popular NASCAR drivers. Squire Gabbard Photo.

Side oiler got its name from large oil passage running along left side of block that fed oil directly to main crankshaft bearings. Conventional system routed oil indirectly from top to crank through cam bearings. Drawing courtesy Ford.

Ford men were learning that output power was only one side of stock-car racing. Staying power was another. And having a top pit crew was extremely important. Along with the Wood brothers, Holman & Moody gave Ford two of the best racing organizations. At the time, Ford was considered the underdog, and NASCAR crowds loved to see the big guys, mostly in Pontiacs, get knocked off. Lorenzen became the top driver for Holman & Moody after Turner had been banned from NASCAR for trying to organize drivers. Marvin Panch was the Wood brothers top mount.

The learning process took some time. In a few years, Ford's engineers set the goal that an engine should last 200 hours at full throttle. But in 1962 form, the 406 fell short at only 39 hours on a track like Daytona. When "Fireball" Roberts hit 159 mph in Smokey Yunick's Pontiac on the Florida highbank, the Ford contingent realized they might as well pack it up—their Fords had neither the power nor durability to win.

Ford teams had 11 engines at Daytona, and it was a good thing they did. It wasn't long before a block cracked. The engineers managed to keep the problem quiet, and replaced every engine that showed signs of its block cracking. But when the flag dropped, the Fords had to stay together for almost four hours. Winning was not to be. "Fireball" led from start to finish, and one Ford after another dropped out with blown engines. The only placing was Lorenzen's 5th, which came about because a fuel-line problem wouldn't let his car run flat out.

Between Daytona in February and Atlanta in April, Ford's engineers came up with a fix for the block-cracking problem: *cross-bolted* main-bearing caps. Bolts were inserted through the side of the block's deep skirt, three per side, and threaded into each of the three center main-bearing caps. Thus strengthened, Ford stockers now had staying power, even if they remained down on power. And with a little reduction in power-robbing aerodynamics, Ford had a chance at being competitive.

The aerodynamic ploy was the introduction of Ford's famed *fastback*. At first, the newly shaped top was bolted onto convertibles. Later it went into production on a variety of 2-door models, quickly becoming a Ford styling favorite. But for now, they were rare. In the 1962 model year, a local Atlanta dealer had a fastback Ford on his showroom floor. However, aside from that single car and the others like it on the track, you couldn't have found another anywhere. The competition screamed, and NASCAR made the Ford teams race with convertible cross members in the chassis rather than lighter sedan frames as was first tried.

At Charlotte in May, the protests were so loud that the fastbacks were banned entirely. The Ford teams had to quickly prepare some older cars to run. Regardless, it turned out to be a Pontiac-Ford duel. Fortunately for Ford fans, Pearson blew the engine in his Pontiac with about 40 miles to go. Stacy shot by to win a thrilling race at record speed of 125.552 mph, giving Ford a very visible win. Then Lorenzen won at Atlanta in a rain-shortened race where his "quick pit" strategy resulted in a win over Banjo Mathew's Pontiac. Even though things were looking good, it would be 20 more races before a Ford finished in front again. Staying power had improved, but horsepower was still down. And the rules limited advantages gained with fastback tops.

In preparation for the 1963 season, Ford engineers bored

Fords from the '30s and '60s show changes in styling that took place during this period.

Competition Proven *was the mark of Holman & Moody, the Charlotte, North Carolina, Ford wizards that built Fred Lorenzen's famous white and blue No. 28 Fords. Faithfully restored '65 model Holman-Moody built stocker weighed in at around 4,000 pounds, but could reach 170 mph on the high banks. Squire Gabbard Photo.*

and stroked a cross-bolted 406 to give 483 cubic inches. Tests showed it to be both strong and powerful. The car averaged 164 mph for 500 miles of testing on the Bonneville Salt Flats, reaching a trap speed of 182 mph in the process. Ford would be tough with this combination, but the NASCAR rules committee ended any such plans when it first announced an engine-displacement limit of 6.5 liters (396 cubic inches) for 1963, then increased the maximum to 7 liters (428 cid).

Ford engineers set to building engines to this specification. The result...the soon-to-be-legendary 427. Complete with cross-bolted mains, mechanical lifters, special heads, intake manifold and cast-iron exhaust headers, and a side gallery oiling system—giving it the name *side oiler*—the FE engine evolved into a strong NASCAR power plant capable of well over 450 *reliable* HP.

Ford was so confident of its new engine that the decision was made to market the 427 as a showroom option. In *8v* form (two 4-bbls), the 427 with 425 horsepower began a legacy of fast Fords for street, strip and track performance. This engine, with wedge-shaped combustion chambers, found 4978 buyers in 1963. These full-size Fords carried gold Thunderbird emblems on the front fenders, rather than silver, and displayed the figure **427** instead of **390**. The 427 was soon a cult symbol of nationwide proportions.

The 1963 NASCAR season opener was at Riverside, California, a road-racing circuit very different than the usual down-South highbanks. Cars had to handle unbanked left and right turns. Setting up a car for that sort of race was difficult because neither Holman & Moody nor the Wood brothers had road-racing experience. To get some sort of edge, Ralph Moody brought Dan Gurney onto the team for his experience at Riverside in sports-car racing. Once Gurney learned the car and the crew settled into the new style of racing with full-size cars, Gurney went fastest in qualifying

lap and proceeded to win the first Riverside 500.

In fact, Gurney won the first four Riverside 500 races. Parnelli Jones' Ford won it in '67, its 5th running. Gurney won again in 1968 at record speed, then Richard Petty won the 1969 Riverside 500 during one of his rare Ford drives, setting an average speed record of 105.498 mph. That mark stood until David Pearson's Mercury bettered it in 1977 at 107.038 mph. Pearson's record was set on the first 500-kilometer rather than 500-mile Riverside Grand National race.

Highlighting the '63 Grand National season was Tiny Lund. He led a grand Ford parade in the first five places of the Daytona 500, coasting across the line out of fuel for a win. What was most satisfying to Ford fans was the failure of Chevy's new *porcupine-head* engine at Daytona. (The engine had no production connection; although it made Chevrolets fast, it didn't last.) No doubt, Ford's clean sweep of NASCAR's feature race had some effect on a GM decision. Following Daytona, Chevrolet's complete withdrawal from stock-car racing was handed down by top management—a re-statement of the 1957 AMA ban that would haunt Chevrolet fans for years to come.

Another super win was the blistering pace "Fireball" set in the 1963 Southern 500, an average speed record of 129.784 mph that wasn't surpassed until 1967.

Ford won 23 of 55 Grand National Division races after Riverside in 1963. That record led the 19 Plymouth and eight Chevrolet wins. Ned Jarrett won eight Grand National races, Lorenzen took six and "Fireball" got four. Lorenzen became the first driver to top $100,000, and Ford cars won 51% of NASCAR prize money that year.

That was *Total Performance*, NASCAR style. With all this Ford success, Joe Weatherly still ended up as the Grand National Champion, driving Pontiacs and Mercurys.

Fearsome foursome of 1965: Fred Lorenzen, NASCAR, No. 28 and 427 Ford. Squire Gabbard Photo.

Basically stock steel-bodied Galaxie fastbacks with special front and rear suspensions, NASCAR stockers of 1965 were a lot more stock than those of today. Squire Gabbard Photo.

By 1964, Total Performance was recognized everywhere—and it meant Ford. Ford—30, Dodge—14, Plymouth—12, Mercury—five and Chevrolet just one, was the NASCAR Grand National finish that year. The Dearborn machine had made good its word by flattening Chevrolet. That was the story for the next several years, when Grand National racing was a face-off between Ford and MoPar.

From 1965 through the '67 season, Ford won 68 Grand Nationals, Plymouth took 51 and Dodge rolled to 25 victories. Chevrolet? Only six!

Plymouths in the hands of Richard Petty during '67 were almost untouchable as "The King" won 27 races, 10 in a row, for the greatest individual season on record. But Cale Yarborough came back to end that in the Wood brothers Mer-

---

1963 Ford Galaxie window sticker

1963 FORDS . . . America's liveliest, most care-free cars

GAL 500XL SPORT HRTP 8		3268.00
710x15 TIRES NYLON WSW		52.80
427 8V HI PERF 3 MOS OR		461.60
4000 MI POW TRN WARRANTY		
FOUR SPEED TRANSMISSION		34.80
RADIO AM		58.50
TINTED GLASS		40.30
2 SPD ELEC WRP&WASHER		20.10
SEAT BELTS		16.80
PADDED DASH & VISOR		24.30
REMOTE CONTROL MIRROR		12.00
WHEEL COVERS	NC	
BACKUP LIGHT & CLOCK	NC	
AIR CLEANER & OIL FILTER	NC	
COOLANT & ANTIFREEZE	NC	
TRANSPORTATION CHARGES		
TOTAL		

Extra Value AT NO EXTRA COST
You don't pay any more for the values built into a new Ford . . . values that mean less trouble, more driving fun.
VALUE . . . Ford's twice-a-year maintenance schedule frees you from the bother and expense of frequent servicing. Service is scheduled only twice a year, or every 6,000 miles. You'll go miles between major lubes . . . miles between oil changes, and minor lubes . . . and brakes are self-adjusting.
VALUE . . . no-charge extras—like 36,000-mile (or 2-year) coolant—antifreeze . . . and Full-Flow oil filter.
OUTSTANDING VALUE . . . Ford's new warranty. Ford Motor Co. offers a 24-month, 24,000-mile warranty. Virtually all parts are covered for the full two years or 24,000 miles . . . and no strict, pre-established service routine is required to keep this warranty valid. These are values that make Ford a better buy, now, and will result in more trouble-free driving pleasure in the future.

$4065.10

Single Holley 4-bbl on top of side-oiler 427 was good for about 525 HP. Squire Gabbard Photo.

Fred Lorenzen's office of 1965. **THINK! W.H.M.?** *was fast Freddie's reminder to take it easy and means,* What the Hell's the Matter? *Squire Gabbard Photo.*

Holman-Moody preparation of Ford's 9-inch rear end including converting it to a full floater and controlling it with four shocks and a Watts link. Note line running from bottom of center section; it goes to a cooler. Squire Gabbard Photo.

cury of 1968. Cale and LeRoy Yarborough split wins at Atlanta, David Pearson won twice at Bristol and again in the Rebel 400. Cale then took the Southern 500, Daytona 500, Firecracker 400 and others to become NASCAR's leading money winner with $136,786.

By now, Ford fastbacks and side-oiler 427s had become greatly admired by Ford fans—and feared by competitors. However, the engine was not the last in the FE engine saga that began in 1957. There was more to come with 428s, but let's not leave the 427, yet. Ford engineers developed a lightweight valve train for the 427, allowing it to rev to 7000 rpm. With other tweaking, the 427 output was increased to 500 HP in 1965. It was to prove an outstanding racing engine in all sorts of Ford race cars, from the GT-40 Mk II and Mk IV wins in Europe to drag racing.

With that sort of power and superb stock-car chassis development, Lorenzen won six in a row, an unprecedented streak of major wins in NASCAR history. Ford walked away with 48 Grand National wins that year. Along with Lorenzen and Panch wins, Ned Jarrett and Junior Johnson (Chevy man turned to Ford) won 13 races each and Dick Hutcherson won nine. They captured the majority of Ford wins that year. Jarrett was Grand National champion. He and Lorenzen came close to evenly splitting over $160,000 in winnings.

To illustrate Ford's rise to stock-car racing supremacy, from 1957 through '67, Ford won 202 Grand National races compared to 113 for Plymouth and 106 for Chevrolet. During the 1964 through '67 seasons, Chevrolet won only seven Grand Nationals. Ford had made good its bid for "total performance," and GM was out of business on the high-banks.

SUPER STOCKS

During the first few months of the 1961 model year, several manufacturers introduced optional high-performance engines that displaced over 400 cubic inches. Along with them came parts and technical information designed for one purpose: to win drag races. Although thousands of fans packed into stock-car races, most were not able to see the cars up close, and the majority of racing enthusiasts could get only as close as their radios for the big races.

On the grass-roots level, drag racing was the auto-enthusiast's sport in America. It was at 1/4-mile strips across the nation that fans could see the cars up close, watch them win or lose in exciting straight-line competition, then head to new-car showrooms to buy their favorites. Manufacturers recognized the "win on Sunday, sell on Monday" advantages of wins in drag racing, too. It was this market that GM went after.

The beginning of the cubic-inch and horsepower wars was over stock-car racing. But by 1961, high-performance equipment was more of a promotional scheme for professional

Mid-size '63 Fairlane offered the ingredients of what became muscle cars with Ford big blocks. Altered wheelbase cars ran A/Factory Experimental (A/FX). Courtesy Ford Motor Co.

racing rather than for public consumption. Drag racing was not as well organized, although on the move toward becoming more just than hotrodding. As new high-performance engines became more available, sanctioning organizations accepted them for Super Stock classes.

That brought on a spectacular rise in the sport's popularity, as baby-boomers made their market segment the largest. Fast cars was the name of their game, and super stocks quickly became very exciting racing. Enthusiasm ran high. In a few years, racers could buy complete factory-built drag cars and a host of equipment for going faster and quicker than ever before.

By the mid '60s, there weren't enough high-performance cars and equipment to meet demand. Still later, when the youth-market wave passed and government emissions and safety regulations took effect, manufacturers had trouble marketing their cars. High performance waned in the early '70s, making a full cycle. In 1961, the golden age of drag racing was just emerging. By 1971, it was about to end for another decade. In the early '80s, the factories came back with a rush of high performance.

In 1961, Chevrolet went after the youth market with 350-horse, 348-cid engines that looked good, then topped off their line-up with the new 360-horse 409 option. Small-chamber heads and an 11:1 compression ratio, along with forged aluminum pistons, were hot stuff in those days.

Chrysler's "Golden Lion" 413 was new that year. It cranked out 350 HP at 4600 rpm. Although the 413 MoPar was the biggest-displacement performance engine—except for the 430-inch Lincoln—neither was a true high-performance

power plant. The 413 was built to power the massive Imperial and didn't have any special internal features, just tremendous torque. The 300G series cars did receive two 4-bbl carbs, though, and a factory rating of 375 HP at 5000 rpm. But they were also very heavy cars that didn't lend themselves to the youth image.

Pontiac, because of Knudsen's urging, was the industry leader in performance. Knudsen recognized the advertising value of successful stock-car racing, then exploited it to the fullest to place Pontiac near the top of new-car sales. Pontiac offered only one engine, the 4-bolt-main 389, but in progressive horsepower steps and internal refinements from 215 to 348 HP in stock form. Three types of cylinder heads were available, and the Trophy 425-A was the high-performance leader. High-performance cam kits teamed with one 4-bbl or a 3-deuce setup were available. And cast-iron headers, among all sorts of factory equipment, showed that Pontiac was heavy into Super Stocks, an outgrowth of stock-car racing.

Ford for 1961 had two 390s, one for standard cars and a high-performance version. The latter did battle with Chevy's 409 and was able to hold its own pretty well. The standard engine was rated at 300 HP at 4600 rpm with excellent torque, 427 lb-ft at 2800 rpm. The performance version with a single Holley 4-bbl pegged power at a healthy 375 HP with the same torque, but shifted the peak up to 3400 rpm. A 4.05 X 3.875-in. bore/stroke combination gave the 390 an over-square design resulting in smooth power band and good revving capability.

The highest-performance 390 had a different block. It had

thicker main-bearing webs with cast-in reinforcing ribs. Also, an extra boss was cast in the block for an oil passageway that ran the length of the block above the cam. The boss was fitted with an oil-pressure relief valve that bled off oil at pressures above 55 psi. This ensured that all oil passages were pressurized to at least 55 psi, thus making sure all moving parts in the engine received adequate lubrication. This technique proved highly successful. The pressure-relief valve prevented Ford's full-flow oil filter from over-pressurizing and blowing out the filter gasket.

The 375-HP 390 received larger oil galleries for increased flow. Additionally, the hydraulic-lifter galleries were blocked off because solid lifters were used. The same cast-iron crank was used in both engine designs. And both received the same standard production rods and pistons. The 375-horse 390 received far more rigorous inspection, and parts were selected for optimum clearances.

Small-chamber heads were the same as those used on the high-performance engine of the year before, the 300-horse 352 built for drag racers and stockers. Intake and exhaust valves of 2.030 and 1.560 inches, respectively, were also the same. Breathing was more than adequate, and the 1960 high-performance cam was carried over from the 352, but valve springs were selected for operation to 6500 rpm.

A different cast-aluminum intake manifold with 10% larger passages was installed on the 375. In mid-year, Ford introduced a three 2-bbl intake manifold and progressive-linkage carburetor option that produced 401 horses at 6000 rpm. Torque rose to 430 lb-ft at 3500 rpm.

Ford was also conscious of producing good-looking engines. The cast-aluminum oval air cleaner, similar to what became famous on later Shelby Mustangs, and a log-type fuel line on the 3-deuce system, made Ford enthusiasts drool. Ford's big-diameter cast-iron headers were another item that gave Ford fans even more special equipment to brag about.

National Hot Rod Association finals of 1961 held at the newly opened Indianapolis Raceway Park showed just how popular the Super Stocks had become. There were all sorts of cars, but the crowd, numbering around 40,000, cheered loudest for the Super Stocks. Hayden Proffitt pushed Mickey Thompson's Pontiac to Optional/Super Stock victory with 110.29 mph in 12.55 seconds. Don Nicholson wasn't far behind with a 110.29 mph in 13.25 seconds in his 409 Chevy. Ford wasn't quite in the picture, yet.

On the west coast, Ford diehard Les Ritchey had established Performance Associates in Los Angeles, and was soon a base for Ford performance. "Gas" Ronda of Covina, California, was another who raced Fords to fame. As Ford's factory commitment to drag racing grew, there were many more names that became well known. In the east, Bob Tasca, a Ford dealer in Providence, Rhode Island, was doing the same in local drag racing. As of 1962, though, Ford drag racing was still thin.

It was for the NHRA Nationals of that year that Ford made a move to prepare 10 lightweight Galaxys with new 406 FE big blocks. They were not all that successful, but it was a start.

Chevy's 409 was basically the same as the previous year, but with some attention to increase power to 380 HP with a single 4-bbl and 409 HP at 6000 rpm with three 2-bbls. Cylinder heads were changed for better breathing—intake ports made 1/4-inch taller—and combustion chambers were decreased from an NHRA minimum legal displacement of 90.15cc to 83.55cc. Thus, actual compression ratio was increased. Improved optional intakes, single and dual 4-bbl carbs were offered to buyers, and Chevrolet introduced its version of cast-iron headers.

Chrysler's new red-hot 413 engine used a dual 4-bbl induction setup on an enclosed cross-ram intake. This was the *Ramcharger* 413. With its sensational up-turned cast-iron headers, Plymouth and Dodge fans had an engine of high visual appeal that was both tough and powerful. It came in two versions, differing only in compression ratio, 11:1 and 13.5:1. The latter produced a whopping 420 HP at 5400 rpm and maximum torque of 470 lb-ft. The milder engine was rated at 410 HP at 5400 rpm with 460 lb-ft of torque. Standard on Ramcharger-equipped MoPars was a very efficient exhaust system with cut-outs. Thus, Chrysler was serious about drag racing and went a long way to supply a wide range of parts and equipment to racers.

Pontiac's Indian was up to 421 cid and was tough. Four-bolt-main blocks were improved versions of the high-performance 389 of the year before, with more material cast in at critical points for added strength. Pontiac remained the industry leader in heavy-duty parts, and its new engine cranked out 405 HP from a compression ratio of 11:1 with a single Carter four-throat carburetor. The 421 received all-new heads with larger valves, now with 2.02-inch intakes and 1.76-inch exhausts. Dual 4-bbl-carb intakes were available, and exhaust manifolds were cast of aluminum. Pontiacs provided tough competition in 1962. The 421 was a top runner, especially at top speeds where Fords tended to run out of "breath."

Ford's cross-bolted-main 406 of that year was an outgrowth of stock-car racing as described earlier. Basically an improved hi-perf 390, it had 0.080-inch larger bores or 4.13 vs. 4.05 inches. Blocks for the 406 were cast from different patterns than those for standard engines in that they incorporated the heftier reinforcement and oiling features of the 375-HP 390. The major change was cross-bolting the number-2, -3 and -4 main-bearing caps. This prevented the inner two bolts on those caps from loosening which, in turn, prevented the block from cracking while under heavy stress loads of high-speed racing. Cross-bolting solved that problem and was used later on the legendary side-oiler 427.

The 406 had the same oiling setup of the solid-lifter 390, but the oil-pressure relief valve was upped to 70 psi rather than 55. Stronger—and heavier—connecting rods were used in the 406, requiring heavier crankshaft counterweights. The cranks were still nodular cast iron with the same journal dimensions as the 390, but were grooved for better oiling. A different harmonic balancer was used to dampen harmonics that could produce stresses high enough to break the crank.

The 406 also got new cylinder heads. Exhaust valves were

The 427-powered lightweight Galaxie fastback of '63 was a lot of car. Donald Farr Photo.

While A/Factory Experimental lightweight Galaxies thundered down the quarter-mile, B/FX cars also made a good showing. Courtesy Ford Motor Co.

increased to 1.625 inches and combustion chambers were reshaped. The 2.03-inch intake valves were the same as used on all previous big Fords. Compression ratio varied up to 11.4:1, and new exhaust manifolds were available for the 406. They, too, were cast-iron headers, but of a new shape.

Like the 390, the 406 also came in two versions, the 385-HP single 4-bbl-carb model and the tri-power at 405 HP. The single 4-bbl was a 600 cfm Holley, the three-carb model was rated at 900 cfm, again using progressive linkage to open the end carbs under full acceleration.

These were the sort of cars that Les Ritchey and Ford engineers prepared for NHRA's 1962 showdown at Indianapolis. A new class had emerged, Factory Experimental, and Mickey Thompson took A/FX with a V8-powered Pontiac Tempest at 115.68 mph in 12.66 seconds. Don Nicholson won B/FX in a Chevrolet at 113.63 mph in 12.93 seconds while Tom Strum took C/FX in another Chevy at 95.84 mph in 14.71 seconds. Stock Eliminator went to Hayden Proffitt's Chevy over the Ramchargers Dodge at 113.92 mph in 12.83 seconds. Top Super Stock class winner was Dave Strickler in another Chevy at 113.35 mph in 12.97 seconds, and from there on down, not a single Ford was class winner except in I/Stock. The A/Stock winning Ford was later disqualified for engine modifications. After running an A/S Mercury during the season, Tom Strum picked up the NHRA World Points Stock title after switching to a Chevrolet at Indianapolis.

The irony of Ford's quest to return to being the hotrodders' make was that GM had taken the wind out of Ford's sails with the 1957 AMA ban on factory racing; it was still being felt in 1962! But, by the end of that season, Dearborn brass was determined to change things for 1963.

FORD COMES BACK

The beginning of factory Ford's re-entry into drag racing in 1962 had not been auspicious. The late-in-the-season start was really a warm-up for 1963, the year Ford got moving. For the first time in years, Ford Motor Co. was first on the new-car scene with a package that got buyer's attention.

The '63-1/2 fastback Galaxie was a nicely styled car with lots of appeal; Chevrolets were almost ugly; Dodges and Plymouths were ugly. Chevy was hanging onto the 409; Chrysler would not re-introduce the Hemi until the next year; and Dearborn stunned the market with its new 427, a genuine fire-breathing performer that pushed Ford to the top of street performance, stock-car performance and drag performance alike.

The Atlanta assembly plant was tabbed to produce 50 special lightweight Galaxies equipped with high-performance 427s, topped with two 4-bbl carbs, rated at 425 HP at 6000 rpm. These cars received all sorts of weight-cutting items: fiberglass doors, hood, trunk lid and front end pieces; aluminum bumpers replaced steel, and all other items not necessary for racing were omitted. Thus stripped, a Galaxie lightweight topped the scale at around 3450 pounds. With Ford's soon-to-be-famous top-loader 4-speed transmission—also lightened with an aluminum case versus cast iron—lightweights were capable of running in the low 12s at around 118 mph.

Although very impressive, the fast Fords were just a little off the pace through the traps compared to other makes, which also had their own lightweights. Consequently, the lightweight Galaxie program didn't win big. However, winning was not the primary goal: Exposure was. But to win the NHRA Winternationals at Pomona, California, or the Nationals at Indianapolis would have been much savored icing on Ford's cake. The company's new image of high performance was paying off handsomely in sales, and Ford fans would've liked the wins.

A second version of the production 427 with a single 4-bbl carb was rated at 410 horses. Either setup made full-size

Cross-bolt main-bearing caps are indicated by bolt heads in side of block just above oil-pan flange. Cross-bolting made the 427 block strong. Ford was so confident of this engine that they offered it in Galaxies, selling 4978 in 1963. Courtesy Ford Motor Co.

With the muscle cars of the '60s, drag racing, that unique American motorsport, became a favorite. Ford's 427 wedge was a strong performer. Courtesy Ford Motor Co.

Fords into truly hot street cars. Steel-bodied fastbacks came in two versions: the Galaxie 500 and the 500XL, both known as the *Sports Hardtop*. All totaled, 100,500 Galaxie 500s were sold, and another 33,870 500XLs with a higher trim level found buyers. As mentioned in the "Fastbacks & Sideoilers" section, 4978 big Fords were 427 powered.

In production form, twin Holley 540-cfm carbs sat on top of a new cast-aluminum intake, and attention to good looks produced a variety of chromed pieces that made the engine compartment of a 427 Galaxie a handsome showcase of Ford power.

The stock factory rating of 425 HP was considered under-rated by most drag-racing fans; the competition engine with dual 600-cfm Holleys, higher compression ratio and other goodies certainly were.

At first, the only real competition for the 427 was from Pontiac with the 421. By the end of the year, it was just about all MoPar. However, at Pontiac, Knudsen was beating the Indian's drums with a new twist: Put a big engine, the 389 in this case, in a mid-size car and call it a *GTO*. The Mickey Thompson and Royal Pontiac V8 Tempest A/FX cars led the way. The theme proved to be a huge success that became the basis of the muscle-car outrage later. Notable among those was Ford's 427-powered ultra-drag machine, the *Thunderbolt*.

Frank Zimmermann was brought in to manage Ford's Special Vehicles program. He immediately set about organizing formal drag racing. The Fairlane Thunderbolt for '64 was one of his first projects. Second was the formation of the Ford Drag Council, composed of Les Ritchey and other top drivers. Each driver represented a dealer in a selected geographic area, to work the region for Ford exposure. The lightweight Galaxies and later Thunderbolts were their cars.

Restyled for '64, Fairlanes were handsome Sports Coupes. They became the basis of the lightweight, 427-powered Thunderbolts. With two 4-bbl carbs, engines produced about 525 HP.

The Thunderbolts were designed at Ford and built by Dearborn Steel Tubing. Eight of the first Thunderbolts were finalized by Ford and test driven for proper tuning on Ford's Dearborn proving grounds before shipment to their pre-scribed dealers. One was retained at Ford for testing purposes. Each car ran under 12.20 seconds in the quarter at over 120 mph. When sent out to barnstorm the strips of America, the A/FX T-Bolts were the class of drag racing. They were conceived as highly modified mid-size Fairlanes to show Ford engineering in the interest of promoting sales. Although 50 were required, 127 were eventually built. As a

Bill Lawton's famous Tasca Ford Thunderbolt from Rhode Island leaves the line against a Falcon Sprint. Factory Ford team competing in Winternationals at Pomona consisted of Don Nicholson, Tom Sturm, Ronnie Sox and Bill Shrewsberry. Factory stock eliminator was a match between Sox and Nicholson, Sox winning with 11.49 at 123.45. Sturm had previously won the 1963 A/Stock national points championship in a Mercury.

SOHC Hemi 427 made Bill's Speed Shop '57 'Bird a fast machine. Courtesy Ford Motor Co.

result, they ran in Super Stock rather than A/FX. These cars were fitted with either a strong 4-speed or a special Ford automatic built expressly for drag racing.

Thunderbolts were spectacular drag cars. The mere idea that they were factory built gave Ford immense prestige among fans who saw that Ford Motor Co. was serious about being their *Total Performance* company. Very purposeful looking, with their wide racing slicks at the rear, narrow tires up front, bubble hood to clear the high-rise induction setup, aluminum bumpers and ram-air ducting from the inner two headlights, the Thunderbolt in action with the 427 blasting through open exhausts was a sight to behold and hear, the sort that brought a lot of admiration from drag-racing fans.

Thunderbolts were built with many weight-reduction features to give about 3200 pounds. The ram-air 8V 427 was listed to be a production high-riser with 425 HP. But everyone seeing them run guessed more correctly that they surely developed about 500 horses to reach the low 12 seconds in the hands of Ritchey, Gas Ronda, Butch Leal, Bill Lawton, Hubert Platt and Phil Bonner. One interesting facet of the story is that, for just $3900, a full-spec factory-prepared Thunderbolt was available to any drag racer through Ford dealers. What a deal!

With the return of Chrysler's 426 Hemi, winners for most of '64 were still MoPar, but the Thunderbolts figured strongly in NHRA national competition by taking six of seven Divisional Championships. The Winternationals came down to a Thunderbolt shootout between Ronda and Leal. Ronda won with an 11.78/123.40 blast, just one of his many wins leading to his NHRA Top Stock Eliminator World Championship title that year. "Right out of the box," he pushed the George Newtell Downtown Ford Thunderbolt to 11.90 at 121 and turned a best of 11.60 at 124.38. His all-time

best Thunderbolt run was a healthy 11.47/125.34 after he switched to Russ Davis Ford sponsorship, the dealership he worked for. All the red cars he subsequently raced wore the Russ Davis banner throughout the remainder of his drag-racing career.

At the Nationals at Indianapolis, Leal took Super Stock honors with a thrilling 11.76/122.78 run against a '64 Plymouth. With that, the Thunderbolt saga was left behind for independents as Ford began concentrating on the more glamorous GT-40 and Indy 500 efforts in 1965. But Dearborn didn't leave drag racing behind. Instead of concentrating on Super Stock, factory racing centered on A/FX. That class generated more interest on the part of both fans and auto magazines that gave Ford drag racing a lot of exposure.

Although the 427 wedge proved to be an outstanding performer, A/FX racing in '65 was with the new Single Over Head Cam (SOHC) 427s, mostly in Mustangs, that were the forerunners of the present-day *funny car*. This new engine had shown 654 HP on Ford's dyno and was a side-oiler with a single chain-driven overhead cam on each bank. Like the original 427, it was intended for stock-car racing, but was not allowed by NASCAR. This was because it was a non-production engine. The next year, the SOHC was optional at a cost of $1963. The SOHC 427 produced substantially more power and proved to be Ford's ultimate drag-racing engine until the return of Ford in the '80s with the BOSS 429 introduced and highly improved for modern Pro Stock drag racing. It also proved to be the Chrysler Hemi's only real threat. Chevrolet didn't have an engine that could compete at this level. So, just as stock-car racing became a Ford versus MoPar showcase, so did drag racing.

Of all the Thunderbolts built, 19 are said to be accounted for today. And while the SOHC 427 (now ultra-rare) took off

Chain-driven single-overhead cams and hemi combustion chambers gave 427 cubic inches more power and higher rpm than wedge-head engine. The SOHC engine was never installed in production, but was available through Ford for racing. It produced almost 700 HP with carburetors on dyno as shown. Courtesy Ford Motor Co.

Lincoln-Mercury Division went into endurance runs and gained several notable achievements: A drive from the tip of South America to Alaska is one; the African Safari Rally of '64 was one that wasn't. Here, one of the cars crosses the equator over a mile high in Kenya. Courtesy Ford Motor Co.

in new directions for Ford, the 427 wedge—so well developed in the fast Thunderbolts—took over as Ford's most spectacular racing power plant. As the tale of the side-oiler unraveled over the years, it found a home in a variety of cars, from the NASCAR machines already seen to the king of sports cars—the sensational 427 Cobra—and twice in the LeMans-winning Gts. These endurance-racing Fords are the cars that sent shock waves through Europe's racing elite when they were beaten by a cast-iron stock-block engine found almost everywhere in America.

MUSCLE FORDS & MERCS

While Zimmermann was pushing Fords into the forefront of drag racing, Fran Hernandez at Lincoln-Mercury was working on Mercury. His plans produced Comets for all sorts of competition, including a 100,000-mile endurance run at Daytona, a durability trial from the southern tip of South America all the way to Alaska, and for a team of cars that competed in the 1964 East African Safari.

Then came drag racing, but Hernandez needed another man to handle it. Al Turner was given the task of shaping up Mercury drag cars. Between the two, the factory Comet team became the best and most successful in the country in terms of total wins. Although the Comets were similar to the Thunderbolts in concept, there were subtle differences. Thunderbolts raced with 7-inch rear-wheel widths and ran in Super Stock, while the Comets ran 10-inch rears and raced Factory Experimental.

At least 50 Comets were built with specifications similar to the Thunderbolts. Four were kept as factory cars for drivers Don Nicholson, Tom Sturm, Ronnie Sox and Bill Shrewsberry. Their cars proved quicker than anything on the circuit,

African Safari drivers Kim Mandeville and Peter Walker are cheered on by admirers. The Mercury team had five cars. Ford Motor Co. also participated in the Pure Oil Performance Trials of 1964 at Daytona with a Falcon, Comet, two Galaxie fastbacks, a Mercury Marauder fastback and a Fairlane. Courtesy Ford Motor Co.

Thunderbolts included, for a simple reason: Air intakes on the Comets were located at the leading edge of the hood. That configuration was better for picking up air than Ford's "bubble" hood because the intake was in a higher-pressure area. The advantage of about two-tenths of a second showed up best when Sox blasted an 11.08 in a warm-up for the

Nicholson set 11.05-second A/FX class record in this Comet. He lost only one match race in the '64 season, to teammate Ronnie Sox. Donald Farr Photo.

Mercury Cyclone styling became more sleek in '65 and gained tremendous recognition with the factory Comet drag cars of Jack Chrisman and Don Nicholson. Squire Gabbard Photo.

Winternationals at Pomona. That time was so superior that many factory-backed competitors didn't even unload their cars when it came showdown time. Predictably, the final round came down to Sox and Nicholson, with Sox winning with a 11.49. In exhibition races throughout the season, the pair remained unbeaten except when running against each other.

By 1964, performance was king, especially in the youth sector, and Mercury Comets fit perfectly. Not only were these fastbacks appealing in style, they were a size that fit the image young buyers wanted. Smaller cars with powerful engines, the more power the better as it turned out, became

the measure of a car in the '60s. Whether Ford or Mercury, if it had a 427 side-oiler, it was likely to be King Kong. Simply put, there were very few pure-stock engines that could match it.

Factory drag racing was big in those days. And one-upmanship would not allow other makes to let the Comets and Thunderbolts get all the publicity. Dodge, for one, added a new twist by building two special cars for one purpose: to be loud and fast to wow the fans. These were not Super Stocks or A/FX cars; they were nitro-burning, super-charged full-bodied cars, a type that was even closer to what eventually became the Funny Car. Hernandez called them *chargers*; the name stuck.

Jack Chrisman, the owner of the Shrewsberry Comet, answered the Dodge ploy with a better one. He soon became king of full-bodied racing on America's drag strips. Where the Chargers went, he went and beat them at their own game. Eventually, Dodge pulled the cars off the circuit, but by then, Chrisman and his Comet—called the *Super Cyclone*—were favorite attractions that commanded $1000 per weekend. Fans flocked to drag strips when the show was in town, and got to see the best drag-racing action available.

The Super Cyclone was a factory lightweight with further attention by Chrisman to make it lighter throughout, yet strong enough to take a blown, nitro-burning full-house 427 wedge engine mounted in the standard location. By today's standards, such a car is only mildly interesting; in 1964, it was incredible. A full-bodied car running under 10 seconds at around 160 mph was absolutely sensational!

This famous Comet has come to be recognized as the first true Funny Car when it received a blown, injected SOHC

Comet Super Cyclone, another illustrious home for Ford's famed 289. Squire Gabbard Photo.

Connie Kalitta, the first to get Ford's SOHC hemi 427, ran 7.85 seconds at over 200 mph. Ford engineers estimated engine produced 1607 HP at 8,500 rpm in AA/FD form. Kalitta turned a 7.17/218.43 to win the '67 Winternationals. Courtesy Ford Motor Co.

427 set back in the chassis a couple of feet. It took some development to get the *cammer* right, but when it was, the Super Cyclone in 1965 was awesome—a formidable drag-racing machine by any standard.

The story of the cammer began with Connie Kalitta of Mt. Clemens, Michigan. He received the first SOHC for tests in his AA/Fuel slingshot dragster and was mainly responsible for the improvements that made the engine a winner. In the winter of 1965 at Phoenix, he became the first man to break the so-called "200-mph barrier" in the quarter. It was done on the very first run of his cammer Ford fueler that cranked

out something over 1600 horsepower.

When the mighty MoPars came back with improved hemi power developed to beat the Ford cammers, Hernandez wanted something even better than the Super Cyclone. Again it was Chrisman who did the trick, and again it was Chrisman who astounded the drag-racing world. The new car was really a short wheelbase AA/Fuel dragster with an all-enclosing fiberglass body that looked like a Comet. The stock hood profile was retained by keeping the fuel-injection air intakes below the hood line to make the car appear stock. It ran first with a full body. Initially known as the *Mercury*

"Sneaky" Pete Robinson was the second drag racer to get Ford's SOHC hemi and faced Don Prudhomme in the NHRA Springnationals at Bristol. Prudhomme won Top Eliminator with a sensational 6.92 at 222.76. Prudhomme was the first drag racer to run under 7 seconds and turned in successive 6.99-, 6.97- and 6.92-second blasts in the finals. Courtesy Ford Motor Co.

The best efforts of Ford drag racers were generally overshadowed by lower-budgeted factory Mercury teams. One of the best was Jack Chrisman who pioneered funny cars. Here he is in his famous Cyclone GT-1 match racer exhibition car. Chrisman's best run of the time was an 8.32 at 184 mph during the Hot Rod magazine meet at Riverside. Courtesy Ford Motor Co.

Throughout the 1966 season, the factory Mercury Comet drag-racing team won 86% of their races. No other team came close. "Dyno" Don Nicholson wound up with an astounding record of 130 wins against 10 loses and had a match racing streak of 30 wins in a row. Courtesy Ford Motor Co.

Cyclone GT-1, because of Kendall oil sponsorship, it was later called the *Mercury Comet GT-1* when the top was removed. Only the cockpit opening was covered; otherwise it was topless.

In this form, the car was Mercury's lead exhibition vehicle, and when Chrisman turned 184 mph in 8.32 seconds, Comet domination was underway. Don Nicholson and "Fast Eddie" Schartman got similar cars, and with two stock-bodied Comets handled by other drivers, the Comet team proceeded to win 86% of its races in 1966. Nicholson was most successful with a record of 130 wins to 10 losses. Consistent times under 8.20 seconds in his 1750-pound missile gave Mercury tremendous popularity. Match racing the MoPars and exhibition runs drew huge crowds of spectators who came away with a healthy respect for the fast Comets.

Schartman and Ed Rachanski also raced factory-sponsored 427 pushrod Comets (20 were built). Although not as successful as hoped, the Comets were tall performers that really caught on with young buyers.

Along with these were 20 much less expensive 289-powered B/FX Comets. While the A/FXers were factory built, the B/FX cars were dealer options. These were assembly-line, steel-bodied Comets with regular serial numbers that went through Ford man Bill Stroppe's shop in Los Angeles. Here, they received extensive attention to weight reduction, topping each car out at about 2600 pounds. Engines were stock HiPo 289s; buyers provided the engine-performance hardware. Among them were Carroll Shelby's well-developed line of goodies for his Cobra and Shelby Mustangs.

Complete Weber equipped 289s were available that produced 395 HP at 7000 rpm. With further development for drag racing, the 289 was said to reach upwards of 450 HP with Webers. In this form the Comets were potent indeed, as shown by Doug Nash, who set a B/FX record of 11.30 at just

"Dyno" Don's Eliminator II of 1967 was powered by a fuel-injected SOHC Ford cammer. Car weighed 1875 pounds and ran consistent 8.10—8.70-second quarters at 175 mph. Early in the '67 season, Nicholson was running under 8 seconds. Courtesy Ford Motor Co.

under 125 mph in the quarter.

Fairlanes and Comets were mid-size cars in 1964 and '65, and while Fairlane styling got worse in '65, Comet lines got better. As a result, Fairlane sales sagged in spite of drag-racing successes, but Comet popularity improved when showroom Comet Cyclone GT fastbacks appeared. Comet sales no doubt benefited from all the ink the factory teams received, and the Cyclone GT combination of performance and styling was attractive to young buyers. With a 4-bbl Super 289 V8 rated at 225 HP, dressed with chrome-plated

Eight Falcon Sprints made up the Ford factory team for the 1964 Monte Carlo Rally. They were prepared in London, England, then won the most rigorous and prestigious rally in the world. Ford entry No. 49 took four trophies. Cars ran dual 4-bbl carbs and were among the first to give Europeans a taste of Ford's throaty V8s. Courtesy Ford Motor Co.

valve covers and other items, and an optional 4-speed and console between bucket seats, the rakish Cyclone GT was an attractive package with good performance. Mercury was leading the way in youth-oriented styling in this size car while Ford's new Mustang, introduced late in 1964, was a smash success. Small-bodied cars with hot engines were the rage.

One such combination was the inexpensive Falcon that had not built a solid reputation among the youth set. Introduced in the 1960 model year, Falcon began as a low-buck transporter, but with the coming of Ford's Total Perform-

ance program, when they received Ford's new small-block V8, Falcons became "hawks" with muscles and clawed their way up to become more interesting.

Along with the nicely styled Futura came the hot Sprint of 1963 in either a handsome fastback hardtop or ragtop. With the standard 260-cid *Fairlane* V8 and a 4-speed, the Falcon Sprint was a modest-priced car that offered good performance. In base 2-bbl 164-HP form, it was no fireball. But as HiPos with 260 HP—predecessor to the HiPo 289—it was hot.

Restyled from the initial bullet shape to a fastback box in 1964, Falcon drag cars largely took back seat to the factory T-Bolts and Comets. But they offered one feature not available in longer wheelbase cars: a short wheelbase that placed the engine closer to the rear for better weight transfer. Thus, Dearborn Steel Tubing was tapped to turn out two 427-powered A/FX Falcons that went to Holman & Moody for development to test the idea. Was a short wheelbase really better?

The cars were offered to the two most successful dealerships campaigning Fords. Dick Brennan won the honor of running the "Romy Hammes Ford" Falcon, and Phil Bonner was even better with the "Daddy Warbucks" car from Archway Ford of Baltimore, MD. These Falcon Futuras were fitted with fiberglass front fenders, front bumper, deck lid and a bubble hood with rear air intakes typical of Ford drag cars of the time. Their *high-riser* 427s with twin Holley 715s were said to produce over 550 HP at 7400 rpm from a compression of 14:1.

The same body style was carried over for 1965. By then, the norm for drag racing was wilder than ever as the top cars went more and more toward being Funny Cars. An example was the heavily modified Tommy McNeeley-sponsored fastback Falcon run by Hubert Platt, the "Sad Sack IV" from Texas. This car was similar to the Brennan and Bonner

1965 Sprint reflects change from rounded lines of '63 model to the squared-off look. Falcon Sprint was a quick, small fastback powered by 260-cid small-block driving through a 4-speed transmission. Squire Gabbard Photo.

Falcons, but had a solid-axle, leaf-spring front suspension and a nitro-burning 427.

These were fast Falcons. They were most often not winners, although sensational match racers. Factory Comets of Chrisman and Nicholson were the top guns, and MoPar hemis were making things tougher all the time. And, although Ford was still gaining on the lost ground brought about by McNamara's shutdown of Ford racing in accordance with the 1957 AMA ban, on the grass-roots level of street racing, Chevrolet had become the hotrodders' make.

By the mid-60s, the Ford Y-block was gone. It had never proven itself against Chevy's small-block. The expensive 427 side-oilers were being matched by Chevrolet's 396 and 427, which were brought over from truck service and developed for the performance enthusiast. Although the new 260-289-302 series of engines and the new 428 were excellent engines with a fast-growing assortment of hotrod parts and equipment from Ford, Shelby American and other aftermarket suppliers, it was all too little, too late. Ford had lost its once dominant position as the hotrodders' make.

The reason? It was simply that time had caught up with Henry Ford's lead, established with the flathead V8. Every make had more powerful OHV V8s by the '60s, and McNamara had helped their popularity along by taking Ford out of the performance race for a long time. Ford had not maintained a steady supply of similar engines over the years, as had been done with the Model-T 4-banger and flathead. In the days of those engines, there were few others for the hotrodder to choose from at the low-dollar level. But after the mid-50s, other makes had caught up. There were simply a lot of others to choose from.

Chevrolet gained ground steadily on the grass-roots level, as the small-block went from 265 cid in 1955 to 283, then 327 and 350 cubes by 1967, and on to 400 cubic inches—all with the same basic castings. Millions of small-block Chevys were in service all across America. Parts could be found in junk yards and speed shops everywhere. In the '70s, Ford management took the company out of the performance picture again. As a result, the Chevy small-block dominated all types of racing. Most of all, hotrodders had little to choose but Chevrolet.

As an example of Chevrolet's popularity growth from 1960 through '67, the total number of entries in NHRA's Summer Nationals was 7405 in from 46 to 92 classes. Chevrolet entries totaled 4303 cars, or 58% of the total. Ford entries came to 742, just 10%. Chevys won 296 class victories during those years, compared to Ford's 37. Thus, spectators were seeing a lot more of Chevrolet than Ford. Even though Ford was heavy into top class drag racing with name drivers who received a lot of press coverage, when spectators went home after a day of drag racing, they were most likely thinking about Chevys.

By 1969 and the early '70s, Ford had launched another line of engines, the 351 Cleveland (351C) and BOSS 302, a small-block with 351C type heads. When the BOSS 302 was dropped after 1970 with only two years in production, and when the BOSS 351 was dropped in '71 after only one year, Ford didn't have a performance engine. The 427 and BOSS 429

The 429 Cobra Jet and Super Cobra Jet Mercury Cyclone of 1970 continued the performance image of Ford and Mercury intermediates, but Dodge and Plymouth aero-wedges were the fastest cars that year. Courtesy Ford Motor Co.

were gone; the small-block 302 was still around and had been expanded to create the 351 Windsor (351W), but neither was a truly high-performance engine; the 428 Cobra Jet (CJ) and Super Cobra Jet (SCJ) were memories, and Ford high-performance parts development was nonexistent. There was little to be excited about from Ford, so the doldrums soon set in again.

In contrast, Chevrolet maintained its performance-parts availability and even promoted their use with annual publication of the *Chevrolet Power* manual that outlined how-to performance building for all applications, from drag racing to road racing to hot street setups.

It is true that the hotrod kids of the '60s had become family men or women of the '70s, so high-performance was not as significant a sales factor. OPEC also put a scare into everyone as gasoline prices skyrocketed during the "energy crisis" mid-70s, but GM held onto its performance interests while Ford bailed out. The typical car of the time became more of a necessary household appliance rather than a toy for fun. Econoboxes abounded. With them came the dark age of the automobile.

With the passing of the baby boom, manufacturers had to wait until the babies of the baby boomers came of age in the '80s for excitement to return to the automobile. With the return of good times in the '80s, Ford offered some of the most sophisticated and exciting cars ever. Ford Motor Co. went racing again, as we shall see in the final chapter. But once again, Chevrolet remained dominant at the grass-roots drag-racer level while Ford cleaned house in the top ranks.

INTERMEDIATES

The great surge of interest in high-powered cars that marked the '60s as the golden age of performance matured toward the last of that decade. Young buyers wanted lighter, smaller cars with as much engine as was available. As a

Ed Terry's 1966 427 Fairlane 500 out of Hayward Ford in California ran in NHRA Super Stock/B but, like most other intermediates, Super Stock was becoming a Mustang showcase. Courtesy Ford Motor Co.

Scoop extends to leading edge of 427 Fairlane hood. Change from earlier "bubble" hood, which picked up air at rear of bubble, increased air pressure at carburetor to improve quarter-mile times. Mercury Comets were first to use setup. Manufacturer's plate—**M** for manufacturer—indicates degree of Ford factory involvement in racing during this period. Courtesy Ford Motor Co.

result, the Mustang was a huge success. In larger models, but still not full-size sedans, the factories responded with intermediate-size cars with optional engines of around 400 cubic engines.

Ford produced one of the first true muscle cars with the 1964 Fairlane Thunderbolt. A muscle car came to be defined as an intermediate with a powerful engine, although any car with a powerful engine fell into the muscle-car category. The Mustang became one of the most sensational performers that America had ever produced.

Continuing with that theme, the 1966 Fairlanes and Mercury Comets were completely redesigned. These sporty, sleek two-door hardtops that looked the part of fast Fords were definite improvements over the earlier boxy models.

Fairlane styling changed from '63 to '64, and again in '66. The '67 GT-A model, foreground, continued the smooth lines introduced that year. Bucket seats with console, four-speed transmission and 335 HP from the 390 GT engine resulted in a stylish, strong-running Ford.

The 425-HP 427 side-oiler with two 4-bbl carburetors was an option in '67 Fairlanes—a tight fit and lots of performance. Squire Gabbard Photo.

Interior of '67 427 Fairlane: Floor-mounted shifter controls Ford's famous top-loader four-speed transmission. It could handle punishment dished out by the 427. Squire Gabbard Photo.

Super Stock Fairlanes ran fast and furious in '67. Courtesy Ford Motor Co.

Their swept-back rear pillars and graceful body lines produced a striking design that appealed to the public.

Fairlane and Comet suspension improvements included stronger, higher-rate springs for the rigors of high performance. And their engine compartments were widened to accept bigger engines. The previous Galaxie designation of 500 and 500XL was shifted to the Fairlane line. And new for 1966 were the GT and GTA big-block-powered cars. The GT was the manual-shift version, three- or four-speed, while the GTA—A for automatic—received Ford's new Cruise-O-Matic Sport Shift, the C-6 built for either manual or automatic shifting.

Both cars received Thunderbird Special 390s that came with a performance cam, more efficient cast-iron intake and other refinements that boosted output to an advertised 335 HP at 4600 rpm from the standard 315 horse 390.

Hardtop or convertible GT and GTA Fairlanes, along with similar Comet Cyclones, were nicely styled on the inside with bucket seats, console and sporty steering wheel, a well thought-out grand-touring package that put Ford and Mercury street performance in a class with the best standard-engine cars of the time.

Unfortunately, Ford did not offer additional performance equipment for the 390, so its single 4V 335 showroom horses found the going tough against other makes that offered more powerful versions of stock engines. The 389-cid Pontiac GTO, 400-inch Olds 442, Chevelle 396 and 401-inch Buick GS were strong street cruisers that kept Ford from winning much in the street wars.

The stars of the muscle-car outrage were the street Hemi

Jerry Harvey in Paul Harvey Ford 427 Fairlane was a favorite in Ford's intermediate. Courtesy Ford Motor Co.

Plymouth and Dodge intermediates with a factory rating of 425 HP. To counter the MoPar and GM problem, a limited number of 427-powered 500 and 500XL Fairlanes were produced. Offered in single-4 (410 HP) and dual 4-barrel (425 HP) configurations with Ford's tough top-loader 4-speed, the 427 Fairlanes were truly hot street machines straight off the showroom floor. Unlike the Thunderbolts that were meant for factory drag racing, these Fairlanes were street bombers that gave Ford a healthy measure of respect among grass-roots fanatics of the muscle-car era. Today, they are among the most sought after Fords ever built.

Knowing that the best air-scoop design was that for the earlier Mercury Comets, the hood of the 427 Fairlanes had a prominent intake at the leading edge. This feature alone became a cult symbol that immediately identified the car as a 427. Everyone who knew what the 427 Fairlane could do maintained a healthy respect for the cars. In those days of skinny tires, any big block could ignite rear rubber almost at

John Elliot, just 17 at the time, on his way to winning the '68 NHRA Winternationals Super Stock crown in the Sandy Elliot 427 Comet. Factory rated at 410 HP with a single 4-bbl, John ran a best of 12.57 at 113.48 mph. He went on to almost win the Eliminator title, but blew the rear axle at the line in the final round. He had already beaten Wiley Cossey's B/S Chevrolet, the 1966 Winternational Junior Stock Eliminator. Courtesy John Elliot.

will; a 427 Fairlane could simply shred the tires in one pass.

Lower-powered versions of the cars continued with the 289 on down to the standard 6-cylinder. The 289 versions weighed around 2850 pounds; the big blocks topped the scales at upwards of 3350 pounds. The gain of nearly 500 pounds showed up in widely different handling as the big

Holding the Super Stock trophy, John Elliot was the first Canadian to win a major NHRA national, and did so as the A/Stock Automatic national record holder. Sandy Elliot Ltd. was the oldest Ford-Mercury dealership in Canada. Courtesy John Elliot.

Available in '68 Fords, Fairlanes and Comets, was the 4-bbl 427. Note how cross-bolts engaged main-bearing caps. Courtesy Ford Motor Co.

"Fast Freddie" Lorenzen's Fairlane at Riverside: Fords won six of the top 11 NASCAR races in '67. Mario Andretti won Daytona in a Ford averaging 146.926 mph. Lorenzen's Fairlane was the only other car on the winning lap with Andretti, and Fords led 161 of the 200 laps. Lorenzen was Ford's top major race winner, with a career total of 12 superspeedway wins through the '67 season to lead all drivers in top Grand National Division victories. By that year, Ford had won 41 of 101 NASCAR races on its major tracks: Daytona, Darlington, Atlanta, Charlotte, Riverside and Rockingham. Overall, from 1955 through '67, Fords won 201 of NASCAR's 667 races. Courtesy Ford Motor Co.

blocks were straight-line warriors while the small-blocks had much better road manners. But it wasn't good handling that attracted the attention of muscle-car buyers. Simply put, it was straight-line "fast" that counted.

On the nation's drag strips, Ford's 427 was again a proven weapon in 1966, but rule changes caused some problems that forced drivers to compete in factory experimental rather than stock classes, against all sorts of full-bore drag machines like the SOHC Mustangs and Comets. It wasn't until the following year, 1967, that the 427 was once again placed in the stock classes.

Another aspect of the intermediate story involves stock-car racing where the shorter wheelbase, narrower Fairlanes gave Ford stockers an edge in aerodynamics over the full-size Galaxies. Rule changes for stock-car racing settled on holding MoPar Hemi engines to a single 4-barrel, and allowing neither Ford's SOHC 427 or the 8V 427-wedge high riser. However, the similarly equipped medium riser produced as much power as the high riser, so Ford engines were not at all hampered even though the MoPars had the potential for substantially more power.

Independent builder Bud Moore was the first to successfully exploit the intermediate-size stocker. He showed it to be the future of stock-car racing when Darel Dieringer drove the Moore prepared Comet to victory in the 1966 Southern 500, averaging 114.83 mph. Clearly, the smaller cars had an edge that could be exploited. The first Fairlane NASCAR victory was taken by Lorenzen in the Old Dominion 500 at Martinsville, Virginia, where he averaged almost 2.5 mph more than Junior Johnson's big Ford win of the previous year. "Fast Freddie" went on to win the American 500-miler at Rockingham, North Carolina, with an average

Formula-1 World Driving Champion and Indy 500 winner, Jimmy Clark, tried stock-car racing. The one and only time was at Rockingham. Courtesy Indianapolis Motor Speedway Museum.

almost 3.5 mph faster than Curtis Turner's winning big Ford the year before.

For 1967, few changes were made in the Fairlane and Comet lineup. The GT and GTA remained, along with the 500 and 500XL models, but the 390 was replaced with the 289 as the standard engine in the GT series. The 427 wedge was still offered and, although the SOHC was finally looked upon with favor by NASCAR, the faithful side-oiler was continued as the mainline stock-car racing engine.

However, a new development for the 427 was the advent of *tunnel-port* heads and 8-barrel intake that increased airflow to combustion chambers, giving 30 HP more. Previous 427

Available in the '69 Cyclone and Torino was the 428CJ backed up by a C-6 automatic. Courtesy Ford Motor Co.

The 351 Cleveland was a very durable engine with tremendous performance potential.

FORD ENGINES

Perhaps the lesson of the 1957 AMA ban was learned well, as Ford Motor Co. ventured heavily into engine research and development to keep pace with competitors. By the mid-60s, Ford performance in stock-car racing had well out-stripped all GM cars, and the highbanks was a Ford versus MoPar show. AA/Fuel drag racing was also exclusively Ford versus MoPar in the major NHRA national events. By 1967, Ford's SOHC 427 engine split two each, with Chrysler Hemi-haulers in the top four NHRA events of that year.

However, Fords were almost non-existent in Super Stock class wins. A few Chevys were sprinkled in among the MoPars as most Super Stock class winners wore the pentastar. It was in these types of classes—the racing that fans most identified with—that Ford effected a turn-around. Beginning in 1968 with the Cobra Jet Mustangs, Ford made a push that by 1970 bagged the majority of Super Stock wins, page 132.

This was done through aggressive engine research and development to produce reliable engines that, in many cases, became serviceable passenger-car engines. The 427 side-oiler is an example. That engine won two straight LeMans 24-Hours victories and so upset the French rules committee that it and all over 5-liter engines were banned. Within the framework of the under 5-liter rule, Fords won two more LeMans 24-Hours victories with small-block V8s that were also modified passenger-car engines.

How it was done involved engines that have become legendary over the years; the 427 side-oiler, Hi-Po 289, BOSS 302 and DOHC Indy (and Formula 1) engines are good examples. It also involved engines that have been forgotten, like the SOHC 289, 3-valve SOHC 302 and Calliope 427, all produced in the mid-60s.

W. D. "Bill" Innes rose from Chief Engineer of Ford's Engine and Foundry Division to Vice President of Manufacturing. He became the driving force behind Ford's experimental engine development. The Ford motto, *Total Performance*, was no nonsense; it was a solid commitment to competition, and to be competitive required a solid commitment to engine R&D.

Bill Gay replaced Innes as Chief Engineer, Engine and Foundry, and was responsible for the Indy V8 that put America's foremost race on a decidedly Ford course after winning three in a row by 1968. Tom Landis, Special Engine Engineering Dept., pointed to future Ford engines having three valves per cylinder—two intake and one exhaust. However, we know now that future Ford engines retained two valves per cylinder and that four per cylinder has become rather common in a variety of cars in the mid-80s.

Looking back to 1968, the experimental engines that didn't make it involve simple reasons; they didn't fit the requirement of economical production. Still, the idea of an SOHC 289 is intriguing. Using the stock 289 block, heads fitted with a single

The 289 grew up to be a 302. The 302 has lots of hotrodding potential. Many Windsors were produced, making them readily available. This basement-built job is a good example of low-cost power for use in a vintage road racer.

GR-7 Can-Am Car is based on Mk IV chassis with unique bodywork and power by a three-valve heads, twin in-block camshaft Calliope. Note divided, unsprung wing. Outboard wing supports mounted to suspension uprights. Courtesy Ford Motor Co.

Gilmer-type belt-driven overhead cam succeeded in one performance objective: a higher, more reliable rpm range. Dyno tests showed around 300 HP at 6500 rpm. However, intake ports were not modified to take advantage of pushrod absence, so airflow characteristics were not improved over stock. Retooling heads meant also retooling the intake manifold. So the gain achieved did not offset the cost involved and benefits obtained. A simpler approach was an engine of larger displacement, the quickest way to more horsepower.

Thus, the three-valve SOHC 302: Born of the SOHC 427, the SOHC 302 never got far along in characterizing the engine, although most parts were tested and design parameters were well developed. The 3-valve, tunnel-port head achieved what the SOHC 289 didn't, but the advantages of the engine were not obvious since the standard internal-cam tunnel-port 302 showed good results in Trans-Am sedan racing in early 1968. Ford's eye toward racing was also tempered with the knowledge that rules frequently were changed when a particular advantage tended to dominate. See "Ohio George" Montgomery section, page 122, for an example.

Another example was the fate of the three-valve per cylinder, dual-overhead-cam *Calliope* 427. Ford won the 24-Hours of LeMans in 1967 with the standard 427-side-oiler-powered GT Prototype class Mk IV. Even before the LeMans rules committee "outlawed" the engine, Ford was developing the

Calliope for another thrust at LeMans in 1968. Then the rules changed; prototypes were limited to 3 liters (183-cu.in.) maximum, and the Calliope had no place to race other than Can-Am.

That ruling also caught Enzo Ferrari by surprise; he was developing his 330 P3 and P4 prototypes with large-displacement engines. The red machines had made the '67 24-Hours a close and exciting race, finishing 2-3, a few miles behind the winning Ford. New rules allowed cars in Sports Car class to run up to 5-liter (305-cid) engines. Ford's GT-40 had been built in sufficient quantity to qualify for that class. A single GT-40 won twice, proving that Ford had a better idea, even without the exotic Calliope.

The Calliope was developed to produce 630 HP at 6300 rpm, about 130 HP more than the tunnel-port 427 in the Mk IV. What made the engine unusual was its over/under, in-the-block dual-camshaft layout. Without an endurance racing program to continue on, the Calliope was tested in a modified Mk IV chassis built for Can-Am racing. This car, the G7-A, actually raced a time or two. But the overall Calliope program came to a halt when the prototype of what became the BOSS 429 was developed, page 120.

intake manifolds routed the intake-manifold runners between the pushrods in the conventional manner. The tunnel-port design gave a straighter shot from carburetor to combustion chamber through large round ports, as opposed to rectangular. To accomplish this, rather than routing the runners around the pushrods, they were straightened and the pushrods ran through the center of the large, round runners. The ports were sealed with tubes through which the pushrods operated.

The tunnel-port setup was a racing-only engine and was not offered in Fairlanes or Comets. In fact, they were not strictly NASCAR legal—and Chrysler screamed about it—but were allowed anyway and, in this form, the venerable 427 was more potent than ever. At the start of the '67 season, Ford fielded the smallest number of stockers in years.

In the season opener at Riverside, favorite Dan Gurney went out with mechanical problems, but hard-charging Parnelli Jones came through to victory with the Holman & Moody Fairlane. Ford advertising was quick to act on this win and openly advertised the 427 Fairlane. Mario Andretti captured the February running of the Daytona 500 in a Holman & Moody Fairlane. Lorenzen took 2nd for a Ford and Holman & Moody 1-2 sweep. The next super-speedway contest at Atlanta in April saw Cale Yarborough and Dick Hutcherson with another 1-2 Fairlane victory.

At this point, it was clear that the smaller Fairlanes powered by tunnel-port 427s were going to clean house in stock-car racing. Consequently, Chrysler threatened to quit altogether because NASCAR rules let Ford run new-technology heads and intakes in smaller cars while MoPars could run only 404 cubes with single 4-bbls rather than dual 4-bbls on a 426-cid Hemi they built in production. Then, in another change of rules, MoPars were again the equal of Ford's intermediates, and Richard Petty went on to take his Plymouth to the greatest season ever in NASCAR racing with 27 wins. Ford accounted for only 10 wins that year.

On the strips, the 427 Fairlanes and Comets found the going tough. By 1967, they were classified as Super Stock/B. Because of this, in all four of the NHRA national showdowns, not a single Super Stock class was won.

However, at the NHRA Winternationals at Pomona, the Top Fuel Eliminator was Connie Kallita in an AA/FD SOHC Ford rail with a sensational 7.173-second, 218.43-mph blast. And the factory experimental class was all Ford. S/XS went to Don Nicholson's Comet (8.56 at 170.45 mph), A/XS was taken by Hubert Platt's Mustang (8.49 at 171.42), B/XS saw Bill Lawton's Falcon a winner (8.79 at 168.22) and C/XS was grabbed by Ken McLellan's Falcon (10.86 at 127.47 mph).

At the Springnationals held in Bristol, Don Prudhomme's AA/FD SOHC Ford dragster posted an even more sensational 6.92-second record dash at 222.76 mph, and factory experimental was Ford in three out of four classes. Another Comet, the STP-Steffey-Rupp machine, took the class (8.30 at 166.09 mph), Tom Grove's Ford took A/XS (Experimental Stock) (8.29 at 170.13), B/XS went to Shirl Greer's Dodge and C/XS fell to Jerry Harvey's Ford (10.92 at 127.47).

The Nationals at Indianapolis saw Don Garlits and Chrysler taking Top Fuel Eliminator. It was not a good day for Ford

The wedge-head, ram-air 428 SCJ powered Cyclone Super CJ was Mercury's answer to the Ford Torino. Courtesy Ford Motor Co.

because almost all eliminators were other makes. Only George Montgomery's AA/Gas Mustang—see the Mustang section for this car—came through. The Super Stock/B win by Ed Terry's '66 427 Fairlane was disqualified for having parts that were not registered with NHRA, although they were legal super-stock items. The class then went to a Plymouth.

Round four, the World Finals in Tulsa, was another dark day for Ford, as Jerry Harvey's 10.76 second win in C/XS was one of very few Ford wins.

Drag racing had grown tremendously by 1967. The competition was fierce. All sorts of organizations had sprung up; even Hot Rod magazine held its own championship at Riverside. The only super-stock Ford win went to Don McCain with a 12.42 at 116.42 mph run in SS/C.

Ford's intermediates captured a fair portion of stock-car racing action, and were successful in the marketplace where Fairlane 500, 500XL, GT and GTA production reached 158,978 in 1966. Only about 60 were 427-powered. Production the next year was off considerably as big-block Mustangs, new for 1967, took potential Fairlane buyers. Comet sales declined in '67 as Lincoln-Mercury featured the new Cougar and let the Comet slide.

New for '68 were redesigned Fairlanes that were almost full-size cars. The smaller size was gone and a new name appeared, Torino. In fastback form looking somewhat like a scaled-up '67 Mustang, Torinos became very popular, both on the street and on stock-car highbanks. By all measures, the Torino/Fairlane was a family sedan, even if the top model was called the GT and came with bucket seats, console and floor shift.

Also new for '68 was Ford's 302 small-block V8, a stroked 289. In Torino/Fairlanes, the 302 was relegated to grocery getting while the aged 390 hung on for another year. Rated at 325 HP in top form with a single 4-barrel carb, it, too, was no storming Ford. Beginning the year was the tough 427 detuned to 390 HP at 5600 rpm. But it was soon dropped as an

LeeRoy Yarbrough on his way to winning the World 600 at Charlotte: His Cyclone Spoiler II averaged 134.361 mph to win NASCAR's longest race. Yarbrough won six major NASCAR races in either Fords or Mercs. Courtesy Ford Motor Co.

For 1969 NASCAR season, Ford introduced the aero-nose Talladega and Mercury Cyclone Spoiler II to do combat on the high banks. The Talladega got its name from the new ultra-fast Alabama International Motor Speedway at Talladega. Cars were not big sellers due to their austere appointments, but made up for it on the tracks with 26 wins and another Manufacturers' Championship for Ford. Courtesy Ford Motor Co.

option and replaced by the new 428 Cobra Jet.

The 428CJ was under-rated by the factory, 335 HP at 5400 rpm, although the same engine in big Fords, milder yet, was advertised at 340 HP. Lower ratings helped Fords in drag-racing classifications. In later years, it was learned that the Cobra Jet actually produced around 410 HP. Basically, the Cobra Jet is the same two-bolt-main FE big block that had powered big Fords since 1966, but with 427 heads and intake for improved breathing. The combination worked very well, and the new styling accounted for a huge increase in Fairlane sales.

Mercury was still a Ford challenger, but instead of one name on those cars, the Mercs wore Comet, Montego or Cyclone. The fastback Cyclones proved to be almost 2 mph faster in Daytona testing. With factory cars in both NASCAR and USAC stock-car racing, the aerodynamic cars were formidable rockets. Racing showed them to be almost 8 mph faster than factory cars of the year before. At Daytona, the fast Fords took four of the top-five positions. Cale Yarborough won, averaging 143.251 mph.

Chrysler was still complaining about being required to run a single 4-barrel against the two 4-barrel Fords; NASCAR gave in. Even so, Fords won 20 events to top all makes, 16 by David Pearson, who took the drivers' championship. A.J. Foyt drove Jack Bowsher's Torino to the USAC crown, and Benny Parsons took the ARCA title to give Ford top honors in all three stock-car series.

1968 was a very good year for Ford Motor Co. Its three stock-car-racing crowns were joined by the Cobra Jet super-stock championship Mustangs that dominated NHRA drag racing. In Europe, the Gulf-Ford GT-40 team also won the 24-Hours of LeMans and World Championship to give Ford its greatest year.

AERO-BOSS

Even though winning in a big way, Ford engineering wasn't standing still. A lot of behind-the-scenes work was

going on at both Ford and Chrysler. Ford had better chassis development while Chrysler could get more power from their 426 Hemi. Time was passing the 427 by as a new movement brought about a new engine to fend off the aged, but ever-so-strong Hemi.

The *Blue Crescent 429*, better known as the *BOSS 429*, was more powerful and more modern. It was developed from the 385 series of 429 and 460 engines of 1968 that went into big Fords, Thunderbirds and Lincolns. With its massive new semi-hemi heads, the BOSS 429 was the most advanced engine on the Grand National trail. Although an excellent engine, it was raced for just two years; the 427 remained competitive after six. That wasn't due to a fault with the 429; it was a sudden change of direction at Dearborn. Ford wasn't racing any more as of late 1970, and the doldrums set in again. Today, the BOSS is back in all sorts of racing.

However, for the two years the BOSS 429 roared around the big ovals in factory cars, it was a strong winner, especially 1969. Better aerodynamics was the main feature that year. As Ford and Chrysler steadily upped the stakes, Chevrolet was left in the dust. Chrysler was on the aero trail and marketed a special-edition Dodge, the Charger 500, built in just enough numbers—500—to qualify as a production car. However, its special treatment wasn't enough.

The BOSS 429 in new aerodynamic packages, the Ford Talladega and Mercury Cyclone Spoiler II, was practically unstoppable that year. David Pearson won his third driving championship in a Holman & Moody Ford—1966 and '68 were the others—and LeeRoy Yarbrough became king of the super-speedways in Junior Johnson's Ford.

One got away, though, as Richard Brickhouse in a Dodge won the inaugural Talladega 500, the namesake of the Ford stocker. Cale's Cyclone won at Atlanta and LeeRoy's Ford scorched the World 600 at Charlotte with a 134.361-mph average. He drove a Mercury to win the Rebel 400 and a Ford to win the Southern 500, both at Darlington. Then the Daytona 500 fell before his Ford, and he also won Daytona's

To commemorate the '69 model year, Mercury brought out the red and white Cale Yarborough Special package on the Cyclone Spoiler—without aero-nose. It was followed later in the year with this blue and white Dan Gurney Special. Courtesy Ford Motor Co.

Ford's factory team for '69: David Pearson (front), won his third championship for Ford ('66, '68 and '69) and later became the second leading all-time NASCAR winner with 105 victories to Richard Petty's 200 earned through 1985. To the left, Cale Yarborough later won three straight championships and became third all-time NASCAR winner with 83. Upper left, the King, Richard Petty—in a rare Ford year. Upper right, LeeRoy Yarbrough. Lower right, Donnie Allison. The car: Talladega. The engine: BOSS 429. Courtesy Ford Motor Co.

sequel, the Firecracker 400. Donnie Allison's Ford won the second 500 miler at Charlotte. Once the Ford Talladega, a Torino with an aero nose, was legalized by NASCAR, there was no stopping the Fords and Mercurys. Ford built 754 Talladegas and 519 Cyclone Spoiler II Mercs, and took another championship in '69 with 26 speedway victories.

In response, Chrysler upped the stakes for 1970 with the wildest stocker ever, the "winged wonders from Chelsea"— the Plymouth Superbird and Dodge Daytona. These cars received extended and highly aerodynamic front ends along with stabilizing struts and a wing at the back. Ford was no match for these super-slick MoPars that became recognized as the most stable high-speed stock cars of their time.

Buddy Baker was the first man ever to exceed 200 mph on a closed course. He did so in a winged Dodge going 200.447 mph at Talladega. Eight months later, Bobby Isaac went even faster, 201.104 mph. Even so, it was Donnie Allison's '69 Talladega that won the 1970 World 600. LeeRoy Yarbrough's '69 Cyclone won the second Charlotte feature that year. The Talladega and Cyclone Spoiler II, built only in 1969, were still strong as shown by David Pearson's Ford winning the Rebel 400 at Darlington and Allison's winning average of 162.2 mph in the Firecracker 400 at Daytona. A.J. Foyt won the road-racing classic at Riverside in a Ford and, as the 1970 season closed, it had been a pretty good year. But the great factory racing went away when Bunkie Knudsen was ousted as Ford boss.

Although factory money dried up, the great tradition of stock-car racing went on in spite of factory pull-outs. The good ol' boys didn't forget how to build cars and go fast. What happened in Dearborn was that Ford soon found itself in the same position it was in a decade before—losing ground to Chevrolet. But now there were other concerns. The oil barons of OPEC saw a way to concentrate the world's

BOSS 429 production engine was Ford's heavy-weight fighter in 1969 and '70, and has returned with SVO Motorsport aftermarket equipment today. Called the HO Cobra Jet, the engine was rated at only 375 HP at 5200 rpm. Basically a 385-series 429 with canted-valve heads, the crescent-shaped combustion chambers resulted in the name Blue Crescent being used to refer to the engine; semi-hemi was another name. Courtesy Ford Motor Co.

In the BOSS 429's only Can-Am racing experience, the light-alloy 494-cid engine was special. The aluminum chassis and body was built by Alan Mann Racing—serial number AMR/CA/1001—in England, and prepared and campaigned by Holman & Moody to compete with Chevy powered McLarens, Chaparrals and Lolas. The car was well developed, but unsuccessful in Ford's limited bid to oust Chevrolet from Can-Am racing. Fuel injection gave the engine around 740 HP that was delivered via a Hewland LG600 5-speed transaxle to 24-inch-wide Goodyears. Acceleration of 0-100 in 5 seconds and 195 mph maximum was not enough to win. Driver Frank Gartner is shown here in the car's first race, which was at Riverside. World Champion Jack Brabham took a third at College Station, Texas. That was about it for the BOSS 429 in Can-Am racing. Courtesy Ford Motor Co.

wealth in their own hands, and racing took a nose-dive as costs and fuel "waste" came into question.

Thus, any form of racing became suspect for a time, but with the passing of another decade, Ford would be back with fast, aerodynamic Thunderbirds. Until then, from 1973 through the '82 season, Ford won the Talladega 500 only twice: Buddy Baker's Ford win in '75 that was 18 mph off the pace of the previous year, and Neil Bonnett's Mercury win in 1980 at a healthy average of 166.894 mph. Atlanta International saw only three Ford wins in its 20 races during that period. Mercury won four; Ford won only once in Charlotte's World 600, Bonnett's 1982 win. His win in the Southern 500 of '81 was Ford's only Darlington win for a decade. Bobby Allison's win at Daytona in '78 looked good

Modern Ford Collector has a lot of interesting Fords to choose from. Fast Fords have always been popular.

when he averaged 159.730 mph, but that was the only Ford win in the 500, and Ford was winless in the Firecracker 400.

That's the way it went. Ford rarely won in stock-car racing; GM cars won more than half of the races entered. Mercury won a few along the way, more than Ford did. It wasn't until the coming of the aero-Bird and Ford's renewed commitment to racing that Fords again returned to taking the checkers on the highbanks.

FORD DIEHARDS

After 1970, Ford racing fell back to diehards who were "hung out to dry," but were able to show a good deal of Ford performance in spite of little support from the factory. Factory performance parts inventories steadily declined and the excellent beginnings shown in the BOSS 302, 351C and BOSS 429 engines rapidly tapered off to nothing. The 428 and 429CJ, and the more powerful SCJ variants, were strong runners in the early part of the '70s. However, without continuing factory involvement in heavy-duty-parts development, Ford enthusiasts had little in the form of true new-car performance to brag about or stocks of parts to buy for building faster street machines.

In contrast, Chevrolet continued its performance-parts program. They also kept in print and regularly revised their *Chevrolet Power* manual, thus keeping "bow-tie" racers up to date on how to make their Chevys perform better for many types of competition.

The 1970s were generally a dark time in the legacy of performance cars. Without factory involvement, the enthusiasm shown by fans for road racing declined to races with few spectators. Fords in drag racing showed some bright spots, though, and the Hemi MoPars that emerged as nearly overwhelming in 1971 and '72 found the going tough as the decade progressed. By then, aftermarket suppliers offered all sorts of parts, including aluminum engine blocks and heads. Highly competitive cars could be built from mail-order sources and builders could build practically any type of race car.

Ford of Europe sparkled in mid-decade with the last Ford win at LeMans, the culmination of the glorious Gulf-Ford association that Britisher John Wyer had developed in the late '60s. In America's SCCA road racing, the potential of Carroll Shelby's 427 Cobra was shown when a private-entry 427 Cobra won the 1973 SCCA A/Production National Championship. Chevrolet Camaros won A/Sedan championships eight years in a row, but the potential of the BOSS 302 Mustang was brilliantly shown by Texan Danny Moore when he won the 1979 A/S championship.

Moore was one of a few Ford diehards who continued the Shelby GT-350 legacy and raced his '65 GT-350 to Southwest region B/Production championships in 1969, '70 and '71. He then purchased an ex-Bud Moore BOSS 302. After a thorough rebuild, the car was entered in the Sebring 12-Hour, where the Moore/McCullough team finished 6th overall, completing 210 laps at an average speed of 91 mph. Although a strong finish only 16 laps behind the winning Porsche, the Mustang ended up 2nd in class behind the class-winning Camaro, two laps ahead.

"Winged wonders" from Chelsea eclipsed everything that came before them, including aero Talladegas and Cyclone Spoiler IIs. Buddy Baker, shown, became the first man to turn a closed-course average speed of over 200 mph—200.447 mph at Talladega. Note long nose and wing. These were available on production 1970 Dodges and Plymouths. Courtesy Ford Motor Co.

In the Southwest region, Moore campaigned the Mustang through 1979 to win the regional championship. In 1978, the team finished 2nd in the National run-offs at Road Atlanta, and sights were set for the championship the next year. The season went well and the old BOSS 302 Mustang, running a 351, was gridded 4th at the start. At the flag, Moore shot into 3rd behind two Camaros. The lead car blew its engine on the second lap and the second Camaro had a flat. Suddenly, Moore was in the lead, where he stayed to take the checkered flag, the first Ford win in almost a decade. There were only two Mustangs in the field dominated by Camaros, and the second Ford finished 7th overall, with a 305-inch engine—an excellent showing indeed. Through 1980, this finish was among the slim highlights of Ford racing.

In 1980, SCCA's B/Production class saw a few Mustangs around the country. That was the last year of A/Production, so B/P became the top class in '81. The 1980 run-offs at Road Atlanta saw Phil Bartelt of Milwaukee running an ex-Bud Moore BOSS 302 to 4th overall after tieing the Central division. It was about then that Ford Motorsports came alive and Ford Motor Co. got back into racing. The Dearborn giant was awakening from a slumber that had kept Ford fans asking "why?" for a long time.

Just as in road racing of the '70s, only a few Fords were competitive in drag racing. The records show that Chrysler's domination of about all of the top classes in the early years left few wins for other makes. One diehard that always seemed to be competitive was Don Nicholson, who campaigned a strong Maverick in Super Stock. The field was light at the AHRA Grand American held in January of '71 at Lions drag strip in Long Beach, CA. Nicholson worked through the entries to take Super Stock Eliminator with a 9.81-second pass. Kenny Lughton's Chevy big-block-powered '56 T-Bird took Competition Eliminator in the amateur ranks with 9.97 at 132.93 mph.

Ford's Torino GT with 429 SCJ engine was a real muscle-car street bruiser. Super Stock *magazine tested a Torino Cobra, coming up with 13.63 seconds at 105.9 mph in the quarter.*

AHRA re-factored Super Stock class by changing the 7 lb/cubic inch rule that included hemi, cammer and wedge engines. But when wedges were given a 6.8 lb/inch break, it instantly gave them a chance and Chevys rolled up a number of Eliminator titles. Throughout the AHRA season, not a single Ford won Eliminator after Nicholson's initial victory. There were strong Fords, though. Wayne Gapps' BOSS 429 Maverick running 9.7s is an example, but top wins were few.

The International Hot Rod Association (IHRA) had been established by then, and was holding its own races that would become the major drag races in the southeast in a few years. Unfortunately, that year had no Ford Eliminators in the IHRA Pro-Am at Rockingham, and Spring Nationals at Bristol.

NHRA had already divided the pros and amateurs into ProStock and Super Stock and Stock Eliminators. And just as 1970 had been a good Ford year, Canada's super-consistent Barrie Poole in Sandy Elliot's '69 notchback Mustang nailed down a SS/H class win, then snuffed Jim Clark's Hemi to win Super Stock Eliminator with a fine 11.28/121.62 win in the Winternationals at Pomona. Ford teammate, John Elliot, Sandy's son, put his Mustang into the winner's circle, taking SS/F laurels. Both the Elliot cars held class records, Poole with low elapsed time (e.t.) in SS/H and John with low e.t. in SS/F.

And, then, one of drag racing's great names to be, Bob Glidden, won SS/H in the Springnationals held in Dallas, with an 11.53-second pass. Nicholson's Maverick put on its best showing of the season by downing the ProStock field in a succession of strong runs. Don put away the first adversary with a 9.68, then downed "Grumpy" Jenkins' Camaro on a 9.64 pass. He also out-muscled Don Carlton's MoTown Missile Dodge with a 9.66, took out another round on a 9.71 pass and faced off against Mike Fon's Rod Shop Dodge in the final. The Mr. Gasket Co. Maverick hauled in the MoPar

with a strong 9.63/141.73 Eliminator victory.

Except for Ken McLellan's '69 Mustang Super Stock Eliminator (11.56/117.95) in the NHRA World Finals at Amarillo, TX, that was it for the 1971 season. Although Fords were not much of a threat that year, the big losers were the fans. Rule changes and other confusion were introduced. But, unlike the growing problems in road racing, drag racing survived as an exciting form of auto racing, and a few Ford diehards kept the make alive over the next few years.

Some of these diehards include Larry Fullerton in his '72 Mustang, who won Funny Car Eliminator (6.58/222.32) in the NHRA World Finals of '72, and Don Nicholson, who raced a ProStock Pinto in '73 to win two NHRA ProStock Eliminator titles—9.33/145.16 in the Winternationals and a sensational 9.04/150.50 blast to win the Gatornationals. Pintos were tough ProStockers, as shown by the short-wheelbase bombers taking four of seven NHRA Eliminator titles in 1973. Glidden posted a win in the U.S. Nationals (9.08/151.26) and Wayne Gapp won the World Finals (9.17/149.00). Two of the remaining three ProStock national eliminators were two MoPars, the other a Chevy, showing that Chrysler domination had waned.

Bruce Sizemore won Modified Eliminator in his H/Modified Production Maverick (11.31/117.95) in the Summernationals in Columbus. This was significant because, other than ProStock, Fords were usually not top contenders. ProStock cars had emerged as drag racing's most popular crowd pleasers, and the little Pintos gave Ford fans a lot to talk about.

Fords in 1974 drag racing returned another four of seven NHRA ProStock Eliminator titles, and Bob Glidden was the hot shoe. Glidden took the first Ford ProStock Eliminator win of the season at Columbus during the Springnationals (9.11/153.06), followed by Wayne Gapp's Maverick winning the Grandnationals (8.90/145.39) at Quebec, Canada. The same day, long-time drag racer Shirl Greer won the Funny Car title with a '73 Mustang turning 6.51 at 198.67 mph. Glidden was back in form, taking the U.S. Nationals (9.01/151.26) and the World Finals (8.89/153.84) for a grand Ford finish.

Ford looked good at the Nationals. Along with Glidden's victory, Dave Condit's '73 Mustang won Funny Car Eliminator (6.24/212.76), and Dave Majors won Competition Eliminator (9.07/146.10) in his 1923 Ford E/Altered rod. Marcel Coultier showed that Super Stock Mustangs were still a threat when his SS/FA '68 Mustang rolled onto the winner's deck for SS Eliminator (11.30/114.50) during the Winternationals. Then Bruce Sizemore came through again, putting his I/Gas Pinto on the Modified Eliminator winner's deck (9.83 at 138.24 mph) during the Grandnationals.

Except for the "Grump" and his single Chevy Monza ProStock Eliminator title in the NHRA Springnationals, 1975 ProStock racing was all Ford. To lead off the season, Glidden's '70 Mustang and Gapp's '73 Maverick rolled to the line for the first of two all Ford ProStock finales, 1st in the Winternationals—Glidden winning at 8.79/154.10—and 2nd in the Gatornationals—Glidden winning again 8.96/152.80. "Grumpy" Jenkins broke the string in the Springnationals, but Wayne Gapp took the next three Nationals in a row: Grand Nationals (8.91/152.28), Summernationals (8.80/154.63 to shut out "Grump's" Vega) and the U.S. Nationals (8.83/153.32).

During the U.S. Nationals, Raymond Beadle put his '75 Mustang bodied Funny Car past Don Prudhomme's Monza in the eliminations (6.61/226.70 compared to 6.26 at 224.44). Ricky Barrett won Modified Eliminator in his C/Gas Pinto (9.28/136.57). With Gapp's win, Ford captured three of eight NHRA Eliminator titles at Indianapolis, not a bad showing at all.

Capping off the season, Glidden came back in form in the World Finals at Pomona by taking his Pinto past the "Grump's" Vega, but did so with an identical e.t. of 8.85 seconds. The timing computer picked the winner in the thousandths of a second range. That gave Glidden the win, and Ford all but one NHRA National ProStock championship!

Bruce Sizemore once again played spoiler with his I/Gas Pinto, taking the Grand Nationals Modified Eliminator (9.83/138.24); he did the same at the World Finals (9.74/138.24). Later, Sizemore won U.S. National Modified Eliminator again at 9.76/137.40.

1976 began like the year before, with Glidden and Gapp squaring off for another all Ford Winternationals (Glidden won 8.82/155.70). But after that, the ProStock Fords were shut out the entire season. However, Sizemore once again captured Modified Eliminator at the Springnationals, with his quick Pinto running 9.88 at 135.95 mph.

1976 might have been slim, but in 1977, Ford came back with another season of four out of seven ProStock Eliminator titles. Nicholson won the Springnationals (8.78/153.06), Glidden the Grandnationals (8.63/156.52) and the World

Finals against Nicholson in another all Ford showcase (8.55/157.34 to 8.69/155.97). Nicholson and Glidden faced off against each other at the U.S. Nationals, with Nicholson's Mustang II taking that one (8.73/154.10) from Glidden's Pinto.

Glidden found the combination in '78 and was the man to beat. All NHRA final rounds saw his Fords—first a Pinto and later a Fairmont—on the line. He only let two slip by. He won six of eight ProStock National titles and began with the Winternationals running 8.67 seconds and 156.52 mph in his Pinto. He had the Gatornationals won, but fouled, one of very few times, and let Frank Iaconio's slower Monza win. The Cajunnationals, new that year (8.65/150.75: Pinto), the Grandnationals (8.55/144.46: Fairmont), the Summernationals (8.61/146.81: Fairmont), the U.S. Nationals (8.61/146.81: Fairmont), and the World Finals (8.61/156.25: Fairmont) were all Bob Glidden wins. Ford read that Glidden was king of ProStock drag racing in 1978.

But 1979 was an even better year for Glidden, this time winning seven of eight major Nationals. The loss was another foul, rare as they are for Glidden racing, and all victories came at the wheel of a Plymouth Arrow. After years of racing and winning with Fords, Glidden switched to the MoPar, proving that it wasn't the Fords that won so much as it was his car preparation and driving.

In the final chapter, Ford ProStock drag racing in the '80s, with Glidden being the NHRA master and Rickie Smith the IHRA star, illustrates that Ford Motor Co. was serious again about racing and winning. The classic Ford-Chevrolet battles are on again. And, in many ways, the '80s parallel the '60s. Cars became exciting again, and Fords are once again quick and fast.

5
THE SHELBY ERA

Cobra & the Man

The man who made it happen, Carroll Shelby. SAAC photo.

The man whose picture was on the cover of an issue of *Sports Illustrated* magazine in 1957 as the Driver of the Year was probably the type who believed he could do anything. Years after this article appeared, after enlisting the aid of a corporate giant and having revived a failing old-line British auto firm, he beat the premier sports cars of the time with better cars that purists claimed were really just hot rods, then won America's only World Manufacturers' Championship with them and humbled GM's heralded Corvette along the way. He then took a team of cars and drivers to Europe's most celebrated race and won it twice, back-to-back, and it indeed appeared that Carroll Shelby could do anything.

For most people, owning a few interesting cars is about as far as they might go. Others might drive and win lots of races. Still others might build cars admired around the world, and a very few might change the course of history. But rarely does someone do it all and become a legend in his own time. If all this sounds like a Hollywood script, remember that it's all for real: Shelby really did do it all!

Shelby's driving of the early '50s caught the eye of John Wyer at Aston Martin. As a result, Shelby joined the British team for both the experience of driving and to learn more about building cars. As Aston works drivers, he and Roy Salvadori drove Europe's premier sports/racing car of 1959— the Aston Martin DBR1—to win the 24-Hours of LeMans, and contributed significantly to the marque's World Sports Car Championship that year. What Shelby really wanted, though, was to learn more about how to build and market the sports car he would eventually produce.

When "Total Performance" became Ford's corporate motto, the company didn't have a sports car; Shelby's day had come. The Thunderbird had gone luxury by then, and there was little chance of designing a sports car from the ground up with the expectation that it would be a big winner quick enough to help sales. And who in Dearborn could have imagined that a retired racing driver with an ailing heart— who taught high-performance driving at Riverside, and who had a Goodyear tire franchise in a corner of Dean

Built to beat Corvette and Ferrari on road courses, Cobras were almost invincible and laid waste to the plastic car and Italian sophisticates.

HiPo 289 was the runningest engine of its time. Not only did it power a lot of street Mustangs and Fairlanes, it was the engine that made the Cobras and GT-40s go.

Moon's speed shop in California—had the answer?

Shelby's answer was the AC Cobra, an aluminum-bodied two-seat roadster from England. It combined the advantages of Ford's new small, lightweight Fairlane V8 engine and nimble handling in a lightweight sports car. His idea became Ford's answer to their sports car dilemma, and it gave quick results.

A sports car of his own make was a long-standing goal for Shelby, and it came about because Britain's AC Cars found itself without an engine when the old faithful Bristol in-line—basically a pre-war BMW design—went out of production. Ford happened to announce its new small-block V8 at about the same time. When the news of the two unrelated events reached Shelby, his goal suddenly became possible.

His timing was perfect, as was his promotion. After briefly meeting a member of Ford's performance staff at Pike's Peak in August, 1961, Shelby called on the man in Dearborn to discuss his plans and to acquire a few of the new Ford V8s. At the same time, phone calls to AC Cars fired their interest. Things were looking better, and when engines were exchanged—one resulting in the first Cobra prototype that ran very fast—Shelby was in business.

On February 2, 1962, Shelby and Ford Motor Co. signed an agreement that Shelby would use POWERED BY FORD on all his cars in exchange for engines and other mechanical parts. AC Cars was delighted to keep their AC Ace in production, but now slightly re-styled and modified to accept the V8 and an American 4-speed transmission. It was carrying a new name, too: *Cobra*.

The first car to arrive in California from AC Cars was dubbed *CSX1001* for Carroll Shelby Export, serial number 1001. Subsequent Cobras also received CSX serial numbers.

By late '63, Shelby's creation was receiving lots of auto-magazine ink for their racing exploits. An early Cobra made the cover of *Road & Track* magazine, whose editors called it "America's Sensational GT Car," and "a 150-mph car built for production racing." In January of '63, Corvette hot shoe of the previous year, Dave MacDonald, and Britisher Ken Miles turned in the Cobra's first win—a 1-2 finish in an SCCA divisional race at Riverside. The racing legacy of Carroll Shelby's Cobra had begun.

Both Shelby and Ford recognized the potential of the car, and major efforts were soon underway to build both street Cobras to be marketed through selected Ford dealers around the country and racing Cobras to win as many SCCA and USRRC road races as possible.

The United States Road Racing Championship (USRRC) was new that year. At first, the little roadsters had teething problems. But they soon became tough, and began winning consecutive races. Private-entry cars scored wins and the factory Cobras became almost invincible. Team drivers rarely had any real competition, and Corvette racers entered a sad phase. From 1963 through '68, nothing but Cobras won the top production sports-car racing classes.

The 2020-pound AC Cobras rode on a 90-inch wheelbase. Beautiful wire wheels added a lot of good looks to the cars, and their obvious sports-car lines were simply sensational. Initially, street Cobras were powered by stock HiPo 260 Fords, but HiPo 289s rated at 271 HP became the engine most remembered in the cars.

AC Cobras were expensive at $5995, but with production held to 200 or so cars a year, they were exclusive transportation. Fast, nimble and quick were the fortes of the Cobra. And with two-turn lock-to-lock steering along with a near

Cobra Daytona Coupes in pits at LeMans, France: This was the big one, the race these cars were built for: the face-off between American iron, Ferrari V12s and Jaguar in-line 6s. Courtesy Ford Motor Co.

ideal 48/52% front/rear weight distribution, they were superb-handling cars.

Most other cars of the time couldn't exceed much more than 115 mph, but at that speed a Cobra was just reaching its 3rd-gear potential. At 7000 rpm in 4th, it topped out at 153 mph! Quick meant that a Cobra reached 0-60 mph in 4.2 seconds and 0-100 in 10.8. And the quarter-mile came up in 13.8 seconds at 112 mph.

The AC Cobra was also known at the time as the *Ford Cobra* or *289 Cobra.* What made them so remarkable was that they were available right off the showroom floor. With only a single 4-bbl carb and in such a lightweight package, the combination of Shelby's magic with Ford's engine and AC's construction produced the most exhilarating car of its day, a milestone car forever identified as Carroll Shelby's sports car.

That story goes on to include hot Shelby American built engines producing nearly 400 HP, and a brilliant racing record that would make an excellent "great American success story" for Hollywood movie moguls. A twist to the AC Cobra saga is that the car Shelby really wanted to build was more like the later 427 Cobra than the 289. Although the 289 was by far the biggest winner, whatever the 289 did, the 427 did better.

THE GREATEST AMERICAN SPORTS CAR

When the first Cobra was shipped from AC Cars on February 2, 1962, and received later in Los Angeles, all it needed was an engine, transmission and body paint. Shelby and Dean Moon of "Moon Equipped" hot-rod-parts fame, spent less than eight hours fitting an engine received from Ford, a HiPo 260. A Borg-Warner 4-spd transmission backed the 260. Once completed, Shelby and Moon roared off through the Sante Fe Springs oil fields near Moon's shop. The car proved to be faster than Shelby had hoped for, and he no doubt began to see the reality of his earlier threat, "Someday I'll blow your ass off," to Enzo Ferrari taking shape.

Once the word got out that Shelby had a hot new sports car, auto magazines lined up to test it. The first to get a shot at the car got a silver Cobra. Because there wasn't time to paint it, Shelby and friends used several dozen boxes of steel-wool soap pads to polish the car's aluminum body.

Road & Track was next. They got a yellow Cobra. In fact, this was the same car, but now painted. It so impressed *R&T* that the car made the cover. *Sports Car Graphic* magazine tested the car, now painted red, and proclaimed that, "Its acceleration...can only be described as explosive." With such coverage, the Cobra suddenly became an established marque, even if there was only one car. Each magazine got a different color car—first silver, then yellow, red and so on, as Shelby and Company repainted the same car, giving the impression that they were turning out dozens of the cars.

The Cobra generated great excitement, and Shelby was quick to promote special racing versions that were said to be even faster than the impressive street cars. No other car so overwhelmed the sports-car arena as the Cobra. Magazines heaped praise upon its stunning performance as both a docile street machine in traffic and a 150-mph bullet in a single package.

When the second car was received from AC Cars in May, 1962, Shelby and Ford had already established a network of dealerships across the U.S. The third car became Shelby's first racing Cobra and his legendary, storybook rise to success was about to take off like a rocket.

Even though the Cobra/AC Cars' front and rear suspensions used an out-dated leaf-spring design from the early '50s, the combination of light weight, power and excellent weight distribution produced a sports/racing machine with superb handling. Throughout their production, Cobras were continually updated as improvements found from racing were incorporated in the cars. Thus, few Cobras were built exactly alike.

Intensive and thorough development of competition Cobras created very sophisticated racing cars. Plus a huge list of options was available to Cobra buyers. It was a true "roll-your-own" sports car for whatever interests, especially racing—Shelby's main interest. He would soon nail Ferrari to the wall, win everything there was to win, and show the world that America and Ford V8 engines could humble the best of Europe's high-winders.

Cobra number CSX1026 took the marque's first win at Riverside in January, 1963. It also raced as a Shelby American team car at Daytona and finished 4th overall. Then came Sebring with NASCAR's famous stock car driver, "Fireball" Roberts, co-driving. The car also won the USRRC at Watkins Glen.

In the beginning—early 1963—there were four Shelby American team cars and six independents racing SCCA, USRRC and FIA (international) races everywhere they could. And because rules were different for different organizations, the cars had to be suitably prepared for each type of racing. In some cases, they even ran in different classes in back-to-back events by changing something, such as removing the windshield.

The purpose of the Cobra was to win races, and Shelby offered independents everything his team cars had, as well as limited factory backing. He even offered racing specials as factory-built competition cars just like his team cars. There were several types. Among them were the "Sebring Cars" (three built), the "Riverside Replica" (one built), "LeMans Cars" (two built), "LeMans Replica" (six built), "FIA Roadsters" (five built), "USRRC Roadsters" (12 built, although six of these were built primarily for SCCA A/P racing), "Daytona Coupes" (six built). In addition, there were 28 known independently prepared Cobra racing cars.

Cobras were the hottest thing going. They left their im-

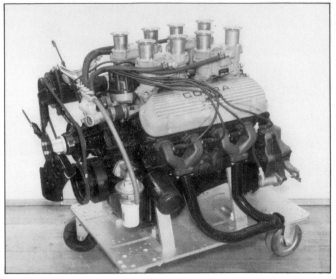

Cobra 289 with Tri-Y *headers: Cobra racing engine produced 380 HP at 6,800 rpm. List price; $2995. Result: 1965 F.I.A. World Manufacturers' Championship. Bob D'Olivio photo.*

print forever emblazoned in the history of American and international racing. In just its second year of existence, the Cobra won the 1963 USRRC Championship and humiliated the Corvette contingent. It was just the beginning.

Although road racing was the heart of the Cobra program, four specials went after another prize—drag racing. The second *Dragonsnake* was a factory drag car, and the third one became the 1963 NHRA A/Sports, B/Sports and C/Sports national record holder. It held those class records at least through 1965, and another owner campaigned the car in 1966 to the NHRA World Championship. Not only were Cobras the top road racers, they were also the fastest production sports cars—all stock and at your local Ford dealer.

Dragonsnake Cobras were offered in four stages as of Sept. 1, 1964:

- Stage I-D, complete, 271 HP — $6795.00
- Stage II-D, complete, 300 HP — 7495.00
- Stage III-D, complete, 325 HP — 8695.00
- Stage IV-D, complete, 380 HP — 8995.00

They carried 23 specific-to-drag-racing options that were intended to allow an owner to field a highly competitive drag car straight off the dealer's showroom floor. The Stage III-D Dragonsnake was set up with four 2V Weber 48 IDA carburetors, among other competition standard equipment. The Stage IV-D, also a Weber-equipped car, was intended for AHRA racing where regulations allowed more development.

The thrill of victory! Gurney/Bondurant Cobra Daytona Coupe No. 5 at start of 24-Hours of LeMans, 1964. Car beat the GT Jags and Ferraris to take a fourth overall and first in GT class after averaging 116.301 mph for 2791.243 miles. Courtesy Ford Motor Co.

The basic street Cobra was priced at $5995 as of November 20, 1963, and came with Ford's new HiPo 289, stronger frame, hand-formed aluminum coachwork, full instrumentation, rack-and-pinion steering, bucket seats and leather interior in black only, limited-slip differential, 72-spoke wire wheels with knock-off hubs, Girling four-wheel disc brakes and body colors in red, maroon, white, black, bright blue, princess blue and silver.

However, that basic street model was only the bottom line. A huge list of options allowed buyers to build a formidable roadster for any occasion. Final-drive gear sets ranging from 4.56:1 to 2.72:1 gave top speeds ranging from around 110 to 180!

Then there were the competition models: The Stage I Competition Cobra was a basic street car with additional equipment "...for the man who wants something a little better than stock," as ads read. They were better-handling cars priced at $6275.00. "For the man who takes his racing seriously," the Stage II Competition Cobra was offered with more factory-installed equipment, including wide magnesium wheels with Goodyear racing tires, flared fenders for wider tires, special steering arms and a hood air scoop—all for $7220.00

If you had to have more, there was more: the Stage III Shelby American team-car replica. It was identical to the team cars that won the Manufacturers' Championship, the SCCA Class A Championship and Drivers Championship. These cars were personally tested at Riverside by Ken Miles,

the top Shelby American team driver. The cars were guaranteed to equal the best lap time of the team cars—the GT lap record—and complied with SCCA and FIA Class III GT regulations.

The Stage I and II cars could be ordered with one of three stock 271-HP engines: the II-R engine with dual 4-bbl carbs and extras for $254.75 more; the III R engine, a fully prepared racing engine with dual 4-bbls for an additional $1,904.71; or the full-spec IV-R engine with Webers, that put the top price for a Cobra at $9,500. This was the car that blew away Ferraris, Jaguars and Corvettes alike.

Specials such as the LeMans cars and replicas, FIA roadsters and especially the Daytona Coupes, won many international GT races. In 1964, they came within a whisker of beating Ferrari for the FIA World Manufacturers' Championship, the first time any American sports car had been so competitive. Cobra would likely have taken that title if Enzo Ferrari had not brought his influence to bear on FIA officials to cancel the last race of the season, one that Shelby's cars were favored to win—the win that would have made good, "Someday I'll blow your ass off!"

No doubt the most interesting Cobra is the Daytona Coupe. They are easily the most valuable today, and were the result of Shelby's and Ford's desires to beat Ferrari. Ford wanted to see Cobras campaigned in Europe on the high-speed endurance circuits like LeMans, where the cars raced perhaps 3,000 miles for 24 hours. In such racing, aerodynamics was seen to be important, and open roadsters were not

Daytona Coupe and the man, Carroll Shelby, at debut of car—Daytona 1964—where car received its name. SAAC photo.

Daytona Coupe Interior. Bob D'Olivio photo.

well suited for the task. Thus, Pete Brock at Shelby American designed a beautiful coupe body for the leaf-spring-chassis Cobra.

Under FIA rules, a coupe body could be raced on a conventional Cobra Chassis and power train even though it was not a regular-production item offered to the public—as long as the chassis and drive line remained unchanged.

The Daytona Coupe remains the most exotic of the Cobra line. It was developed for the sole purpose of ending Ferrari's stranglehold on the GT World Championship. The aerodynamic coupe body gave the 380-HP Cobra a top-end speed increase of 20 mph and an unanticipated increase in fuel economy. With the proven reliability of the basic car, they more than matched the best Ferrari could muster.

The first Daytona Coupe was completed at Shelby American in January, 1964. During shakedown trials at Riverside, it reached 165 mph on the long back straight to show it had a potential of 185 mph at LeMans. It was then prepared for its first race, Daytona—thus the origin of its name. While running the Continental with a comfortable lead, a pit-stop fire sidelined the car, ending its chances for a first race victory. Gurney and Bob Johnson salvaged a 4th in a team roadster behind three GTO Ferraris after the coupe burned. Fortunately, it had only minor damage and was back in action at Sebring, where Bob Holbert and Dave MacDonald easily won GT class, finishing 3rd overall ahead of the Lew Spencer/Bob Bondurant and Jo Schlesser/Phil Hill roadsters.

Holbert and MacDonald ran 1,087 miles at an average of 90.6 mph around 209 laps on the flat 5.2-mile Sebring course. They finished just 26 miles behind the winning Ferrari prototype after 12 hours of racing. For a GT car to perform so well was a worrisome point for Ferrari. As the season pro-

Powered by Ford Cobra Daytona Coupe engine with Weber carburetors: Built on AC Cobra leaf-spring chassis, coupe body made car faster. Bob D'Olivio photo.*

gressed, it was clear that the Daytona Coupe was superior to the much heralded 250 GTO Ferrari. In a twist of fate, the 250 GTO never actually qualified for FIA Grand Touring class racing because only 40 were built. The way Ferrari got around the GT rules was by saying the GTO was nothing more than a rebodied 250 SWB (short wheel base) Berlinetta, which it was not.

Cobras were at home on drag strips when converted to Dragonsnakes. CSX2093, shown here, held NHRA A, B and C/Sports national records in 1963, '64 and '65. Ed Hedrick bought car and won the 1966 NHRA World Championship. In '67, Hedrick won the NHRA Winternationals (11.71/117.49) in B/SP, then won the Spring Nationals (11.65/117.80) and closed out the season winning the U.S. Nationals (D/SP 11.92/106.38) and the World Finals C/SP (11/87). His Cobra won all four top NHRA events in class that year.

The Daytona Coupe showed the way to winning. Three more chassis were readied at Shelby American for coupe bodies, but they were built and fitted by Carrozzeria Grand Sport of Modena, Italy—Ferrari's home town. All totaled, six were built.

Roadsters and coupes were raced in a variety of international races. Dan Gurney and Jerry Grant won the GT Over 3-liter class of Sicily's grueling Targa Florio Enduro. The Schlesser/Dickie Attwood team won the same class of the Nurburgring 1000Km in Germany. In the French classic, the 24-Hours of LeMans, the Daytona Coupe performed magnificently in the hands of Gurney and Bondurant. They finished 4th overall and led the GT class ahead of a GTO.

No Cobras placed at Spa where the GTO took a 1-2-3-4 sweep. Suddenly, Ferrari was back in the running. The red machines then placed 3-4 in the Reims 12-Hour, without a Cobra placing again. Then, Gurney showed the Cobra's mettle by taking a 1st GT finish at Goodwood, and finishing 3rd overall in the RAC Tourist Trophy in a Cobra 3-4-5 sweep ahead of the nearest GTO. Ken Miles looked really impressive in the Bridgehampton Double 500, finishing 3rd overall to lead the GT class—but it was to no avail. By the end of the season, Ferrari saw the future and did political maneuvers to save another World GT title because his cars were beaten. A loss in the final race was avoided when he managed to have it canceled.

In 1965, there was no stopping Shelby's well-prepared machines. All six coupes were complete, and raced under Guardsman Blue team color with twin white "LeMans" stripes running the length of their bodies. Four Daytona Coupes ran the European races that year and scored nine wins, eight seconds, three 3rds and one 4th. Ferrari was nailed to the wall and quit, while Carroll Shelby's Cobra works won America's only World Manufacturers' Championship (1965). The Ford-powered Cobra proved to be the most formidable production-based sports car you could buy.

The leaf-spring Cobras—654 were built—scored USRRC championships in 1963 and '64, the 1965 FIA GT World Championship, 1964 ARRC A/Production national title, and SCCA A/Production national championships in 1964 and '65. Add to that the drag-racing titles and records set by 289-powered "Dragonsnakes," and what you have is proof that the little Cobra was indeed "the greatest American sports car!"

ON THE SALT

Daytona Coupe Cobras are best known as the cars that ended Ferrari domination of international GT racing. What they did in road racing has been well documented. However, as land speed-record cars, their accomplishments are not well known, but deserving just the same. And it happened in the same year, 1965.

After the Shelby team made history by winning the World Manufacturers' Championship, Craig Breedlove and Bobby Tatro smashed International Class C (183 to 305 cubic inches) speed records on Utah's Bonneville Salt Flats. Their record runs were during November. The car they used had been on tour around the country as world champion and received little more than a new 289 engine.

Breedlove became best known for establishing the out-right land speed record of over 600.6 mph in the "Spirit of America—Sonic 1" jet car on November 15, but before that, on the 5th, he and Tatro drove a Cobra Coupe for 12 hours at high speed to set 16 national and seven international records. After three hours, Tatro set the new mark of 159.98 mph. After 200 miles, he had reached an average 161.65 mph. Then Breedlove set the fastest time of 165.59 mph. Overall, the car ran 1,801 miles for 12 hours and averaged 150.09 mph—including pit stops, another astounding accomplishment in the Cobra saga.

The Shelby American Daytona Coupe ran pump gas and Goodyear Blue Streak tires as used in road racing. It proved the Cobra concept at speeds that set new world marks as the fastest car of its type flat out.

BIG BROTHER

When it comes time to point to the most awesome production street machine ever made, it will be the 427 Cobra. Never has there been a car so overwhelmingly popular. In its days of dominating racing, they were virtually unbeatable, and the history they made is a lasting tribute to the marque—so much so that many kit-car builders today offer their versions styled more or less to look like the 427 Cobra.

As time goes on, it is becoming increasingly easy to lose sight of just what the real 427 Cobra really was. Along with all the other Shelby cars, the Shelby American Automobile

427 Cobra, the most sensational and lasting sports car ever built.

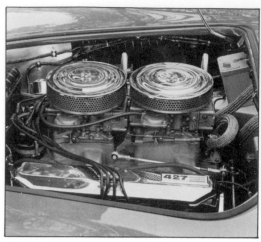

Factory under-rated by about 100 HP, the 427 side-oiler was advertised at 425 HP. Standard final-drive ratio of 3.77:1 gave S/C 427 Cobra real street performance: 0 to 100 to 0 in 13.6 seconds with a top speed of 175 mph, all for a list of $7495.

Club has gone a long way toward documenting as much detail about the cars as possible. Production of the 427 Cobra officially began on January 27, 1965, and ended in March, 1967. Like the 289s, their basic construction was by AC Cars in England. All 427s exported to the U.S. received serial numbers reading CSX3001 through CSX3360. The cars were shipped to Shelby American in Los Angeles for final assembly, then marketed through the established Ford dealer network handling Shelby cars, or directly from Shelby American, Inc.

The reason for building the NASCAR 427 side-oiler-powered Cobra was to compete in international racing with Ferrari, who was building a production car he hoped would regain the world GT title lost to the 289 Cobras. Another aspect was that GM was attempting to make their plastic cars go faster with 396- and 427-cid engines, so the 427 Cobra had two main adversaries. However, it turned out that FIA paid more attention to Ferrari's practice of building a few cars and calling them production models, and did not accept the new car. Also, Carroll Shelby's new weapon was not accepted because too few had been built. Thus the 289-powered cars were still Shelby's GT rivals against the Italian machines, but Ferrari got mad and pulled out of FIA. If he couldn't win, he wouldn't race at all. And the 427 Corvette didn't materialize as a real threat, either.

Of the three types of 427 Cobras built—the competition, semi/competition and street model—only about 56 were built with genuine 427 side-oilers. Those engines were expensive, and with perhaps 550 HP on tap, they fulfilled Shelby's dictum that "Too much is just right." When street versions were offered, they received "police interceptor" 428-cid engines that looked outwardly like the 427. The 428 produced around 410 HP, although Ford factory cars with the engine were rated at 335 HP. On the street, there was

Full-competition 427 Cobra was homologated with single 4-bbl Holley and air box. Car took four consecutive SCCA A/Production national championships: 1965, '66, '67 and '68.

very little real difference in the cars, as both big blocks made the big Cobras formidable machines. The 428 was $410 cheaper and more available, thus an acceptable alternative to the side-oiler.

The full-competition 427 Cobra received the NASCAR medium-riser engine with aluminum heads and a single 780-cfm Holley 4-bbl. Perhaps only a dozen or so were sold as full competition cars. The S/C Cobras were very much like the racing version and fitted with a competition body: wider rear flares, front oil cooler and chin scoop, hood scoop, front brake scoops and ducting, and quick jack pads front and

The S/C and full-comp 427 Cobra dash. The 180-mph speedo was out of the way to the right.

Slip into the S/C 427 Cobra, a man's car—the hairy-chested beast of sports cars.

rear. They received 427 low-risers mostly fitted with two 4-bbl Holleys on aluminum intakes. The battery in both full-comp and S/C models was located behind the passenger seat. S/C Cobras were fitted with differential oil coolers, a 42-gallon fuel tank, front anti-sway bars, 3.77:1 final gearing and competition-style dash layout. The speedometer was positioned off to the right, out of the way of useful instrumentation. Halibrand pin-drive magnesium wheels with three-ear spin-on nuts, 7-1/2-inch wide at the front and 9-1/2-inch wide at the rear, were fitted with Goodyear Blue Dot tires. Street cars received "sunburst" alloy wheels of the same dimensions. List prices ran about $9,800 for the competition 427 Cobra and $7,495 for street models.

In addition to these, a 427 Dragonsnake could have been yours for $10,485. Drag-racing engines were balanced and blue-printed 427 high-risers with aluminum heads coupled with lots of special engine work. NHRA approved equipment was also included.

When the 427 Cobras went to work, they dominated SCCA A/Production racing, winning the National Championship in 1965, '66, '67 and '68, then again in 1973. Both the 1968 and '73 wins were without a factory supplying anything––there was no factory support then. Shelby shut down his plant in 1967. Another series of coil-spring Cobras—known as the *Mk III* chassis—was built. These were the *AC 289* cars completed by AC Cars and marketed in Europe. They carried COBxxxx instead of CSXxxxx serial numbers. Thirty-two cars were built in this series.

The 427 Cobra was and remains "the world's quickest production car," regardless of claims by other manufacturers. That was proven with 0-60 mph times of 3.8 seconds, 0-100 in 10.6 seconds and 0-100 and back to a dead stop in 13.6 seconds. No other cars short of factory-built racing cars produced in just enough quantity to qualify as "sports cars"

have ever matched the 427 Cobra.

Handling was superb, with enough power on tap to make the car do whatever the driver wanted. Even though 427s were heavier than their 289-powered predecessors (2529 pounds compared to 2020), ultra-modern coil spring chassis design of the 427 cars gave them characteristics well beyond the best of any other car of the time.

Ford's GT-40 development program supplied much of the technology that went into the 427 Cobra. Both the GT-40 and 427 Cobra were overwhelming successes, but in different classes. The 427 Cobra began as a prototype leaf-spring roadster stuffed with a 460-HP 427. Ken Miles raced it first at Sebring, but crashed in practice.

The second prototype was a special 1,600-pound lightweight 289 roadster with a flip-up front end and 427 engine. It was blindingly fast, but didn't finish its first race either, Nassau in December, 1964. While on the track, though, nothing could touch it.

The 427 engine first specified for the production Cobra was the side-oiler, cross-bolt main-bearing-cap cast-iron block with aluminum heads, aluminum water pump, magnesium 4V intake manifold—later changed to aluminum—and fabricated tubular exhaust headers and side-pipes. The transmission was a Ford cast-iron top-loader 4-speed with competition gears.

In comparison, the frame tubes of the 427 Cobra were 2 1/2 inches farther apart from side to side than the 289 Cobra frame tubes, and were made of 4-inch-OD main tubes rather than 3-inch . Thus, the 427 body was wider by about 5 inches, and the car sat a little lower than the 7-inch ground clearance of the 289. Wheelbase was the same at 90 inches, and only the doors, hood and trunk lid, windshield and interior were the same for both cars. Body sheet aluminum was thicker on the 427: 0.050-inch as opposed to 0.045.

427 Cobra in action.

The last Cobra national championship was taken by Sam Feinstein in this car (CSX3009), the 9th 427 Cobra built. Car had previously won the '66 ARRC with Ed Lowther at the wheel.

When production 427 Cobras became a reality after only three months from concept to finished car, they were fitted in some cases with out-of-the-crate NASCAR 427 side-oilers with two 600-cfm 4-bbl Holleys. "Advertised" horsepower was 425, but they produced closer to 550 HP.

One part common to both 289 and 427 Cobra was the Salisbury third member manufactured by Jaguar. It proved to be capable of withstanding the 427's torque, although the half-shafts that drove the rear wheels were beefed up for the 427. After they were received from AC Cars with unpainted aluminum bodies, the cars went through final assembly and were painted white, Rangoon Red, Guardsman Blue, Ivy Green, charcoal or silver.

As a footnote, the last two 427 Cobras built were specials with twin Paxton superchargers and Lincoln automatic transmissions—one built for comedian Bill Cosby, a long-time friend of Shelby's, and the other was the last 427 Cobra built, one for the boss himself. These engines produced over 800 HP, making the cars "rockets on wheels!" If you want to hear about these cars, get hold of Cosby's comedy album entitled "200 Miles Per Hour."

As for potential, a drag-prepared 427 Cobra set the NAS-CAR AA/Sports Production record of 10.3 seconds at 133 mph. In NHRA drag racing, the Dragonsnake was campaigned by Gus Zuidema for Harr Ford of Worcester, Massachusetts, and set both ends of the A/Sports class record of 10.38 seconds at 138 mph. In A/Modified with tunnel-port heads, the same car held the A/M class record with stats of 10.12 seconds at 146 mph. And an independently prepared 427 Cobra reportedly set a quarter-mile record of 9.70 seconds at 142 mph.

Thus, there is little to say other than the 427 Cobra was an absolutely formidable machine with tremendous potential. It was both a well-mannered roadster for gentle cruising on nice afternoons and a championship rocket when turned loose.

MUSTANGS

Lee Iacocca says the best thing he did while at the helm of Ford was killing the Cardinal, Ford Motor Company's answer to the Volkswagen Beetle. In its place he championed a car already well along in development, the Mustang. That project began as a design study of a two-seat sports car known as the *Mustang I*, which was a revival of the original Thunderbird concept.

Chief Engineer Herb Misch, stylist Gene Bordinat and engineer from Ford Research Roy Lunn were responsible for the Mustang I. Lunn, who would later figure highly in Ford's domination of world-class racing, laid out the Mustang I's design objectives.

Famed sports-car builders, Troutman and Barnes, widely known for their Scarab and Chaparral sports/racing cars of the late '50s, were given the job of building the prototype on a tubular chassis, then fitted it with a stressed aluminum body. An integral roll bar was part of the design of this roadster. Many of its components came from the Cardinal prototypes, including a 2-liter (117.5 cid) 60° V-4 rated at 90 HP. The car was looked at as the Ford sports car to compete with the European 4-cylinder cars of the early '60s.

The Mustang I was first shown in October, 1962, at the United States Grand Prix at Watkins Glen. Dan Gurney drove the car around the circuit, and later magazine road tests gave the car high marks. But Iacocca wasn't satisfied. The car could not be volume produced profitably in the Mustang I form. Thus, further design studies resulted in concept cars such as the XT-Bird, Allegro, Stiletto, Torino and Cougar before the Mustang II finally arrived. It ultimately became the production Mustang.

The new sporty Ford took the industry by surprise. Here was a car of sports-car styling and appeal, but with seating for four. It was the car Iacocca wanted Ford to build, and it was a smash hit by all modern standards, out-selling all predictions. And it was basically a styling job because most

Shelby G.T.350 for 1966 was little changed from '65. Quarter windows rather than vents and functional rear-brake cooling ducts were main differences. SAAC photo.

chassis, engine, suspension and drive-line components came from the Falcon and Fairlane. Thus, the Mustang was a highly profitable car.

The 1965 Mustang was officially introduced at the New York World's Fair on April 17, 1964. Ford Motor Company blanketed the country with advertising on prime time TV, where an estimated 29-million viewers saw the car, and in every major newspaper.

The handsome coupe was base priced at $2,368. Public demand ran so high that Ford dealers were deluged with orders. First-year production was pegged at 100,000, but it only took four months to reach that goal. In its first 20 months, Mustang sales soared to almost 681,000. During the 1966 model year, the car went over the one-million mark. The new Mustang set all sorts of industry records and, for the first time in years, Ford Motor Company had an ace that Chevrolet didn't have.

Mustangs came in basic body styles—coupe, convertible and fastback—and there was nothing like them on the market. They were the beginning of the *ponycar* revolution of smaller, high-style personal cars that soon became a major segment of the auto industry.

The concept Ford product planning laid down was to provide base Mustangs and let buyers select options they

Mustang coupe, the heart of America, sold 1,001,716 from introduction through '66 model year.

Cobra dress-up option for 289 gave Mustang engine compartment handsome good looks as well as thrilling performance. The Mustang was an excellent car in many ways.

The mark of the hottest '65—67 Mustang, the runningest engine of its time—High Performance 289 with 271 factory-rated horsepower. This was its symbol.

option that developed 0.95 HP per cubic inch and 312 lb-ft of torque at 3400 rpm. Quick winding was the forte of the Hi-Po. Some features included from the factory were special high-compression, small-chamber cylinder heads; solid lifter, high-lift cam; free-breathing intake and exhaust manifolds, and lots of potential for more power.

POWERED BY FORD was the heart of Carroll Shelby's Cobra equipment with this engine. Many types of high-performance parts were available through most Ford dealers and through Shelby American.

Shelby American's August, 1966 performance-equipment catalog included dozens of parts, ranging from drag-racing and full-competition cylinder heads—$349.50 and $425 a pair, respectively—to a dual 4-V high-riser induction system priced at $249.50. And, at the top of the carburetion price list was a set of four Weber 48 IDA carburetors on a cast aluminum COBRA-lettered intake manifold for $595, scatter-shields, exhaust systems, clutches and gear sets, and everything else needed to build a street, strip or road-racing bomber.

Cobra lettered and chrome-plated engine accessories gave Ford 260-289 owners lots of show-and-go goodies from which to choose. For the racer, Shelby listed a selection of complete engine assemblies, including the single Holley B/Production Competition G.T.350 road-racing engine for $2645 (350 HP at 6750 rpm) and the Weber-equipped 289 Cobra Racing engine for $2995 (390 HP at 6750 rpm) and the Weber aspirated 289 Cobra High-Rev racing engine for $3195 (395 HP at 7000 rpm) produced 1.37 HP per cubic inch. Its total weight of 530 pounds gave this cast-iron engine an output of 0.75 HP per pound. In peak drag-racing tune of around 450 HP, specific output rose to 1.56 HP per cubic inch and 0.85 HP per pound, showing that Ford's new technology engine did indeed have a great deal of designed-in potential.

What is really surprising about the 289 was that, in every

wanted. That made the cars personalized to taste and were, therefore, more appealing. Fitting the sports-car idea was a selection of high-performance options, including the newly updated thin-wall small-block V8.

Originally a 221-cid engine for the Fairlane, it went to 260 cid with 260 HP in hottest form as seen earlier with the Falcons, then to 289 cid with 271 HP, which was basically the HiPo 260 with more displacement. These Hi-Performance 289s were the runningest engines available in anything. They've since become the legendary *K-model* Mustangs, which came from the first letter in the alphanumeric serial number designation of the high-performance package that included the HiPo 289 engine.

Other 289s included the 200-HP 2-barrel and the 225-HP 4-barrel engines. Top was the single 4-bbl Hi-Po 289, a $442

Shelby Mustangs are strong vintage road racers today and one of the most popular and desirable cars ever built.

Shelby G.T.350 dominated SCCA's B/Production class. Rated at 350 HP at 6800 rpm, these 530-pound small-blocks were available from Shelby-American for $2645.

'66 G.T.350 Cutaway.

form—from low-buck Mustangs to SCCA B/Production champion G.T.350 Shelbys and world championship Cobras—all were powered by engines whose crankshaft ran in 2-bolt main-bearing caps!

The new Mustang with 289 power made a sensational combination, one that created intense desire to drive. It was a personal car with appeal, found only in Ford showrooms.

If Ford's own High Performance 289 Mustangs were not enough, Shelby produced his own hotted up G.T.350s that were, without doubt, *the* runningest cars on the road in the mid-60s. During this era, the story of Ford racing is largely the story of Carroll Shelby, and he has become a legend. Today, his cars and Cobra equipment he offered are highly sought-after collector items.

1966 Shelby G.T.350 is a highly desirable Mustang. This beauty says it all!

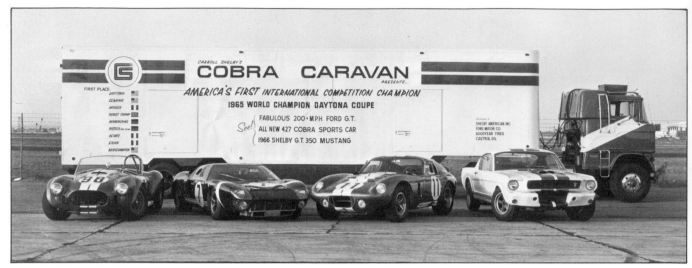

Shelby-American line-up of champions: 1965 promotional photo featured the new 427 Cobra, SCCA A/Production national champion; GT-40 MkI, future world champion; Cobra Daytona Coupe, world champion; Shelby G.T.350 Mustang, SCCA B/Production national champion. SAAC photo.

Looking back at that period, Mustang was the beginning of a new era in American automobiles, and Carroll Shelby was the center of operations that brought Ford resounding racing success, first in America, then on an international scale. Except for Henry Ford himself, probably no single person in the history of American automobiles has had such a lasting impact as Carroll Shelby.

From the beginning of this century, the Ford name on cars has always been appreciated because of the efforts of one man who reached for excellence in quality and durability at a fair price. And like him, the Shelby name that went on special-edition Ford Mustangs has come to be recognized for high performance at a fair price.

Unlike both Ford and Shelby, the name *Chevrolet* has no particular meaning other than a name on cars from GM. The meaning of the name has become rather lost in time and generally suppressed by Chevrolet historians who aren't thrilled to learn that the Chevrolet brothers were the Carroll Shelbys of the 4-banger era who made their name everlasting with high-performance Fords.

PONYCAR WARS

Ford's 1967 Mustang was no longer alone in the ponycar market. New for that model year were Chevrolet's Camaro and Pontiac's Firebird sistership. The Plymouth Barracuda received a major facelift in an effort to compete, and Mercury entered the market with its high-style Cougar. Thus, Mustang had stiff competition, which showed in a significant drop in sales, from 607,568 in 1966 to 472,121 in '67. For comparison, Camaro sales reached 220,917, less that half of Mustang sales.

Mustang updates for 1968 could not fend off the rise in sales of competitive personal-size cars. For instance, Camaro volume rose to 235,151, still well behind Mustang sales of

Shelby Mustangs are still exciting cars and faster than they were 20 years ago because of advances in tire, handling and engine technology. This example shows faithful commitment to the Shelby legacy in form and function.

317,404. The new Javelin and AMX from American Motors offered buyers still more choices. Plymouth Hemi Barracuda Super Stocks soon "owned" NHRA Super Stock/B class drag racing, drawing high-performance car buyers into MoPar showrooms as a result. Cougar buyers wanted more style and class than offered in other cars of the type, and Ford's own newly introduced Torino attracted buyers who wanted a larger performance car. Thus, competition in the personal and performance car market of '67 was intense.

For 1967, Mustangs were updated with new sheet metal, a more refined interior with greater attention to GT styling treatment, and a new engine. Previously, the 289 was the largest available, but for '67, the track was widened to accommodate the larger FE big-block engine. This was largely in response to a demand for more straight-line go at the

Mustang takes roar of Ford's V8 to Europe and the Tour de France, a 3800-mile high-speed event around France. It took several days as a test of the versatility of cars and was composed of road sections, racing circuits (LeMans and Monza, for instance) and rally sections (the Monte Carlo). Ford had run three Galaxies in the Tour de France in 1963 without finishing, due to driver error in two cars and a mechanical failure in the other, and had gained a great deal of experience with the eight Alan Mann rally Falcons that ran the Monte Carlo Rally. Sweden's Bo Ljungfeldt drove his Falcon to finish second overall and first in class. Ford factory Mustangs were the entries of 1964 Tour de France in Touring class as opposed to the GT class. Four were prepared and entered by Alan Mann, three for drivers Peter Harper, Peter Proctor and Ljungfeldt, and the last for Ford of Europe driver Henri Greder. In GT class, Shelby's Cobra team needed to win the Tour to beat Ferrari for the World Manufacturers' Championship, but wasn't able to. In Touring, the Mustangs dominated. Proctor and Harper finished with a commanding 1-2 victory after winning 13 of 17 speed events. This was the first major win for Mustang. Courtesy Ford Motor Co.

Shelby G.T.350 Mustangs from '66 (right) and '67 (left). The '67s were wider with a wider track so engine compartment would accommodate big-block engines. Courtesy Ford Motor Co.

expense of overall handling. The small-block V8 was still the best all-around engine, but it didn't have the muscle to compete with over 400-cid engines offered in most competitive cars.

The 4-V 390 rated at 320 HP was Ford's mainline sedan engine and was standard in the Thunderbird. It had become available in the '66 intermediate Fairlane and was new in '67 Mustangs. With the *Select-Shift* Cruise-O-Matic transmission—one that could be held in any one of three forward gears—the 390 Mustang was a potent car in 1967 and certainly in the top league of street performance.

The same three basic body styles—convertible, coupe and fastback—were carried over in '67 and were offered in 13 different power teams, from a base 120 HP 6 banger to the 390. With the optional performance handling package, which was standard with HiPo 289 Mustangs, big-block Mustangs covered every conceivable buyer. Factory special-edition Mustangs appeared along with Shelby G.T.350 small-blocks and the new big-block G.T.500, a boulevard cruiser that was right at the very top in street performance.

For '68, a new foe against performance appeared in the form of government safety and emissions regulations. Consequently, Mustangs came in an array of engines including detuned versions and the new mid-performance 302, a stroked 289. The 390 went up to 335 HP and came with either a 4-speed or autoshifter. New was the introduction of the side-oiler 427 for the serious driver, a first for production Mustangs. Under-rated at 390 HP, the 427 came with the Cruise-O-Matic only, which hampered its performance. Both the 390- and 427-equipped cars came with Ford's new floating-caliper power front disc brakes.

Through 1968, Mustang styling evolved from the original 1964-1/2 models. The cars steadily got larger and heavier, and resulted in the first major redesign in 1969. We'll look at the first four years of the Mustang in some detail, including their racing exploits.

RACING MUSTANGS

When the Mustang came along in 1964, Total Performance was well in place and Ford Motor Company, under the direction of Lee Iacocca, saw the sales benefits of Mustang wins. Whether it was European rallying, SCCA road racing or drag racing, Mustangs were to become a force other auto manufacturers had to deal with. And Carroll Shelby was the focus of most of it.

Much of the flavor of those early racing Mustang days has been lost in today's frenzy to collect the finest and most valuable cars. But to recall the colorful involvement of Shelby and his crew should add an interesting dimension to Mustang racing. After some background, we'll look at the color.

A lot has been written about the rise of Shelby American, Inc., in Los Angeles, and of the great American legends in racing that came from the Shelby works. To cover the G.T.350 story briefly, the cars—so named for the approximate length, 350 feet, of the Shelby shop—came from a

1966 High-Performance Mustang window sticker

MUSTANG HARDTOP	$ 2398.43	Ford Motor Company continues to lead in safety . . .
BASE 289 2V 8CYL ENGINE	104.84	
289 4V HI PERF 3 MOS OR		
4000 MI POW TRN WARRANTY	325.55	You're looking at a product of America's leading automotive safety engineers.
FOUR SPEED TRANSMISSION	182.69	
3.89 REAR AXLE LOCKING	295.80	
NO SPIN		
SPECIAL DISC BRAKES	61.90	Both structurally and mechanically, this Ford-built car is designed to provide safer, more reliable and comfortable transportation.
G.T. FOG LAMPS	33.90	
5 6.95X14 NYL TIRES	46.60	
WHEEL COVERS	5.10	
TRANSPORTATION CHARGES	———	
TOTAL	$3454.81	

THE FOLLOWING EXTRA SAFETY FEATURES ARE STANDARD EQUIPMENT ON ALL 1966 FORD-BUILT CARS:

Front and rear seat belts, Padded instrument panel, Padded sun visors, High-strength door latches, Outside rearview mirror, Windshield Washers, Backup lights, Special safety glass windshield, 4-way emergency warning, flasher

Trans-Am notchback Mustang of Tom Yeager, Walt Hane and Peter Feistman on banking at Daytona in '67. Number 66 finished the 24-Hour Continental 16th overall averaging 79.08 mph over 1897.38 miles. This private-entry Mustang was the major Ford Trans-Am entry of 1966 and contested the seven-race schedule to the last race, Riverside, where Shelby-American made its entry into the series. Team driver Jerry Titus won the race and the first Trans-American Sedan Manufacturers' Trophy. Courtesy Ford Motor Co.

period when having fun with cars had peaked in popularity. Looking back at the group of young and dynamic people working at Shelby American, one sees that having fun was indeed a major part of the enterprise, and changing the course of racing was their game.

Once Iacocca set the tone of Ford's involvement in racing, Shelby became the prime source of Mustang performance. The factory Hi-Po 289 Mustangs were tough street machines in their own right, but going full-bore racing required considerably more than Ford built into them. Proper preparation was the task set before Shelby.

Once fully specified, Shelby fastbacks were specially built at Ford's San Jose, California, assembly plant, then suitably modified at Shelby American to produce the most competitive road machines of their time. A total of 562 G.T.350 Shelby Mustangs were built in '65. Turning a factory fastback into a Shelby required a package of special items and a good deal of improving on the Ford product for more speed, better handling and more effective brakes. All such items were made available from Shelby American for any buyer to modify his own car.

The suspensions of Shelby cars were beefed up with heavy-duty parts, lowered and fully developed for racing. And, a huge amount of knowledge was accumulated by the Shelby team that no independent could possibly have achieved on his own. Yet, along with the parts, Shelby American made available the knowledge and even provided financial support for drivers who filed a racing report within 48 hours of a competitive event they were in. If they made it

Ken Miles, the man who would have won the triple crown of auto racing—Daytona, Sebring and LeMans—in 1966, had Ford Motor Co. let him win rather than dictate a photo finish at LeMans that cost him the victory.

Shelby-American ran the '67 Trans-Am under the guise of the Terlingua Racing Team. Here, Jerry Titus, Shelby's top driver, leads Parnelli Jones in the factory-backed Mercury Cougar. Courtesy Ford Motor Co.

Titus and his Terlingua Mustang, the first Mustang built expressly for Trans-Am racing, led the 13-race Trans-Am series of '67 to Ford's second Manufacturers' Trophy. Built for SCCA's A-Sedan class, Shelby-American offered similar 289-powered Mustangs for $5500. Handling was their specialty, but speed was their game—over 140 mph. Courtesy Ford Motor Co.

to the year-end American Road Racing Championship (ARRC), $500 was available.

Shelby's crew tweaked Ford's Hi-Po 289 for an additional 35 HP—271 to 306 advertised HP. Street Shelbys received Shelby American, Inc. serial number plates reading SFM5Sxxx—S: Shelby; F: Ford; M: Mustang; 5: 1965; S: Street; xxx: consecutive serial number—riveted over the Ford serial number on the driver's side inner fender.

Of the 562 Shelbys built in '65, a total of 37 G.T.350 Mustangs were full-spec SCCA road-racing cars that carried SFM5R serial numbers. The *R* meant *Race*, and that was what these Shelbys were all about. G.T.350 Mustangs qualified as SCCA sports cars because they had no rear seat, and proceeded to take SCCAB/Production class honors three years in a row: 1965, '66 and '67. Not only were the Cobras knocking off everything in the top classes—particularly big-block Vettes—but the G.T.350s were cleaning house in their class against the likes of Corvettes, Porsches and Jaguars.

While the G.T.350 Shelbys were working over the sports-car fields, another SCCA style of racing was becoming hotly contested. Owners of standard Mustangs and other similar cars who wanted to go racing found that no class was available. To solve the problem, SCCA announced late in 1965 that a new series was being organized. It was called the *Trans-American Sedan Championship—Trans-Am* for short, and it soon attracted a host of cars, including active factory participation.

The Trans-Am racing series was based on the international FIA Appendix J regulations for series production cars (Group I) and Touring Cars (Group II). Two classes—under 2-liter and 2- to 5-liter (305-cid) powered cars—raced together. That pitted many small foreign sedans with Falcons, Mustangs, Dodge Darts, Plymouth Valiants and Barracudas, and Chevy IIs. Bob Tullius was the big gun that year in his well-developed Dodge Darts. Iacocca saw that something had to be done to put Mustangs in the winner's circle.

He assigned Shelby American to build Trans-Am Mustangs. While the standard Shelby fastbacks were built, a total of 21 notchback coupes came off the San Jose assembly line. They then received R-model updates and were really R-models in coupe form, but not as stark because regulations required them to have complete interiors and window mechanisms, among other production hardware. List price for these full-spec, 2,606-pound Trans-Am Mustangs was $6,414. Unmodified, they came from the Ford San Jose

Jerry Titus, 1967. Courtesy Ford Motor Co.

Carroll Shelby and his '67 G.T.350: Although wider and heavier, the '67s were built essentially on the same platform as earlier Shelby Mustangs. SAAC photo.

assembly plant with window stickers of $3,533.81. For comparison, the list price of a street G.T.350 was $4,547 and $5,950 for the R-model. Just to add a little more spice, list for a specially built G.T.350 Drag Mustang capable of class-record quarter-mile blasts in 1966 was $5,441.50.

The Trans-Am notchback Mustangs are no doubt the most obscure Shelby Mustang and have only recently become known. The Shelby American Automobile Club, curator of Shelby legends, maintains Shelby and Cobra documentation, including production serial numbers for the Trans-Am cars. As of mid-'87, only six of the cars had been accounted for.

The story of these cars is similar to the G.T.350: They cleaned house. The first year of the Trans-Am, 1966, was closely fought with the Tullius Darts looking good right down to the last race of the season. With the championship riding on that race, Iacocca sent the Shelby team into battle. Jerry Titus, editor of *Sports Car Graphic* magazine, was the G.T.350 team driver. With the Shelby team's vast experience in road racing, Titus won the pole position and walked away with the Trans-Am win and first championship in the series.

In 1967, the Shelby Trans-Am team Mustangs were painted *tequila* yellow with *mesquite* black hoods and trim, and raced under the crest of the *Terlingua Racing Team*. With the new Camaro, Firebird and Cougar coupes, and heavy factory involvement, considerable updates were allowed to production cars. But for the second consecutive year, it was Mustang that won the Trans-Am championship—even though Ford Motor Co. put its primary backing behind the Bud Moore built and campaigned Cougars driven by racing stars Dan Gurney and Parnelli Jones.

The Terlingua team name provides a look into the colorful behind-the-scenes activities of Shelby and friends who were having a blast being the premier racing team in the country. The Terlingua name came from a ghost town located on the huge and desolate Chiricahua Ranch that bordered Mexico in the southwest corner of Texas near Big Bend National Park. A friend of Shelby purchased the area for its wild life and intended to sell off parcels as hunting reserves. Shelby bought a large portion of the site, thus planting the seed for the Terlingua Racing Team name.

Some years ago, Rick Kopec of the Shelby Club was determined to find out more about the Terlingua origins. Here's what he found: Shelby friend, Bill Neale, whipped up the black-on-yellow team crest with its rabbit holding up one paw saying, "hold the chili peppers in the chili." Under the rabbit were three feathers that represented the three Indian tribes that had lived in the area: Comanche, Apache and Kiowa. They gave rise to the name for the area, *Tres Linguas* (three tongues), which subsequently was Americanized to *Terlingua*. The sun behind the rabbit stood for the ever-present and searing sun in the region. And the number, 1860, in the upper left corner of the crest was for the first race held in the area, a horse-drawn wagon race over what became known as the *wet-back expressway*.

Shelby and his influential friends installed an entire Terlingua area council, complete with a Commodore of the Terlingua Navy. Shelby was officially the dog catcher. Just for fun, they called Terlingua "the Chili Capital of the World." The motto of the "city"—population nine—was, "Look Backward." The official bird was the buzzard, and the city song was "How Dry I Am."

The chili part of it all became the origin of the multitude of chili cook-offs that are being carried on around the country to this date. But when the first was held in Terlingua—the "World Chili Cook-Off" of 1967—it was really an excuse for

Team Cougar for 1967: These high-style coupes were prepared by Bud Moore Engineering of Spartanburg, S.C. Courtesy Ford Motor Co.

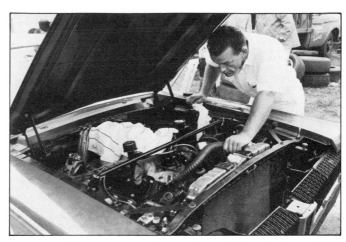

Under hood of '67 Trans-Am Cougar: Power is from highly modified small-block. Courtesy Ford Motor Co.

Shelby Racing Co. ran notchback Mustangs, scoring an auspicious debut at Daytona. Titus and Ronnie Bucknum—car No. 1—finished fourth overall behind three prototype-class Porsche 907 factory cars. Jim McGhee Photo.

a big party and was attended by some 300 people, including representatives from *Time, The Wall Street Journal, The New York Times, Newsweek* and finally, *Sports Illustrated*, who later ran a six-page article on the event!

This colorful side of Shelby racing went largely unknown to most racing fans, who paid little attention to the Terlingua Racing Team crest on the '67-team Trans-Am notchbacks. It ranged much further though, from "chili times" in Terlingua to R-model Shelbys racing in 1965 to factory Cobras, and "on the flanks of four Indy 500 winning cars and in the winner's circle at LeMans, Nurburgring, Targa Florio, Silverstone,

Sebring, Riverside, Laguna Seca and Luckenbach," according to Kopec and SAAC files.

A public relations man once said a good P.R. man could put a ghost town on the map. That was Tom Tierney, a Ford P.R. man at the time; he did it with Terlingua. Carroll Shelby showed the world what a little humor in Texas could do.

FAST STRIPES

Shelby American competition director Ken Miles and G.T.350 project engineer Chuck Cantwell specified special production order Mustangs from Ford's San Jose assembly plant that were the raw materials for the Shelby cars. The Shelbys received aluminum-case Borg-Warner T-10 close-ratio transmissions, large disc brakes up front and large Fairlane station wagon drums at the rear. A *Detroit Locker* rear-axle center section was fitted, and engines were re-moved, balanced, blueprinted and re-assembled after extensive race preparation. Special head work, along with a 715-cfm Holley 4-bbl carb with center-pivot floats and Cyclone 2-inch tube headers completed the engines. Dyno-tuning showed that power ranged from 325 to 360 HP—350 HP was chosen as average.

Extensive suspension work went into the cars, and R-models were further developed. By 1965, Shelby American had a vast amount of racing experience with 289-powered Cobras; this translated into G.T.350 wins.

In that year, Shelby Mustangs became eligible for SCCA B/Production class racing, and captured five of six national divisions to became joint Manufacturers' Champion with Porsche's under 2-liter sports cars. Jerry Titus raced the first G.T.350 built—serial number 5R001—to the Southwest Divisional title, then went on to take the B/Production National Championship as Shelby American team driver. His victory

Titus on Daytona's high banks: the '68 beginning in Trans-Am that ended with arch-rival Camaro and Mark Donohue taking the championship. Courtesy Ford Motor Co.

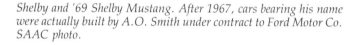

Shelby and '69 Shelby Mustang. After 1967, cars bearing his name were actually built by A.O. Smith under contract to Ford Motor Co. SAAC photo.

in the ARRC at Daytona was over mostly other Shelby drivers, notably Mark Donahue, because these fast Mustangs dominated road racing. They accounted for 10 of 14 entries in class. The 2nd-place finisher was Bob Johnson's G.T.350; 3rd was another G.T.350, making it a 1-2-3 sweep.

Carroll Shelby's school of high-performance driving used an R-model for race-driving training for anyone who wanted to learn the finer points of wheeling a G.T.350 on the race track. Along with Cobra roadsters and GT-40 Fords, the school offered the best cars of the time and the best training available.

In 1966, no factory cars were raced. Instead, Shelby American supported independents. That year, Walt Hane drove the third Shelby built—the '65 ARRC 3rd-place car—to a close-fought victory over Ron Dyke's Sunbeam Tiger, another Ford powered sports car in the Cobra tradition. That year's ARRC was held at Riverside, and the 3rd-place finisher was another R-model, the eighth one built. It was driven to the ARRC B/P National title in '67 by Freddie Van Buren of the Dos Caballos Racing Team from Mexico City.

In the 12-Hours of Sebring that year, the Van Buren/Jett team completed 185 laps, finishing 16th overall after an oil-cooler fitting broke, causing the loss of all engine oil. Clearly, the 289 was a durable engine. After a lengthy pit stop of over 12 minutes for repairs, the car was back out, and finished ahead of a number of European sports cars. At the

finish of the '67 ARRC held at Daytona—Daytona and Riverside alternated as the ARRC site each year—the Van Buren team averaged 101.01 mph for a win that clinched the 1967 B/P championship, three in a row for Shelby's cars.

As late as 1969, the G.T.350 remained highly competitive in the face of considerable Corvette advances, and proved its 1965 technology when other R-models won SCCA's Southeast and Southwest Divisional championships that year. However, highest finishes in the ARRC year-end runoffs were 4th-place in 1968 and '70, but still quite a tribute to the G.T.350, a 1965 product.

In European racing, particularly rally competition and the long-distance Tour de France, Fords were dominant for several years in the '60s. Ford of Britain-built Cortinas just about shut out all competition in their class to take the RAC World Manufacturers' Rally Cup in the first year of the Cortina team, 1963. The British *saloon-car*—European sedan—championship was almost an all Ford Cortina affair that year and, also in 1964 and '65. However, the 1965 victory was by Roy Peirpoint with an Alan Mann prepared Mustang. It was the Mann Fords that won the '65 European touring-car championship after taking the Falcon team to a sensational victory in the Monte Carlo Rally, along with an equally sensational Mustang victory in the Tour de France that year, Sept. 24, 1964. Ferrari had long dominated the Tour de France, and for an American car—particularly a

During the 1968 model year, the G.T.500KR (King of the Road) was introduced.

428 Cobra Jet engine was the major improvement in the mid-year G.T.500KR. The 428CJ had large-port 427 heads and 735-cfm Holley.

production car to win—was a highly acclaimed achievement. Later, one of the Mann Falcons was driven by Frank Gardner to the 1967 British saloon-car championship, showing that Fords in both forms, British and American, were highly competitive with Europe's best. It was a fact that soon became a bitter pill for the continentals to accept. More about this in the GT-40 sections.

In drag racing, Shelby drag-prepared Mustangs competed in NHRA B/Sports Production class and in AHRA classes. A G.T.350 was consigned to noted Ford man Bill Stroppe for development. A second Shelby drag car was run by Mel Burns Ford of Long Beach, California, and it became an AHRA record holder in the hands of Shelby American employee Don McCain.

Shelby Mustangs were raced wherever racing was done and established a huge legacy of conquest, a tradition that lives on today with the Shelby American Automobile Club and other organizations that promote the heritage of the *striped stallions*. These race-bred Mustangs are among the most collectible cars ever built in America and are surpassed only by Shelby's Cobras and the fabulous GT-40 Fords.

The first two years of Shelby Mustang production—1965 and '66—were cars built with only 289 engines. The 1967s were joined by the G.T.500 with FE series 428 big blocks. The G.T.500 received its name for no other reason than it had to have a larger number than the G.T.350; but folklore soon arose that said the real reason was the engines turned out 500 HP. In reality, the 428 was Ford's big-car engine, producing a rated 355 advertised horsepower at 5400 rpm, to quote promotional literature. But that implied what Mustang fans wanted to believe: There was more horsepower than you could ever use. By 1967, Shelby folklore talked of too much being just right, and the G.T.500 served that image well. With twin 600-cfm Holleys, the G.T.500s were thirsty boulevard cruisers that were real attention-getters.

1967 was the last year that Shelby American's Los Angeles facility actually produced cars. Thus, the '67 G.T.500 Shelbys built through about mid-year are the only big-block Mustangs actually built by Shelby's works. His LA Airport facility was closed down, and Ford Motor Co. moved production of all Shelby cars to A.O. Smith, a Michigan-based contractor who continued to build Shelbys through 1969 in what was a hot-water-heater plant. The last Shelbys, 1970 model, were actually updated '69s. With those last cars, the Shelby/Ford decade came to a close. All totalled, 7359 G.T.350 Shelbys were built from 1965 through the 1970 model year. The total for G.T.500s comes to just 7009 built from 1967 until '70. Those 14,368 Mustangs created a lasting legacy surpassed only by Shelby's own Cobra, another great American legend among cars.

Sunbeam Tiger Mk II, foreground, Mk IA, background.

Fairlane V8 of 260 cubic inches tucked away under Tiger's cowl: Standard 2-bbl or optional 4-bbl or dual 4-bbl Holleys made the Tiger Ford fast or faster.

THE TIGER CONNECTION

The Sunbeam Alpine, a traditional British roadster of the early '60s, became a hot sports car with the addition of Ford's Fairlane V8. Just as Shelby had transformed the AC Ace into the awesome Cobra with that engine, Ian Garrad, west coast USA manager for the Rootes Group that built cars through its Sunbeam-Talbot division, approached the 4-cylinder Alpine with the same thought.

Garrad and Ken Miles built the first V8 Sunbeam over a weekend, for around $600, to see if the V8 idea would work. It did, and Shelby American was tapped to fully develop a V8 Alpine for proposal as a production item to the home office in Great Britain. The Shelby car cost $10,000 and sold Rootes management on the idea. Production Tigers were the result. A total of 5,109 were imported to the U.S. out of a production run of 7,083 built between the spring of 1964 and December of '67.

The cars came in three similar forms. The first was the Mk I Tiger with Ford's 260-cid V8 in base 2-bbl form with 164 HP. Top factory and dealer optional equipment for any sort of performance applications was the 4-bbl 260 rated at 245 HP, making the Tiger a hot machine. Next came the Mk IA, with the 260 built by Ford's Industrial Division using a 289 block and head castings.

The final form came as the Mk II Tiger with the 289 engine and optional performance equipment to take the base 2-bbl of 184 HP upwards of around 275 HP. Most Ford performance equipment developed by Shelby American for 289-powered cars also worked on Tigers. And a lot of specialty options, called *LAT* (Los Angeles Tiger), were available to Tiger owners.

These were nicely balanced cars with a 51/49 front/rear weight distribution that helped to give excellent handling. With performance potential easily in excess of 300 HP in racing tune, the cars proved to be threats in SCCA B/Production road racing.

Shelby American drivers Ken Miles and Lew Spencer raced an early Tiger with Rootes factory backing to several wins against E-Type Jaguars and Corvettes, but most Tiger racing was by independent teams. By 1965, Tigers were sporting some new awards, one being AHRA class world record holder with drag racing stats of 12.95 seconds at 108 mph set by Gordon Chittenden, a record the car held for two years.

On road-racing circuits, a Tiger sponsored by Hollywood Sports Cars was driven to victory by Jim Adams in the Santa Barbara Road Races where he averaged 101 mph. Adams then won the next weekend at Mosport Park in Canada, with a flag-to-flag victory over an impressive field, including a Shelby team G.T.350 and a Cobra. This was followed by still another win, this one in extreme heat at the Salt Lake Road Races, over a factory E-type Jag entry.

Another private-entry Tiger was sponsored by Vincent Motors and driven by Ron Dykes to a class win in the 1965 Riverside Grand Prix for A/P and B/P cars. He won B/P and finished 4th overall behind the big Cobras. His clocked top speed of 157 mph showed the potential of a race-prepared Tiger. Dykes successfully raced his Tiger through the following year, winning an invitation to the ARRC run-offs at Riverside to determine national champions. In a wreck-shortened race, Dykes battled it out with Shelby G.T.350R driver Walt Hane, then lost in a close finish—but well ahead of the 3rd place car, another G.T.350R Shelby that went on to win the ARRC and national title in '67.

Endurance racing was a Tiger forte, as was shown by Don Bolton and Arthur Latta. They finished 12th overall in the Daytona Continental 2000 Km of 1965 by averaging 76.81 mph for 956.3 miles.

Perhaps the Tiger's biggest claim to fame took place in Europe where it proved to be a hard-to-beat rally car. Just three weeks after the car was introduced, Rootes factory cars were entered in the Geneva Rally, and took a 1-2-3 sweep of the 1,100-mile event through the wintertime French Alps and parts of Switzerland and Italy.

Top acclaim in Europe is earned by a car winning the Monte Carlo Rally. Rootes works drivers took a 1-2 finish in the GT-over 2,500cc class, and finished 4th overall in 1965. *Road & Track* magazine said, "to our mind, this is the success story of the year."

GALLERY of FAST FORDS

Early Fords

Henry Ford built this car and set a new world land speed record of 91.37 mph on the ice of Lake St. Clair on January 12, 1904. Road & Track photo.

Henry Ford put America on wheels with millions of Model T Fords.

Built from Model-Ts, 4-bangers like this Ascot racer were the fast Fords of the '20s.

The Model A was Henry Ford's answer to sagging sales of "Tin Lizzies." Power was still by a 4-banger.

During the '30s, most bridges in America were narrow and motorists often debated who crossed first. Here are two V8 Fords nose to nose.

"Hard times" made the '35 rumbleseat Roadster a luxury of the times. Only 4896 were produced.

By 1936, the Great Depression was easing and new Fords like this Deluxe Roadster with rumbleseat were favorites. Fewer were built than in '35, just 3862.

Following WWII, Fords like this '46 Convertible Club Coupe were very popular among returning GIs; 16,359 were sold.

Ill-fated but beautifully designed mid-thirties entry for the Indy Classic was a collaborative effort between Ford and legendary builder Harry Miller. Cars all failed with the same malady: steering gear seizure.

Low, sleek handsome styling of "new Ford company" cars, introduced in 1949 and continued through '51, were extremely popular and revitalized the company.

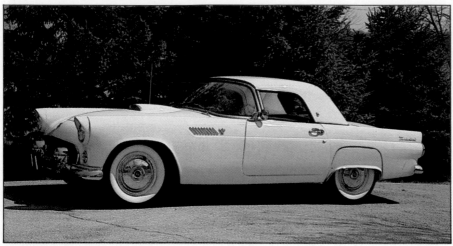

Sensational 1955 Thunderbird proved to be far more popular than Chevrolet Corvette.

1956 Fairlane Sunliner was motoring at its best, a treat for the whole family.

Styling as it has never been since, '55 Crown Victoria was a beauty.

Thunderbird was introduced in 1955 and received updates and an optional "continental kit" in '56.

Long and elegant '63 Galaxie was the first production year for both the 427 side-oiler engine and fastback top. Convertible meant cruising in open-air style.

Fastback for '64 continued the legend of the 427 in street form.

"Fast Freddie" Lorenzen drove this fastback in '65, the year he won the Daytona 500 and, among others, both the World 600 and Miller High Life 500 at Charlotte.

1965 Falcon Sprint was the stylish mini-muscle pocket rocket small sedan of the "Total Performance" era.

One of the few 1967 427 Fairlanes built; they were thrillers. Body style was seen winning stock-car, drag and stop-light races.

Ford's entry into the aero-wars of stock-car racing began in 1969 with the Talladega.

1970 Cougar Eliminator received its name and reputation from the Don Nicholson and Eddie Schartman Cougars. Street models were both high-style and fast Mercs.

Introduced in early 1964 as a '65 model, the Mustang was the most sensational new model of modern times. It remains the most popular.

Mustangs for '67 were widened to make room for Ford's big-block V8. Fastbacks, coupes and convertible body styles were available in 1967.

A group of California Ford dealers conceived the California Special Mustang for '68. With bold styling and performance to match, the CS was a hit.

Mustangs were restyled for '69. MACH 1 was the top showroom machine available with the legendary ram-air 428 Super Cobra Jet.

BOSS 302 and Cougar Eliminator were the performance leaders from Ford and Mercury for 1970.

Although built for only two years, BOSS 302 Mustang made a lasting impression as one of the most aggressive ponys ever.

In the Trans-Am wars, the Bud Moore 1970 BOSS 302 Mustangs were Ford's factory cars, the 3rd T-A win in five years of racing.

BOSS 429 engine was homologated for NASCAR stock-car racing in 1969 and '70 BOSS 429 Mustang.

Last BOSS Mustang was '71 BOSS 351.

Carroll Shelby's 289 Cobra was the greatest American sports car. It overwhelmed the racing world in all categories: international, national and drag racing.

Of all the sports cars ever built, the 427 Cobra earned its royal position among them by being brutally fast, with handling that was literally tailored by your throttle foot.

Cobra roadsters were the force of SCCA road racing in the early to mid-60s, but were surpassed by the 427 Cobra.

Shelby introduced the G.T.350 Mustang in 1965. Like the 289 Cobra, they were sensations as pure performance machines.

G.T.350 Shelby Mustangs dominated SCCA B/Production road racing in the mid-60s.

1966 G.T.350 street cars were only a little more civil than race cars, giving buyers sensational street performance.

G.T.350 and Cobra doing battle: Few marques have been raced as extensively as Carroll Shelby's wildlife.

1967 was the first year for big-block engines in Mustangs; Shelby's G.T.500 was the top boulevard heavy hitter. Small engine G.T.350s like this one carried on the small-block tradition of high-winding performance.

G.T.500 Shelby Mustangs were top luxury cruisers of the late '60s.

1968 Shelby GTs were considered by many to be the middle ground between lean '65-'66 cars and aero-influenced '69-'70 cars that marked the end of a great series of cars. The '68s were purposeful, few-frills musclecars.

Like the 289 Cobra, Ford small-block powered Sunbeam Tiger provided stiff competition and won a string of impressive wins and drag-racing records.

Ford 427 side-oiler big-block and Cobra teamed up to become quickest production car ever.

In full competition trim, 427 Cobra perform-ance was matched by the car's bold and ag-gressive styling.

Ford GT-40, one of the all-time best endurance racers, is shown here in street and Gulf-Ford competition trim. The Gulf backed GT-40s won the World Manufacturers Championship in '68.

In action, the GT-40 was the fastest, most reliable under 5-liter-powered race car of its time. Car established a stunning string of wins.

Mk II GT-40 Fords were the first long-distance racers to receive 427 side oiler. Car won the World Prototype Championship in '66.

Mk IV was an all-American Ford that proved to be the most durable endurance racer of the '60s. Cars set speed and distance records during the 24-Hours of LeMans that were not broken until 1971.

Pantera was the exotic home of mid-engine 351 Cleveland power in a svelt Italian design created by deTomaso as the Mangusta.

Following semi-retirement from illustrious career of campaigning world-class endurance racing cars such as the GT-40, John Wyer returned with John Horsman in the mid-70s with the Cosworth powered Gulf-Mirage cars to win the 24-Hours of LeMans in '75. This particular version of the Mirage is a one-off, and never faced actual competition.

"Racing into the Future," Ford's motto of the '80s, is best expressed in the small Mustang Probe.

IMSA GTO Mustang by Roush Racing was a champion in the hands of Scott Pruett and Bruce Jenner.

Total domination of IMSA GTO class with Mustangs and SCCA Trans-Am racing with turbo-four powered Merkurs became the name of FoMoCo's racing game of the '80s.

Scott Pruett doing chores in the Roush Racing GTX Mustang during 12-Hours of Sebring. Night racing gave drivers a different set of challenges.

"Awesome" Bill Elliott of Dawsonville, Georgia, has become a legend in his own time behind wheel of Coors-Melling Thunderbird.

Ford's return in the '80s has been spelled THUNDERBIRD. On the high banks, 'Birds of Bill, Davey, Ricky and Kyle have been tough to beat. Shown are Ricky Rudd's Motorcraft Thunderbird and Derrike Cope's Bird at Charlotte.

Davey Allison, 1987's awesome rookie, led most major races at times with his Havoline Star Thunderbird. He won a spectacular Talladega 500 victory.

Bob Glidden made a spectacular comeback in 1986 to win his 7th NHRA ProStock World Championship.

Although 15-years old, Donnie Moore's '68 428 Cobra Jet Mustang proved to be the best Super Stock of 1983 when he won the IHRA Super Stock World Championship.

Old Mustangs never die as shown by Rusty Perkins' '70 Cobra Jet that can still get'em up fast.

IHRA '86 ProStock World Champion Rickie Smith puts his Mustang through a 193-mph 1/4-mile.

Kenny Bernstein and his world's fastest Top Fuel Funny Car Tempo set all sorts of records in both speed and elapsed time to become premier TF/FC in 1985 and '86.

Mark Oswald and his '87 Motorcraft sponsored TF/Funny Car lays down a warmup blast.

Bob Glidden warming up those Goodyear gumballs for another 190 + mph ProStock run.

Rickie Smith puts away another Camaro. He set an all-time low ET ProStock record—7.172 seconds—to win IHRA Winter Nationals, then won Spring Nationals!

Carroll Shelby, the only man to have won the 24-Hours of LeMans as a driver, then returned as builder and team manager, and won that French classic two more times. SAAC photo.

CARROLL SHELBY

No single individual has had more influence on the direction American cars have taken or the acclaim they have received than Carroll Shelby. His personal achievements alone, before the advent of his Cobra, are more than enough for a spectacular human interest movie that would appeal to the heart of every American.

Carroll Shelby is a good guy, a winner against all odds, a man who thoroughly enjoyed driving and winning with fast sports cars when he was able, and a man who thoroughly enjoyed building fast sports cars that other drivers won with, when failing health forced his own retirement from driving.

He was 29 when he slid into a borrowed MG-TC and drove his first race in 1952—to victory! Four years later, Shelby was named *Sports Illustrated* magazine's Sports Car Driver of the Year. Again he proved his ability at the wheel by becoming Sports Car Club of America (SCCA) national driving champion that year. Fittingly enough, he repeated both successes the next year, and was named by the *New York Times* as "Sports-car Driver of the Year," in 1957-58.

After beating John Wyer's Aston Martin team and Ferrari factory entries with another borrowed car—a Cadillac powered Allard—in an international race in Argentina, Shelby was hired by Wyer to drive Astons. That association led to teaming with Britain's Roy Salvadori to win the world's premier race, the 24-Hours of LeMans, in an Aston Martin DBR1. That victory was deeply satisfying because it was a major step in Shelby's driving career. In this case, it was also the major step in Aston Martin winning the World Sports Car Championship. Thus, Shelby was at the top of the racing world, an achievement few individuals have attained. And it didn't stop there. Shelby be-

came United States Automobile Club (USAC) national road racing driving champion in 1960.

Shelby was born January 11, 1923, the son of a Leesburg, Texas, postal clerk. From that beginning, his life with cars involved every phase, from poor admirer to convincing cajoler who talked wealthy owners into letting him borrow—to race, no less—their top-caliber cars. Then he became cajoler of an industrial giant.

"I guess if I really look for a beginning, it started down in Dallas when I was still in high school," muses Shelby. "I had an old '38 model Willys that I always used to run around in, and we used to try and out-run the Fords. That thing was the terror of the streets down there—and of the cops and everybody else.

"In a way, that Willys was my first racing car—not the MG-TC. Although, I guess you'd say I started in organized racing with an MG and some specials that were owned by a buddy of mine, Ed Wilkins. Then the war came along. I was a test pilot at Childress, Texas, and eventually ended up being stationed at 19 other places, all in the same state. I didn't actually start getting interested in sports cars until about 1949 or '50."

Racing became Shelby's major occupation, but his real interest was not to continue as a driver. What he wanted to do was build and market his own car. He tried several other lines of work along the way: ready-mix cement, oilfield roughneck, then chicken farming. When the market price for chickens fell, Shelby went racing.

"So that's when I decided that, well, I'd always wanted to be a race driver and why didn't I try? Sure enough, I made a living out of it after two years.

"A guy in Okmulgee, Oklahoma, let me drive his new Jaguar, and then I got a ride in two Allards, both of them with Cadillac engines. When you had one of them in those days you really had something. I won quite a few races.

"Roy Cherryholms of Jacksboro, Texas, finally let me take his Allard down to Argentina to race guys like Phil Hill and Masten Gregory. We raced against four Ferraris down there and damned if all the Ferraris didn't break down. Then Hill's car broke down and Masten's broke, and I was lucky I had this pilot on my crew—Masten's brother-in-law, Dale Duncan.

"He kept that old Allard going with fenders blowing off and every other damn thing going wrong. We even had a fire in the pits, and we didn't have any water so we smothered it as best we could and finally, Dale peed down the carburetor. Damned if we didn't end up winning this big thing for the United States.

"We had won nothing, of course, except a big old cup. Then we took the old Allard down to the dock after the race to be loaded on the boat to be sent back to the U.S. Damned if they didn't drop a great big box on it and smashed it flatter'n hell. Cherryholms never did let me drive any of his cars anymore, and I don't know what became of the cup.

"I met John Wyer in Argentina and that's really where I got started. Getting started there let me build the rep that got the Cobra built.

"As for the idea of the Cobra, I guess that started when Ed Wilkens and I built a flathead Ford special that we raced a little bit. Then the guys around Dallas started putting the little flathead 60 in MGs, and that was a pretty good mating, except you needed a little more cooling capacity. I decided right then that it was stupid to have these expensive foreign cars when you could put an American V8 in easy enough. Then the Chevy V8 came out. You could fit a Chevy in the same hole. That was the germ of the Cobra thing.

"Of course, all that time I was driving I never did have any money. Besides, everybody laughed about my ideas. All the time I was driving in Europe for Wyer, I talked about how much I'd like to build a car combining the best of two worlds. I talked to everybody about it and hung around the Aston shop learning as much as I could.

"Then when I was forced to quit racing in 1960, I got to work. I moved to California and started thinking seriously of building a car. One day I was at Ak Miller's shop when Ray Brock—then editor of *Hot Rod* magazine—came up to me and said, 'Hey, Ford's got a new engine, a little 221-cubic inch small-block V8. Maybe that's the ticket.' Turned out it was.

"My first idea was to build my own chassis, so I had this guy Mike Jones design me a tube-type frame that would work with the small-block Ford engine. I had decided that I wanted a car the same size as the Austin-Healey, only with this 221 engine.

"So I wrote to Ford and said I had this chassis, which I didn't—it was only Mike's drawings and sketches—and Don Frey, who was the assistant general manager of the division then, sent word for me to come on in and talk about it.

"About two days before we were due to meet, I did some projections and figured what it would cost to build a chassis and body and, hell, we saw we'd never be able to do it."

About this time, AC Cars announced that it would be dropping its line of roadsters, the AC Ace, because the 6-cylinder Bristol engine they used was being dropped from production. Shelby contacted AC Cars, and they were willing to work with him. During the meeting with Frey, Shelby had all the ingredients Ford was looking for in a sports car, something they didn't have to counter GM's Corvette. However, Shelby didn't realize until afterwards that what really got him the meeting was what Frey had read about him.

"He could remember reading about me while I was racing and he thought the papers had it right—that I was some kind of Texas millionaire. He didn't know I didn't have a quarter to my name. When Ford decided to dump $25,000 into the kitty, I was suddenly fat, I'll tell you.

"Naturally, there was to be a watchdog and, again, I got real lucky. Ford sent me a guy named *Ray Geddes,* and he had a law degree and a Masters and knew his way around real well. He helped the program stay alive in lots of ways. The people at AC, especially Derek Hurlock and William Hurlock, were helpful when I went over there for six weeks while they were building the first chassis.

"Well, we couldn't have wound up with a more unaerodynamic body shape than we had for the first Cobra. It looked like it was pretty good aerodynamically, just to look at. But, hell, once it passed 140 mph it was pushing so much air that, well, that's the reason we came out with the Daytona Coupe.

"Pete Brock was the pencilman on the coupe, and Phil Remington and he fought like cats and dogs about what it should look like. I guess you would say it was about half-Brock and half-Remington, if you have to say what it really ended up as. There is no doubt, though, that the design concept was Pete's; making it work was Phil's.

"One funny thing happened about the coupe. A friend of mine who was, I think, the world's greatest aerodynamicist, old Benny Howard, took one look at the mock-ups and said it'd never work. But it sure did, so you've got to hand it to Brock that the shape did penetrate the air. The Daytona Coupe was the thing that really got the Cobra off the ground, as far as international racing was concerned. Without it, we never would have been so successful.

"That was the real idea—to go racing. I never wanted to build a lot of automobiles to make a lot of money. All the time my intention was to build 100 a year, because that was what you had to build in order to race. My idea was to build a car that would outrun the Corvette and Ferrari production cars. Ferrari was sitting around lying, because he would build two or three cars a year like the ones he raced and then say he had built 100 and sign the papers off that he had.

"The Cobra turned out to be a real tough car. The only fragile thing about it was the soft aluminum body. We overengineered the Cobra, on purpose. We knew everybody would be hopping them up, and we wanted it for racing anyway. Well, after that first championship, Ford got very interested when they saw we could beat the Corvettes and, even though they'd given me money for racing from the conception, they began talking about going to Europe. That's when Henry Ford II got interested in LeMans, so about that same time . . . well, see, when Henry got interested in something, everybody else had to get interested, too.

"We built the little 289 for four years, and when we learned that Corvette was putting a 427-cubic inch engine in their car, that presented a problem, because our real aim was to blow the doors off Corvettes. Ford had 427 fever, too, so I got together with the man I think is the best chassis engineer in the world, Klaus Arning. He had us a chassis designed off the computer at Ford in just about two weeks. From the time we thought of the 427 Cobra until the time the first one was running over here in the States, exactly three months had gone by, which shows what a little company can do when it makes its mind up. And we never made a change in the 427, never made a change.

"It was Lee Iacocca who really stayed behind us all the way, encouraged us and then he got us into the Mustang program. Well, all of the corporate vultures jumped on the thing, and that's when it started going to hell. It took me five more years to get out of it.

"It was getting more and more apparent that you couldn't make dime one building cars, and it wasn't fun any more, what with so many restrictive legislative rules to go by. Rules that are constantly changing at the whim of the politicians. It's really a tragedy that you see fewer and fewer people doing what we did with the Cobra.

"There're a lot of people who want to build the right thing, but they get a hitch in their gittalong somewhere between their desires and the necessity for compromising. We were lucky. None of us felt like compromising any more than we had to, and we didn't have to too much. The first Cobra was exactly what I wanted it to be, and I thought it sold for a pretty fair price."

The above has been adapted from a Shelby interview in 1971. Not much has happened since; not much more than his cars are even more widely recognized as the greatest American sports cars; not much more than Shelby becoming a legend in his own time; not much more than Carroll Shelby being seen as a truly great American, perhaps the last American hero.

6

STRIPPERS

Drag Strips to the Salt Flats

New Ford Mustang, the car that stole the show when introduced in April, 1964.

1965 Mustang lineup—2+2 fastback, convertible and coupe— appealed to everyone.

Fast Mustangs blistering the quarter mile were a main feature at the drags all across America in the mid-60s. Drag racers pitted their skills and their machines against each other in front of crowds who cheered the performances of Gas Ronda, Hubert Platt, Les Ritchey, Bill Lawton, Jerry Harvey, Paul Norris and other Ford drag racers. It is easy to see from drag-racing records that Ford-powered cars have claimed only a fraction of the available class victories of the time, but when it comes to being the most sensational cars, Mustangs ranked among the top.

Total Performance in 1965 was strong in Mustangs, and when Ronda came to the line the first time in his Russ Davis steed, it was sure to be the same sort of "killer" that his '64 Thunderbolt Top Eliminator World Champion ride had been. Ford Motor Co. chose to go for the most exciting full-bodied cars in '65 and skipped Super Stock. The Russ Davis A/FX Mustang was powered by a fuel-injected SOHC 427, one of several factory team cars that ambushed the competition during the Winternationals at Pomona.

These cars weighed about 3230 pounds and were capable of 10-second blasts. Len Richter ran a similar car bearing the Bob Ford logo. Paul Norris was the Holman & Moody Mustang pilot, and Bill Lawton was in the now-famous Tasca Ford Mustang. The final at Pomona was an all-Mustang shoot-out between Richter and Lawton, with Lawton taking the A/FX win in 10.92 seconds at 128.20 mph. Richter set a class low elapsed time (e.t.) at 10.91 seconds, and Ronda was close with a 10.92.

Mustangs powered by Ford big-blocks were fearsome quarter-milers. Here, Ford star Les Ritchey and his Performance Associates A/Factory Experimental Mustang lays down fast quarter-mile at Pomona. Bill Lawton's A/FX Mustang took NHRA Winternationals Factory Stock Eliminator in 1965 with a strong 10.92 at 128.20 mph. Jerry Harvey nailed down the '66 Winternationals Street Eliminator with his A/FX Mustang (10.68/132.15). Tom Grove blasted the Competition Eliminator field at the '66 Springnationals running 8.97/162.16 in his A/Experimental Stock Mustang funny car. Grove returned in '67 to take Funny Car Eliminator in his '67 Mustang at 8.34/170.13. Courtesy Ford Motor Co.

Gas Ronda in Russ Davis Mustang match racer helped pioneer funny-car class. Courtesy Ford Motor Co.

Gas Ronda and his 427-cammer Ford of '68 turned consistent 8.50s running fuel injection. Most competing match racers were running blowers. Courtesy Ford Motor Co.

Hubert Platt reached national attention with his Georgia Shaker. Here he blasts the Winternationals at Pomona, winning the '67 A/ Experimental Stock with a strong 8.49/171.42 pass. Courtesy Ford Motor Co.

In the AHRA World Finals, Ronda and Norris faced off in another all Mustang finale with Rhonda taking the Super Stock crown. Ronda's red Russ Davis fastback set an NHRA A/FX national record at 10.43 at 134.73 mph, the best for the entire '65 season. That year was the last that saw A/FX cars, as the funny-car movement picked up considerably in 1966 to become the mainline cars. A/FX cars had altered wheelbases, but remained somewhat stock in appearance. Funny cars were obviously different, and with altered bodies, blowers and nitro, they were little more than dragsters with long, low fiberglass bodies derived from production-car styling.

First classified Super/Experimental Stock, these Mustangs generally faced off against themselves and MoPars; Chevrolet didn't have the stuff for this class. By 1966, match racing among the top cars of the time was very popular and drew big crowds. Ronda was a favorite with his Mustang. Holman & Moody built the chassis for this car. The fuel-injected *cammer* was placed about 18 inches back from the stock engine location. Total weight was 2100 pounds, and the combination was enough for Ronda to set a variety of records. One record set was the first unblown full-bodied 8-second time recorded, an 8.96 at about 155 mph, defeating

Don Nicholson and his factory-backed '68 Cobra Jet Mustang. After teammate Al Joniec won Super Stock Eliminator at NHRA Winternationals (12.50 second et), Hot Rod magazine called the Cobra Jet "the fastest running pure stock in the history of man." Courtesy Ford Motor Co.

Gas Ronda, another Mustang Cobra Jet factory driver, teamed with Nicholson, Hubert Platt, Al Joniec and Jerry Harvey in a dominating Mustang Super Stock class. Courtesy Ford Motor Co.

Tom "Mongoose" McEwen's match racer named the *Hemi 'Cuda.* That was truly sensational at the time, and fast enough to shut out Doug Thorley's Chevy II in another match race.

There was much more Mustang drag racing around the country than can be recounted here. For example, Jerry Harvey's A/FX Mustang took the 1966 NHRA Winternationals Street class with a fine 10.68 at 132.15 mph. Mike Schmidt took the Street class Springnationals final that year at Bristol with a '65 B/FX Ford running a strong 11.85 at 119.68 mph.

Mustangs were strong, but not over-powering as was shown by "Fast Eddie" Schartman taking the Super/Experimental Stock win at the '66 World Finals at Pomona with his Comet. And there was Jack Chrisman's blown Comet running a full second quicker than Ronda's non-blown Mustang, or in the mid 7s by '67. Still, his unblown car was tough to beat in class. After turning what was the highest unblown speed—just over 178 mph—it was clear that Gas Ronda and the cadre of Mustangs were top-drawer cars.

By 1967, *Funny Car* became a class all its own, and Mustangs remained top cars. Tom Grove put his Mustang on the winner's deck at the Springnationals with an 8.34 pass at 170.13 mph. Top Fuel eliminator was taken by Don Prudhomme, knocking out a sensational 6.92-second blast at 222.76 mph with his cammer Ford AA/F dragster. Ronda ran consistent 8.50s with his Mustang, still unblown in '67, but by the next year, he was in the blown class.

With a second and more advanced car that year, his was one of more than 60 cars of the nitro funny-car field that turned out for a manufacturers' showdown at Orange County. Ronda set low e.t. of the meet with a 7.26 at 200 mph and

To prove Cobra Jets are still hard to beat, Donnie Moore in his '68 CJ Mustang won the 1983 IHRA Super Stock World Championship, won SS Eliminator in the Pro-Am Nationals and U.S. Open Nationals that year. Squire Gabbard Photo.

put himself in the final round with one of the toughest cars in the country, the "Chi-Town Hustler" Dodge Charger. Both cars left the line in a classic hole shot; Ronda put away the "Hustler," 7.47 at 199.55 to 7.48 at 202.70!

Although Super Stock racing was by now largely ignored by Ford, the new Cobra Jet Mustangs of 1968 were the basis for a sensational Mustang drag-racing team. These were pure-stock cars racing in NHRA Super Stock class. Ford fielded eight factory cars at Pomona. Four were piloted by

Today's Super Stock rules allow few variations from stock, so Moore's CJ is close to 1968 vintage, although capable of 10.20 quarters at 130+ mph. Squire Gabbard Photo.

Sandy Elliot's team of "Border Bandits"—Barrie Poole, Sandy Elliot and John Elliot—was made up of two Mustangs and a Comet. Trophies tell the story. Sandy Elliot was named Super Stock Crew Chief of the year in Car Craft magazine's 5th annual all-star team of 1971. Courtesy John Elliot.

1969 Mach 1 was a Mustang heavy-hitter, a boulevard cruiser capable of neck-snapping acceleration in Cobra Jet form.

428 Super Cobra Jet (SCJ) ram-air, the engine that won drag races.

Gas Ronda, Jerry Harvey, Hubert Platt and Al Joniec. The white Cobra Jet fastbacks took the Super Stock Winternationals by storm with Joniec versus Platt in the SS/E final. Joniec took the class with a strong 11.49/120.6 pass. He then came away with the SS Eliminator victory with an easy 12.50/97.93-mph win. *Hot Rod* magazine gave the new 428-powered Mustangs a big sales boost by proclaiming the Cobra Jet to be "the fastest running pure stock in the history of man."

What turned the 428 into the Cobra Jet that produced a real runner was the addition of larger-valve 427 heads and intake to the more conventional 1967 428 FE big-block. In this form, with a single 4-bbl Holley, factory rating was 335 HP, but actual power was closer to 410 HP, a ploy to keep insurance rates lower for Cobra Jet buyers.

The year 1967 saw another change in drag racing that brought a new force to the quarter-mile. "Ohio George" Montgomery from Dayton had campaigned the "World's

"Ohio George" Montgomery, pioneer drag racer in gas class, was highly successful with his 427-cammer-powered Malco AA/Gas Supercharged Willys, setting many NHRA records. Courtesy George Montgomery.

Rusty Perkins and Scotty's Speed & Custom 428 Cobra Jet convertible running in Super Stock/I pulls a wheelie at Beech Bend International Raceway Park in Bowling Green, Kentucky. Cobra Jets are still hard to beat. Squire Gabbard Photo.

New-style race cars sold new production cars, so Ford wanted Montgomery to switch to a late-model body style. The Malco Gasser '67 Mustang was the result, the first late-model body in gas-class racing. The car caused all sorts of out-cries from competitors who called it a funny car when, in fact, it was built like any other gasser, but wrapped with a Mustang body. "Ohio George" continued setting NHRA records. Courtesy George Montgomery.

Ford's 427 SOHC cammer, supercharged and fuel injected, could turn out 1700 HP, another Dearborn winner in the hands of "Ohio George." Courtesy George Montgomery.

Wildest Willys" in AA/Gas Supercharged class for years, but switched to a '67 Mustang in 1967. It brought about loud protests from competitors who saw the gasser as a funny car, although it was built to gas-class specifications using a Mustang body rather than the more conventional '30s coupe.

The Mustang gasser was introduced at Bristol's "Thunder Valley" and immediately went about setting a string of records. Montgomery built a series of Mustangs during the next few years that continually upset NHRA officials and competitors.

There were five all-fiberglass '67 bodies built. The driver and engine remained in the normal position. George completely dominated all competition by winning his class in the Summernationals, Springnationals, Winternationals and the U.S. Nationals, with speeds and times in the 163-mph/8.70-second range.

George's beautiful blue *The Malco Gasser* was campaigned into 1969 when a new car was needed, and Ford Motor Co. let George use a Mach I prototype to *pull* a new mold for his

George Montgomery AA/GS class winner, NHRA U.S. Nationals, Summernationals, Springnationals and Winternationals, with record after record beginning with an 8.93 at 162.16-mph blast that let competitors know the revolution in gas-class drag racing had arrived. Courtesy George Montgomery.

Montgomery's ultra-slick '67 Mustang AA/GS fastback not only won speed and set records, it also was so well executed that he received NHRA's "Best Engineered Car" award. Courtesy George Montgomery.

The only all-fiberglass '69 Mustang built was this car, George Montgomery's "Mr. Gasket Gasser," a SOHC 427-powered car that set many records in AA/GS. At the debut of this Mustang at the U.S. Nationals in '69, George won the class, then Super Eliminator with a blistering 8.59 at 164.23 mph, and won "Best Engineered Car"— everything he could win at that event. Next, George won the '69 Springnationals Super Eliminator running 8.78/161.00. Courtesy George Montgomery.

new gasser Mustang of that model. The *Mr. Gasket Gasser,* a one-off all-fiberglass drag car was originally intended for the new BOSS 429 engine, but was raced initially with a cammer similar to the earlier car.

Both cars were all-Ford except for Willys frame rails that were required in gas-class racing. Both ran C-6 automatics, Ford 9-inch rear ends and lots of other Ford-built equipment used for factory testing and development. In 1971, a twin-turbocharged BOSS 429 was developed for Alcohol Funny Car, another new class. Its 440 cubic inches cranked out around 1400 HP, and produced a gasser Mustang that was revolutionary in concept and beautiful in execution. The

Turbo-BOSS was nothing short of phenomenal and so superior to the competition that George was singled out for a handicap that made the car non-competitive. The reason was probably that turbos muffle the engine while doing their job, and NHRA officials thought George was holding back because the car ran so quiet.

So much for the welcome that pioneering received in drag racing. What George Montgomery experienced back then is being debated again today with the revival of turbocharged ProStockers.

By the early '70s, Ford Motor Co. had fired Ford Division boss "Bunkie" Knudsen, the force behind Ford racing at the time, and closed the till on factory racing. Carroll Shelby had retired, Ford was out of stock-car racing, factory Trans-Am racing dried up and the decade of doldrums set in again.

BOSS MACHINES

Among the breed of fast Fords that raced across the American road-racing scene, the BOSS 302 Mustang was one of the best. Unfortunately, its existence was short, only 1969 and '70. And like its bigger brother, the BOSS 429 Mustang was also short-lived. Thus, both models had little effect on Ford's on-going attempts to re-kindle its image as the hot-rodder's make, a goal that takes a long-term commitment.

Although the BOSS 302 engine was a superb performer, its brief life span in production was too short with too few built for after-market suppliers to develop any significant line of parts. Consequently, the engine was gone before a substantial hot-rodding legacy developed. A more pressing matter, though, was facing Ford Motor Co.

During 1968, Mustang sales fell for the third straight year and Ford was experiencing an image problem. While the Mustang once had the market segment to itself, by 1968, competition among long hood/short deck personal-size cars was fierce. Buyers had a variety from which to choose. Each

Mercury's answer to the Mustang was the Cougar Eliminator offered in 1970 with four engine options: BOSS 302, 351C-4V, 428CJ and 428SCJ. Only 2200 total were built.

With Ford's Muscle Parts equipment on a big block, a Cougar Eliminator was a handsome machine.

Parnelli Jones and George Follmer gave other Trans-Am teams fits behind wheels of their Boss 302 Mustangs. Courtesy Ford Motor Co.

When Shelby-American closed its doors at the end of 1967, several California dealers got together and created the California Special offered only in 1968. The CS Mustangs were notchbacks equipped like Shelbys for good looks and performance.

manufacturer had similar models, and Ford management was looking for answers.

One came in the form of Semon "Bunkie" Knudsen who was hired away from GM to head up the Ford Division. He had climbed the GM ladder to the top of Chevrolet, then on to a GM Vice-President position. But when he lost his bid to become GM President to Ed Cole, he began looking for something else. In February, 1968 he accepted a million-dollar offer from Henry Ford II. It was a corporate coup that surprised everyone in the auto industry and was the opposite move his father, William S. "Big Bill" Knudsen, did when he left the elder Ford's employ in the '20s, also in a huff, and subsequently set to building up Chevrolet to rival Ford.

Knudsen was charged with the job of gaining ground against Chevrolet and wanted more racy-looking cars with real performance. He immediately set to refining models for the '69 model year to reduce cost, improve styling and to be fast. One of his first successful tasks was a raid on GM styling that brought Larry Shinoda over to head up Ford's Special Design Center. The first thing Knudsen and crew did was to reduce anticipated manufacturing costs. They then applied the racy image of stripes, scoops, spoilers, wings and bold colors and graphics along with *real* performance. Four of the first image cars Shinoda's group developed were the Mach I, the BOSS 302, BOSS 429 and Cougar Eliminator.

Then came this: George with his twin-turbo alcohol-fueled BOSS 429, the engine that strained NHRA to the point that they handicapped the car so much that it wasn't competitive.

"OHIO GEORGE" MONTGOMERY

"I had been quite friendly with Ford through the mid-60s, and it was in the '64-'65 era when we came to terms with parts and pieces. I had some help with the SOHC engine in my AA/Gas Supercharged Malco Willys. About then, the Ford wheels told me to forget about the Willys—'we don't make them' they said—and wanted me to run a Ford. There were no late-model bodies in the class at the time, and the '67 Mustang I built for the engine was the first late-model gas-class car.

"Being an old hard-core gasser, the switch to the Mustang caused a lot of controversy. I ran it first in late '67 at Bristol and received the 'Best Engineered Car' award. It was so superior to the competition that I had to judge my runs by my opponent and had to back off to keep from running away with it. NHRA had actually mis-dialed my index into the *tree* and probably would have re-run the match, but I was so far under the index that they disqualified me.

"Ford had five of the all-fiberglass '67 Mustangs built, and my blue Gasser was a very successful car. The first record I set with the car was on June 15, 1967, when I ran an 8.93 and 162.16 mph to set both AA/GS marks. It turned out that the car also fit into AA/Altered and BB/Altered classes. In June of '68, I set an AA/Altered low e.t. record of 8.82 seconds at National Trials, then ran an 8.77 in AA/Gas Supercharged for another record the same day at Columbus, Ohio, in the Springnationals. My speeds were consistently over 160 mph. In June of '69, I

won the Super Eliminator at the Springnationals in Dallas with the blue '67 Gasser, 8.73 seconds and 162.74 mph.

"In mid-68, I started the '69 Mach I car because Ford wanted me to race a new-model Mustang. At the time, there were only two Mach I prototypes, both hand-built cars Ford was using for design studies. We had a tough time scheduling one of these cars to use to make a mold for the fiberglass car, but we finally got one for a week, and you wouldn't believe the mess we made of it trying to get a mold made from it. We ended up having to repaint it and kept it for a month. Ford engineering was screaming for the car because it was scheduled for other people on down the line. After we made the body for my car, the mold was destroyed, which made my red '69 Mach I *Mr. Gasket Gasser*, a one-of-a-kind car. That was the car I used mainly for national championship races, and the blue '67 was my work horse.

"I had a lot of Willys parts and both cars were built on Willys frames to make them legal for gas classes. There wasn't all that much difference in the way the cars were built and their performance was about the same, but I kept the freshest parts for the '69 car. I won a lot of races with the cars—match races and championship runs included—and set many, many records, usually both ends—speed and e.t.. The most successful single racing I did with the '69 Mustang was its debut at the U.S. Nationals at Indianapolis, where I won the 'Best Engineered Car' award. I won my class, then took Super Eliminator and set a low e.t. record of 8.59 seconds and an 164.23 mph for both ends of the record. The car had only been completed about two weeks, and won everything it possibly could. The highest speed record I set was about 169 mph in the Mach I. At National Trails in '69, I won Super Eliminator again, running 8.78 and 161.0 mph. The last racing I did with the car was in the Gatornationals of '73 and '74 where I won an easy AA/GS 13.58 seconds coasting to a 62.84 mph win in '73, and then set a low e.t. of 8.44 at 167.59 mph to win BB/Altered in '74.

"Ohio George's" turbo BOSS 429 "Mr. Gasket Gasser" as it sits today, the only car of its kind. Note exhaust protruding from front-wheel opening. Car was so quiet that NHRA officials thought George was holding back. They handicapped him 0.500 second when 0.100 second covered the field, testimony to the fear George's Mustangs created. Courtesy George Montgomery.

"These cars were powered by 427-inch cammers, super-charged with fuel injection and were probably in the 900-to-1000 HP range. I ran C-6 automatics in both cars, and the Mach I weighed about 2300 pounds. It was originally built with a BOSS 429 in it, but we didn't have enough parts to complete it as a blown car. At the last minute, I took the BOSS out and put a cammer in and raced it that way for '69. In mid-70, we started some testing with the BOSS, but I didn't do much racing with it as a supercharged engine.

"In 1971, we started the turbo program, but had the rug pulled out from under us when Ford pulled back from racing. We had completed all the ground work, and I knew the potential of the Turbo-BOSS was terrific. So Danny Jones and his Ford people in the racing group, on their own, decided to go ahead with the program without Ford funding. Suppliers were very gracious about it and agreed to continue, even though it was much slower paced.

"The overall results of the turbo program were nothing short of phenomenal. It absolutely dominated AA/Gas Super-charged in two major events I won, and it upset NHRA to the point that they handicapped it so bad that they made it absolutely non-competitive. They didn't know the potential of the car, and it ran so quiet that they thought I was holding back so much that they slapped a 0.50-second index on me. That upset me very greatly that NHRA singled me out and made me non-competitive. I was the only drag racer running turbochargers and the '75 rules stopped turbos, period. I never really ran the car after that.

"The engine in that car was a 440-cid BOSS 429 turning out around 1400 HP. About then, alcohol funny cars were said to be the great salvation of drag racing, and I built a '73 Mustang

Malco Super Gasser II, one of the last efforts by Montgomery until NHRA forced him out. Courtesy George Montgomery.

called the *Boss-Turbo* with another twin-turbo BOSS 429. I spent about two years developing that car, and was getting about 1800 HP out of it. I thought it would have dominated the class. When NHRA found out about it, they did me in again with a stiff handicap before I even got started. I dismantled the car, sold it and my involvement with NHRA after that was very limited. I thought that was really wrong to do before the car was ever brought out, but they were scared of it and afraid that I would do to Alcohol Funny Car what I did to AA/Gas Super-charged. My Mustangs showed a lot of pioneering ideas and development, and were the quickest, fastest and best cars of their type, but NHRA couldn't handle them."

Both the BOSS 302 and BOSS 429 Mustang programs were authorized by Knudsen, and their purpose was two fold. First, Chevy's Z28 Camaro won the 1968 Trans-Am championship powered by an engine more successful than Ford's ill-fated tunnel-port 302; Knudsen wanted a Mustang in the winner's circle. That required a new engine, one that could be volume produced at a lower cost than the racing 302. Secondly, the highly proven 427 tunnel-port had become rather dated, although still competitive, and needed a replacement for wins in stock-car racing.

Thus, both BOSS Mustangs were a direct result of Knudsen's pressing Ford into racing. The origin of the BOSS 302 engine was the recognition that the proposed Ford mainline V8 for the '70s, the 351 Cleveland, was already slated for production. The 351C incorporated large-diameter, canted-valve heads that had significant horsepower potential because of improved breathing and a more efficient combustion chamber than the conventional wedge chamber.

The tunnel-port 302 in the Trans-Am cars of 1968 had not proven very successful and, more significantly, it was not to be a production engine. Its strong 4-bolt-main block had proven very durable, and only slight modification of the Cleveland heads resulted in just as much horsepower as the race-bred tunnel-port head. Thus, when the canted-valve Cleveland heads—so named for being produced in Ford's

Ed Schartman, a Mercury die-hard who won '66 NHRA World Finals with a Super/Experimental Stock Comet, takes Funny Car Eliminator running 8.38/174.08 in a Cougar. Courtesy Ford Motor Co.

'70 model BOSS 302 Mustangs were available with everything under the hood or with the shaker hood—the fresh-air scoop mounted to the carburetor and protruded through the hood.

BOSS 302 in street form, a mean machine and probably the all-round runningest Mustang ever built.

Cleveland heads—so named for being produced in Ford's Cleveland, Ohio, plant—were adapted to the 302, a new engine was born: the BOSS 302.

The story of the BOSS 429 is similar. Ford's 429-inch engine was introduced in the 1968 Thunderbird and became available in full-size Fords; a 460 version was used in the Lincoln. The making of the BOSS 429 engine was accomplished by using newly designed ultra-wide cast-aluminum, canted-valve heads on the 429/460—or *385-series*—block. Like the BOSS 302 and 351 Cleveland, the BOSS 429 heads gave significantly improved breathing, a more efficient combustion chamber and greater power potential.

The BOSS 302 Mustang was, as Knudsen proclaimed, "the best handling street car you could buy." It also had another role, and that was Knudsen's plan for Ford's Trans-Am racing machines to flatten the Camaros on the road-racing tracks of America.

There is little doubt that the BOSS 302 remains one of Ford's all-time best designs for overall performance. When introduced in 1969 as Camaro's adversary, it immediately asserted itself as a tough, high-winding street machine. And on the tracks, all adversaries, including Camaros, found the new Mustang almost unbeatable. Were it not for mid-season bad luck—a crash that almost wiped out the entire factory team—the BOSS 302 Mustangs would no doubt have smashed Camaro as planned. Unfortunately, because of the crash at St. Jovite, Canada, and the length of time it took to get the cars back into top racing form, Mark Donohue's Penske Camaro team was able to take a second Trans-Am championship.

Knudsen's image cars were really factory-built replace-ments for Carroll Shelby's Mustangs. After mid-season 1967, all Shelbys were built by A.O. Smith on contract to Ford. Ford's captive race/performance-car development firm was Kar Kraft of Brighton, Michigan.

For the 1969 model year, Knudsen elected to have BOSS 302 Mustangs built by Ford and BOSS 429 Mustangs built by Kar Kraft. The purpose of the BOSS 429 Mustang was to *homologate* the new engine for stock-car racing. Ford and Mercury were fielding new low-buck special-edition Talladegas and Cyclones that year, page 57, but the cars were built before the engines were ready. Thus, the cars rolled off the Atlanta assembly line with more conventional engines, and when the BOSS 429 was finally ready, a new car was needed. Knudsen selected the Mustang. The huge engine in that car also served to fulfill another of Knudsen's objectives: The Mustang was Ford's image car, and the combination of it and the new monster motor resulted in a real attention getter.

Unfortunately, the street BOSS 429 engine was speedily developed as a detuned version of the NASCAR engine and had some problems that detracted from its public image. The huge intake and exhaust ports weren't practical for a street engine—even a high-performance one—due to the lack of *bottom-end* torque. The cars were rather lackluster and unable to defend their image against 13.10-second Hemi 'Cudas, 13.16-second ZL-1 Camaros, 13.38-second 455 GSX Buicks and 13.54-second Trans-Ams and other cars tested by auto magazines. However, on the high-banks, the BOSS 429 was almost unbeatable and proved to be another Ford stock-car thoroughbred by taking 26 stock-car victories in 1969 and another manufacturers' championship.

124

"Dyno Don" and his Eliminator is up against "Fast Eddie" and his Rattler in an all-Cougar final round. Courtesy Ford Motor Co.

"Fast Eddie" Schartman's '69 Cougar was an excellent showcase for Lincoln-Mercury. His and Don Nicholson's Cougars were the basis of the special-edition production Cougar Eliminator marketed only in late '69 and '70. Courtesy Ford Motor Co.

BOSS 429 Mustang introduced in 1969 came in six colors and featured the 429 Cobra Jet HO, otherwise known as the BOSS 429. KK 429 NASCAR 1451 shown here is one of the best examples in existence.

BOSS 429 Mustang serial-number plate.

On the drag scene, the BOSS 429 was capable of under 14-second quarters in stock form. One magazine test reported a best of 13.60 seconds at 106 mph, but the cars were not able to capture a single NHRA super-stock national event. Kar Kraft built several-drag racing BOSS 429 cars; two were Cougars for Lincoln-Mercury's drag program, and they appeared throughout America and at U.S. military bases in Europe. Match races were big spectator attractions at the time, and Mustangs were run by a number of teams. A variant on the theme was the supercharged BOSS 429s that ran in A/Modified Production.

The potential of the BOSS 429 engine was tremendous. Just as with the SOHC 427, Connie Kallita was one of the first drag racers to get the new engine. He ran two Ford powered cars—an AA/Fuel dragster and a '69 Mustang funny car, both carrying his famous name, Bounty Hunter. Danny Ongais campaigned the Mickey Thompson BOSS funny car while "Fast Eddie" Schartman and "Dyno Don" Nicholson ran the BOSS Cougars in Super Stock. Drag racing, with all its factory backing and monster mills, made the sport into a

Giant valve covers of BOSS 429 "grabbed" your eyes the instant hood was raised. Cars were built with a manually operated ram air hood scoop. The 735-cfm Holley was totally dominated by huge size of the BOSS 429.

Mustang spring towers were modified to make room for BOSS 429. Brake master cylinder had to come off before left valve cover could be removed.

"Fast Eddie" Schartman's Cougar, the Rattler, ran in Super Experimental class in 1968 and match raced anything from anywhere. Courtesy Ford Motor Co.

The Rattler was what is now known as a funny car. Injected and blown SOHC 427 cammer produced under-8 second quarter-miles at around 190 mph. Courtesy Ford Motor Co.

manufacturers' shoot-out that soon gave rise to a new class—ProStock—where the big boys could fight it out among themselves.

Unfortunately, at the Winternationals in '69, not a single Ford took an eliminator win. But at the Springnationals, Fords were strong by capturing three out of eight Eliminator titles. Ongais won Funny Car with a blistering 7.63 at 191.89 mph; George Montgomery's AA/GS Mach I dominated Super Eliminator running 8.78 and 161.0 mph and "Dyno Don" cleaned up Street Eliminator with his A/MP '69 Mustang running 10.49 at 120.96. Then, Ongais and Montgomery took big wins at the U.S. Nationals, taking strong victories in Funny Car (7.47/195.65) and Super Eliminator (8.59/164.23).

In 1969 road racing, two factory teams ran BOSS 302

Mustangs: Shelby American out of California, and Bud Moore Engineering out of Spartanburg, South Carolina. Shelby's illustrious racing record has been well covered over the years, and Moore's experience with the '67 factory Trans-Am Cougar team—the cars driven by Dan Gurney and Parnelli Jones—was the source of his selection to run the BOSS 302s. In 1968, Lincoln-Mercury dropped its Trans-Am racing, and Moore raced the ex-factory Cougars in NASCAR's "Baby Grand" series, officially called the *NASCAR Grand Touring Division*. The well-developed ex-factory team Cougars ran away with the first Baby Grand race—the Sandhill 250 at Rockingham—with Tiny Lund leading a Cougar 1-2-3 sweep ahead of teammate Swede Savage, and Paul "Little Bud" Moore in the third car. Cougars went on to win

Iron man Parnelli Jones and his Bud Moore Engineering 1969 BOSS 302 Trans-Am Mustang. Jones and George Follmer were the drivers on Moore's factory team. Jones won two of the first six rounds of the season, the Wolverine T-A at Michigan International Speedway, and Donnybrooke at Brainerd, Minnesota. Follmer won at Bridgehampton to account for three of Ford's four wins, Sam Posey of Shelby-American won the other, and Ford was well ahead of Donohue's Penske Camaro. Then a crash at St. Jovite took out three of the four team cars. Remainder of season was slim; no more wins. Courtesy Ford Motor Co.

other Baby Grands: David Pearson at Hickory and Lloyd Ruby at Daytona. Lund took the season championship.

The early Trans-Am races that year were dominated by Mustangs as they won four of the first six races. Then came St. Jovite when all four factory Mustangs DNF'd. Afterwards, with only one "good" car, Mustangs won no other Trans-Am race and finished 2nd in points to Donohue's Camaro.

The next year was a new beginning and, true to Knudsen's goal, Mustang flattened the Camaro effort in 1970. In fact, it was the Penske/Donohue Javelins, rather than Camaro, that proved the greatest threat to Ford.

Wild man Parnelli Jones was the lead driver in 1970 with George Follmer in the three-car team of vibrant orange Boss 302 Mustangs. Jones once remarked, "If you're under control, you're not going fast enough!" And that's just the way he drove, even to the extent of leaving Follmer in the dust when there were no other challengers.

Ford's Trans-Am Boss 302s were as tough as the iron men who drove them. They are probably the most bulletproof production-based racers ever built. Testimony to that is the fact that there was only one engine failure and no transmission or rear-axle failures in all of the 1970 season. This was a season that saw the Mustangs winning six of the 11 races, and dominating the points standing with 72 points; Javelin had 59; Camaro, 40; MoPar, 33; and Firebird, 0.

But, then, corporate racing was brought to a halt and

Revenge in 1970 came at the hand of Jones as lead driver of the Bud Moore Trans-Am Mustangs. Jones is shown here on his way to winning at Mid-Ohio, one his five wins that season. Follmer won at Bryar Motorsport Park, giving Ford the Trans-Am championship with six wins in 11 races. Jim McGhee photo.

Knudsen was ousted. Henry Ford II withdrew the factory from all forms of racing in October, 1970. That left the Ford Trans-Am cars at their most competitive until modern times, or 16 years.

One of the three Bud Moore team cars of '70 (foreground) and S.S. Jacobs Co. car campaigned by Follmer for Moore in '71. Without factory backing, Follmer finished second overall in the '71 Trans-Am series.

Jones' 1970 backup car as it appears today.

The cars carried serial numbers 70TA-01 (Follmer's car), 70TA-02 (Jones' lead car) and 70TA-03 (Jones' back-up car). They began life as '69 model fastback Mustangs with Ford factory serial numbers 9F02M212775 (Jones' -02), 776 (Follmer's -01) and 777 (Jones' -3). Even though Jones always ran with number 15 on his car and Follmer with 16 on his, just which car ran which race and driven by whom is not known for sure because the cars were so much alike.

According to Mitch Marchi, one of Kar Kraft's engineers, the cars were received from Ford for extensive modification from production to Trans-Am racing specs. He says there were perhaps 12 total Trans-Am Mustangs built for the 1969-70 seasons: nine in '69 when both Bud Moore and Shelby American ran teams, and three in 1970 when only Moore campaigned the cars. The cars received Kar Kraft's tough full-floater, ear ends and ultra-strong transmissions that were designed and built for 200+ mph laps at LeMans without a failure of any kind.

All drive-line components were Ford's best. They were required to handle the high-winding, canted-valve Trans-Am version of the Boss 302 engine that developed 460 HP from one 4-bbl and a compression ratio of 10.5-to-1. Stopping was just as good with 11.7-inch disc brakes up front and 10.5-inch discs at the rear for a total of 374 square inches of swept area. Panic stops from 80 mph were well controlled and achieved full stop in 180 feet, even for a car with curb weight of 3,240 pounds.

Wheels were 15 X 8 Minilites fitted with Firestone 11.50s on the front and 12.00s on the rear. Turning was just 2.2 turns lock-to-lock, and with a final drive 4.33:1, top speed was over 150 mph at 7500 rpm. Bud Moore claimed his cars could pull 1.1g lateral acceleration, which gave his BOSS Mustangs tremendous cornering ability.

Moore's Mustangs went up against Roger Penske's Traco-powered, AMC-sponsored Javelins (driven by Mark Donohue and Pete Revson), Jim Hall's Chaparral Camaros, Dan Gurney's All American Racer Barracudas, Pete Hutchinson's Keith Black-powered Dodge Challengers, Jerry

Several BOSS 302 Trans-Am Mustangs were raced by independents. Ford engineer Ed Hinchcliff prepared and raced car at right.

Titus' Firebirds and many other strong Trans-Am entries. But the Javelins provided the main competition. The BOSS 302s took the 1970 Trans-Am series by storm—Ford's third championship in five seasons.

Mustangs were strong on the quarter miles that year as well. Funny Cars and ProStockers were the two top full-bodied car classes, but Fords could only take two eliminator victories in the NHRA Winternationals: Barrie Poole won in Super Stock with an 11.26 at 117.34 mph in his SS/H '68 Mustang; Stock Eliminator was taken by Richard Charbonneau's '67 E/Stock Ford with a 12.06 at 117.03 mph.

In the Super Stock classes, Fords pulled seven wins out of 14 classes, five of those in Mustangs. SS/C went to Ken Dondero's '67 Ford with an 11.22 at 122.61 mph.

Ford missed all Eliminator victories in the NHRA Gatornationals in the first year of the Gainesville, Florida, shoot-out. The Springnationals at Dallas was also a thin Ford showing with one Eliminator title going to Ford: John Elliott's '68 SS/F Mustang winning Super Stock with an 11.15 at 109.62. Seven Fords—six of them Mustangs—won victories in 13 Super Stock classes that had entries. Along with George Montgomery's record win in AA/GS, Ford was looking good.

"Sneaky Pete" Robinson's cammer rail took Top Fuel at both the NHRA Summernationals at York, Pennsylvania (8.78 at 196.13), and again at Bristol. "Ohio George" campaigned a new BB/A Maverick to win the NHRA Nationals at Indianapolis with an easy 8.66 at 139.10 mph win. The irony of that meet was Joe Lemley's Modified Eliminator win with a Ford powered J/Gas Chevy II. Seven of 16 Super Stock classes were taken by Fords, six of which were Mustangs. But SS/Eliminator was won by a Dodge. In the NHRA World Finals and Supernationals, Fords came up without an Eliminator victory; Chrysler products showed stronger than ever.

Ford's war-horse of 1970 doing what it was built to do, but doing it today in vintage racing where these loud, fast Mustangs are still favorites.

1970 BOSS 302 with Bud Moore's own "Mini-Plenum" intake manifold produced more power from one Holley 4-bbl than with dual-4s the year before. 460 HP at 7,500 rpm was on tap, but being bullet-proof at 9000 rpm meant more power was there when needed. Throttle return spring wired to oil-filler neck is not the original race setup.

By 1970, the American Hot Rod Association (AHRA) emerged as a competitor to NHRA, drawing huge crowds with its nationals. In the AHRA Winter Nationals held at Phoenix, Tom Grove's cammer-powered '69 Mustang bodied funny car called *The Going Thing* clipped Jake Johnson's Dodge powered Mustang by more than a tenth of a second, or 7.54 seconds at 196.65 mph compared to Jake's 7.67 at 198.23 runner-up blast. Jay Howell's Mustang funny car gave a 7.37/180.00 mph whipping to Gene Snow's 7.56-second Dodge funny car in the AHRA Grand Nationals at Detroit.

Ford super stocks were finding the racing tough against the Sox & Martin 'Cuda, Don Carlton *Motown Missile* and "Grumpy" Jenkins' Camaro. The MoPars left few ProStock wins, but "Dyno Don" ran 0.01-second faster (10.07 at 136.77) than the Herb McCandless Duster to take ProStock in the AHRA World Championships held at Bristol in August, 1970. "Sneaky Pete" also blasted a Ford win with a Top Fuel victory in his SOHC 427 rail.

When the smoke cleared after the 1970 seasons of drag racing and road racing, Ford faded away. Simply put, Ford Motor Co. quit and the results showed in the general absence in top class wins in 1971 and later years. The going was tough, but a few Ford diehards tried valiantly to keep Dearborn going. However, the MoPar Hemi haulers were tough to beat and captured about everything in drag racing. As the '70s unfolded, however, Chevrolet once again emerged as a Ford beater.

Barrie Poole in Sandy Elliot notchback Mustang he raced to two NHRA National Eliminator titles at 1970 Winternationals (SS—11.26/117.34) and 1971 (SS—11.28/121.62 in front of 78,000 fans). Poole was runner-up in a third national final along with nine semi-final rounds. He took two Canadian National Eliminator titles and was the NHRA Division III champion, all in 1970. John was runner-up. The Elliot team also participated in the Popular Hot Rodding National with Poole and teammate John Elliot making the final Super Stock round. Poole's SS/H Mustang won with an 11.33 over John's SS/F Mustang that ran a strong 11.21. Also at that meet was Ralph Wilkins in the Elliot team H/Pure Stock 428 Mercury Cyclone CJ that won Pure Stock Eliminator with a 14.05/102.22 victory, a clean sweep for Team Elliot. Courtesy John Elliot.

BORDER BANDITS

The Sandy Elliot Mustangs became known as the *Border Bandits* when Barrie Poole and John Elliot invaded the 1970 NHRA Winternationals with Super Stock class wins and Poole taking Eliminator. Such success had, of course, begun years earlier when Poole became Performance Advisor for Sandy Elliot, Ltd., Canada's oldest Ford-Mercury dealer.

Poole was responsible for preparing and driving the dealership's cars. He earned that spot because of his consistent wins in a 1966 C/SA Comet Cyclone Convertible with a 390 engine. Thirty-four trophies and one Eliminator title later, *The Collector* Cyclone became a 427 Comet station wagon called the *Collector Too*. At the Springnationals, Poole was the fastest SS/C, but was beaten by "Grumpy" Jenkins in the class final.

In 1968, Sandy Elliot shifted his efforts to a Super Stock/E Automatic Cobra Jet Mustang. During the season, Poole set a class record with an 11.87-second pass, but that was improved at the U.S. Nationals when the car ran a 4-speed in SS/E and set a new class record at 11.32 seconds. That run qualified for the World Finals at Tulsa.

Things began moving in '69 with Poole running a 432-cid 428CJ with a 0.025-inch overbore. The ram-air CJ ran a General Kinetics cam with 320° duration and 0.472-inch lift. Stock 10.8:1 compression ratio went to 11.5:1 with flat-top pistons. Ford lightweight competition valves and dual valve springs along with Ford's 427 adjustable rockers fed cc'd heads. Exhaust was through 2-1/2-inch-diameter Doug's headers. Using a Ford top-loader, Hurst shifter and Line-Lok,

John Elliot and his Cobra Jet Mustang on his way to winning the 1970 NHRA Springnationals Super Stock/F class (11.15/109.62). John then trounced the SS field to take Super Stock Eliminator running 11.29 at 110.97 mph, beating Bob Lambeck in the Dick Landy SS/EA Dodge Charger in the final round. Sponsor Sandy Elliot's Ford of Canada racing team had best overall record of any Mustang team. Cars were built by Barrie Poole. Courtesy John Elliot.

10.5-inch 34-pound Sheifer clutch and a 5.10:1 Detroit locker 9-inch rear axle controlled by traction bars of Poole's own design, made the 3,250-pound Sandy Elliot Mustang the terror of the quarter mile.

Poole's engine work, plus a stock Ford intake and Holley 735-cfm carb and stock 3/8-inch fuel line, produced a solid performer—enough to notch an SS/I record (11.27 seconds) at Dallas during the Springnationals. He ran an unbelievable 11.16 to become the world's fastest Cobra Jet, then posted an SS/H record (11.26) and set a best of 11.11 seconds at 123.40 mph.

Another hot CJ was Ken McLellan's '69 fastback, the *Cobrastang* that ran a best of 11.19 seconds. During the eliminations, Poole put down all but one competitor, then faced off against Ronnie Sox in the finals, but lost in a close one. By season's end, Poole had won Division III ahead of John Elliot. Both drivers qualified for the World Finals. Unfortunately, Poole lost to Sox, who again won SS Eliminator.

By 1970, Barrie had become "Pomona Poole" and was awarded "Racer of the Year" by Ford Canada.

1970 has been described as the best year drag racing ever had. With 17 major events along with several magazine meets, more drag-newspaper shoot-outs and many local events all around the country, there was a tremendous amount of drag racing going on. To dominate Super Stock was such an achievement that Poole and Elliot were named Super Stock Drivers of the Year.

Through that year and 1971 when Poole began campaigning Sandy Elliot's ProStock Comet, the team recorded an astounding record—by far the most successful of any national-calibor team. Both of the Elliot Mustangs made final eliminations in 16 of 17 rounds, either by class wins or by qualifying. The team won three NHRA nationals and was runner-up twice out of 12 semi-final finishes. Adding two Canadian National Eliminator wins, two *Popular Hot Rodding* meet victories and after setting nine national records and leading Division III points three years in a row, Sandy Elliot Mustangs in the hands of Poole and Elliot proved to be the best.

Barrie Poole posing for a photo with Miss Hurst, Linda Vaughn, one reward for winning Super Stock Eliminator with the fastest Cobra Jet Mustang, a record Poole set when he ran a sensational 11.16-second blast. Courtesy John Elliot.

The ProStock Comet Poole built weighed in at 2,700 pounds and ran a 429CJ wedge with aluminum heads and dual Holley 4-V carbs on an intake of Poole's own design. A 4-speed transmission and 5.13:1 final gears were enough to pop a 10.17/136.77 blast on its first run.

Ford won seven of 16 Super Stock classes. MoPars won four, Chevrolet four, but Ron Mancini closed the door on Lorin Downing for a Dodge vs. AMX final taking Super Stock Eliminator.

Ford also won four Stock Classes.

All totaled, 1970 was an impressive year. Super Stock Fords took the majority of class wins in the three top National events given here.

SALT FLYERS

One hot-rodding sport that flourished in the late '50s and '60s, but waned in interest during the '70s, is all-out high-speed trials on the Bonneville Salt Flats. Speed-record attempts at Bonneville go back to the early days of racing, but when the first modern event was held in the late summer of 1949, the sport of going as fast as you can over a 9-mile stretch of dried lake bed grew quite popular. Always a "run what you brung" sort of sport, highest speed cars in the early days quite often were built using surplus WWII aircraft fuel tanks stuffed with an engine, chassis and cramped driving compartment. These rather crude machines evolved into highly sophisticated cars with single and multiple automotive engines. And later, the fastest cars were powered by jet and rocket engines that ran ever closer to the speed of sound, or over 700 mph.

Cars for the salt were called *lakers* in the early days. Those that reached speeds over 200 mph resulted in the driver receiving membership in the exclusive 200 MPH Club. The club grew slowly in the first decade, but by the '60s, lots of cars passed that mark with ease. The number of entries regularly totaled over 150 by then. About 1,000 qualifying runs were made that set speed-record attempts by perhaps 75 cars.

1970 SUPER STOCKERS

Some highlights of the 1970 season should indicate that in street-class Super Stock drag racing in NHRA events, Mustangs were tough to beat.

NHRA Winternationals, Pomona, CA, Jan. 30 - Feb. 1, 1970
Super Stock Class winners:

Class	Driver	Car	Time/Speed
SS/A	Ronnie Sox	'68 'Cuda	10.44/117.03
SS/B	Jim Johnson	'69 AMX	11.02/123.00
SS/C	Ken Dondero	'67 Ford	11.22/122.61
SS/C	Disqualified		
SS/E	Dick Landy	'69 Dodge	11.15/122.00
SS/F	Geno Redd	'68 Mustang	11.30/122.61
SS/G	Ken McLellan	'69 Mustang	12.31/115.23
SS/H	Barrie Poole	'68 Mustang	11.46/99.33
SS/AA	Don Grotheer	'68 'Cuda	10.62/114.79
SS/BA	Jim Clark	'65 Dodge	11.07/125.17
SS/CA	Jim Morton	'67 Ford	11.35/122.95
SS/DA	Lee Cameron	'67 Dodge	11.41/109.35
SS/EA	John Teddar	'69 Plymouth	11.96/105.63
SS/FA	Disqualified		
SS/GA	Bill Allis	'69 Mustang	11.63/114.79
SS/HA	Ken Myers	'68 Mustang	11.34/117.34

Ford won seven of 14 Super Stock classes. MoPars won five, and all General Motors cars were shut out, no wins.

Canada's Barrie Poole took Super Stock Eliminator with a blistering 11.27/117.34 final against Bill Allis, an all-Ford showdown in the end.

Stock Class Winners included five Fords, and Dick Charbonneau's '67 Ford wagon took Stock Eliminator.

NHRA Springnationals, Dallas, TX, June 12-14, 1970
Super Stock Class winners:

Class	Driver	Car	Time/Speed
SS/A	Ed Hendrick	'68 'Cuda	10.75/132.93
SS/B	No Entries		
SS/C	No Entries		
SS/D	George Warren	'70 AMX	11.07/106.63
SS/E	Dave Van Luke	'67 Ford	11.70/118.42

Class	Driver	Car	Time/Speed
SS/F	John Elliot	'68 Mustang	11.15/109.62
SS/G	Ken McLellan	'69 Mustang	11.35/99.00
SS/H	Barrie Poole	'69 Mustang	11.55/98.79
SS/AA	Judy Lilly	'68 'Cuda	10.34/131.77
SS/BA	Tom Crutchfield	'65 Dodge	10.95/124.48
SS/CA	No Entries		
SS/DA	Ed Ward	'67 Plymouth	11.28/120.80
SS/EA	Bob Lambeck	'70 Dodge	11.68/111.80
SS/FA	Stacy Shields	'68 Mustang	11.46/120.00
SS/GA	Bill Allis	'69 Mustang	12.06/115.08
SS/HA	Bob Glidden	'69 Mustang	11.87/116.12

Note Bob Glidden's class win, the beginning of great things.

Ford won seven of 13 Super Stock classes with entries. MoPars won five and all of the General's cars were shut out again.

Again, the Super Stock Eliminator came from Canada. John Elliot's Mustang shut out Bob Lambeck in Dick Landy's Charger.

Fords also took four stock-class victories.

NHRA Nationals, Indianapolis, IN, Sept. 3-7, 1970,
Super Stock Class winners:

Class	Driver	Car	Time/Speed
SS/A	Jim Wick	'69 'Cuda	10.55/131.19
SS/B	Ken Barnhart	'69 Camaro	11.16/121.13
SS/C	Ed Capullo	'67 Camaro	11.39/122.44
SS/D	Lorin Downing	'69 AMX	10.79/126.05
SS/E	Ernie Musser	'69 Chevrolet	11.43/121.72
SS/F	John Elliot	'68 Mustang	11.17/114.64
SS/G	Ken McLellan	'69 Mustang	11.15/122.78
SS/H	Barrie Poole	'69 Mustang	11.26/113.06
SS/AA	Ron Mancini	'68 Dodge	10.41/110.15
SS/BA	Tom Crutchfield	'65 Dodge	10.80/127.11
SS/CA	Jim Morton	'69 Ford	12.37/113.06
SS/DA	Gary Ostrich	'70 'Cuda	11.22/113.63
SS/EA	Ray Allen	'70 Chevrolet	11.37/119.68
SS/FA	Dave Morgan	'68 Mustang	11.60/120.32
SS/GA	Bill Allis	'69 Mustang	11.70/104.52
SS/HA	Hubert Platt	'69 Mustang	11.88/115.08

To introduce the new Mustang, Ford chief "Bunky" Knudsen sent Mickey Thompson and crew along with three '69 Mach 1 Mustangs to the Bonneville Salt Flats. The cars, powered by a 302 or 427, set 295 United States and International speed records. Courtesy Ford Motor Co.

The 9-mile long course for the Nationals was usually divided into four speed trap sections to measure a driver's progress. And of the 13 categories and 93 classes available for land-speed record attempts, the variety of cars was immense. Practically every make of American engine has been put to the test from time to time, and many Ford powerplants have set new class records.

For example, in the 1967 record runs, veteran record setter Jack Lufkin's car driven by Jim Duke ran a 260-inch Ford engine in E Modified Sports to smash the previous class record of 184.284 mph, running 215.568 mph. The engine turned up to 7,200 rpm in those attempts. Lufkin worked for Ak Miller, of Pico Riveria, California, a legendary figure in racing. And, along with fellow employee Jerry Kugel and Red Holmes, Miller's garage was well represented.

In 1967, Holmes and Kugel entered a 1932 Ford roadster powered by a 427 Ford low-riser—running basically stock internals—in two classes: B Fuel Roadster and B Gas Roadster. Kugel set new records in both classes and earned membership in the 200 MPH Club with a 205.560-mph blast in Fuel class, then backed up the run with a 192.893-mph record run in Gas class to better the old record of 183.038 mph.

Another 427-powered salt flyer was the Burke brothers' Studebaker Avanti running Weber carbs on a '63 low-riser and a Ford 4-speed transmission. This car hit 186.04 mph for a record, then produced many 170+ mph runs by crew members who wanted to shake the salt for fun. Finally, the basically stock engine gave up the ghost with a cracked block.

The aged Ford flathead was still running strong in '67 when George Morris' 1932 Ford fitted with a '30 A-Model roadster body set two new records. In X Fuel Roadster, Morris ran a 258-cid flathead set up for alcohol to capture the record with a strong 144.548-mph run, beating the old record by over 22 mph.

One of the great ironies of the '67 Nationals was another Burke brothers entry, a Camaro powered by a Bill Thomas built 427 Chevy. The Camaro was Chevrolet's newest release in the performance-car market, but on the salt the

Danny Ongais, Ray Brock and Bob Ottum drove the 302 car on the salt and set a standing-start mile average speed record of 106.08 mph, which means the car must have been doing around 180 mph through the traps at the end of the mile. The 427-powered car set a class record of 112.45 mph and a final trap speed of over 190 mph. Courtesy Ford Motor Co.

Mickey Thompson's Autolite Special was a twin SOHC 427-powered land speed-record car than ran the salt on October 14, 1968, but wasn't as successful as hoped. Courtesy Ford Motor Co.

Storm clouds over Bonneville and twin SOHC 427-powered streamliner. Car showed extraordinary craftsmanship in the quest for more speed. Courtesy Ford Motor Co.

Burke car was sidelined after only one pass when it got light in the front at over 140 mph and spun, almost flipping in the process. Pulling the chute prevented a crash. Perhaps the 427 was a bit much for the Camaro, considering that in Spanish, Camaro means *shrimp*. In fairness, though, it should be pointed out that another Camaro driven by LeVan Prothero was stable enough to set a record.

Mustang performance on the salt also looked good when Ak Miller posted a 143-mph pass with a 6-cylinder fastback he drove from Los Angeles to Bonneville. Ak fitted his Mustang 240-inch six-banger with a 300-inch truck crankshaft to give 330 cubic inches. After changing to a solid-lifter cam, he ran 148.75 mph, quite a trick for what is generally not regarded as a performance engine.

To highlight more salt flyers, the 22nd Annual Bonneville Speed Week of 1970 saw the running of the Chaffey College entry. Believe it or not, the college taught race-car building. Its class members assembled a '69 Mustang and succeeded in setting a new C/Production record of 172.83 mph. That must have been some college because their cars were seen in a variety of competitive events including Trans-Am racing.

However, for Mustang straightliners, the August and September 1969 record feat was by far the most significant. "Bunkie" Knudsen had once tabbed Mickey Thompson to

Mustang Mach 1 was introduced in 1969 along with the first major restyling Mustang line had received since its introduction in 1964. Courtesy Ford Motor Co.

put some spark in Pontiac sales with high-speed bragging rights—the world land speed record for one—and, when brought to the helm of Ford, Knudsen did the same again. The result was 295 United States and International land speed records set by Thompson and his able assistants, Danny Ongais, Ray Brock and Bob Ottum. They drove three 1969-style Mustangs fitted with either 302 or 427 engines. This was a magnificent achievement for the new '69 Mustangs, and no doubt the high point of Mustangs at top speed.

The 302-powered car fit international Class C regulations. It succeeded in setting 42 endurance speed records, one with an average of 159.97 mph for three hours. Another was the standing-start mile of 106.08 mph, giving an exit speed at the end of the mile of about 180 mph.

In Class B (305-488 cubic inches), the 427 Mustang set the standing-start mile record at 112.45 mph and an exit speed of over 190 mph. Thompson drove this car to a 10-mile fast lap of just over 187 mph, a truly remarkable speed for a production-based car and, no doubt, the beginning of bigger things for Ford. Unfortunately, that came to a close when Knudsen was ousted.

Perhaps Ford's last great effort at the salt was Thompson's SOHC-427-powered streamliner. He returned to Bonneville during the following October with a magnificently prepared twin-engine bullet for the purpose of putting Ford and its tough engine in the record books. Unfortunately, the effort met with bad weather and mechanical problems that limited what might have another great showing for Ford salt flyers. Knudsen's leaving squelched future attempts because Ford Motor Co. dropped out of most phases of competition.

THE LAST BOSS

Knudsen was most influential on Mustang styling of the 1971 models. These cars were the second extensive restyling of the Mustang line and were as big as Mustangs would get. And they carried Ford's last really hot V8, the BOSS 351. Ford stylists were guided by sales that showed buyer interest called for more room and more luxury; engineers were guided by Ford's racing heritage. Although one of the largest Mustangs, the '71s were also among the strongest street performers in BOSS 351 form.

First BOSS Mustangs, the 1628 '69 BOSS 302s, outsold the SCCA requirements of 1,000 units needed to meet Trans-Am rules. The '70 models had to exceed new SCCA requirements of 7,000 units; 7,013 were sold that year. Unfortunately, for the '71 model year, Ford was out of racing, and the production BOSS 351 intended to supersede the earlier cars have no factory racing heritage. A total of 1,806 were sold.

The earlier BOSS 302 cars were rated at 290 HP, although everyone knew they were thoroughbred horses that easily out-performed similarly rated 302 small blocks. The BOSS 351 was described as the *351 4-V high-output* or *351 Super Cobra Jet* because of its ram-air induction and special internals that produced a rated output of 330 HP. Here again, ratings were under actual output, or more like 380 HP.

The BOSS 351 Mustang, called the *SportsRoof* rather than *fastback*, weighed 3,450 pounds, and the HO 351 propelled it through the quarter-mile at a respectable 13.80 at 104 mph as recorded in one magazine road test. In a compilation and comparison of contemporary magazine road tests, *Car Review* magazine listed the 50 fastest production musclecars as

Fastest 351 Ford ever built, BOSS 351 could put the needle to a lot of over-400-cubic-inch cars.

determined by quarter-mile elapsed times and found that the BOSS 351 was the quickest under 400-cid-powered car of the musclecar era. It was also quicker than a lot of over 400-cubic inch cars. In fact, the BOSS 351 was almost as quick as the BOSS 429 (13.60/106). Topping the list was, of course, the 427 Cobra with stats of 12.20/118—a real fireball for showroom-stock performance.

Just as Trans-Am racing was the reason for the marketing of the BOSS 302, it was also the basis of the BOSS 351, a larger-displacement, canted-valve, high-revving engine of similar design. And Larry Shinoda was responsible for the car's bold styling. However, no one could have predicted that Shinoda and Ford chief "Bunky" Knudsen would "leave" Ford late in 1969. Their influence at Ford ended with the BOSS 351, a one-year-only Mustang that ranks as one of the rarest of the specialty Mustangs.

The '71 Mustang rode on a 1-inch longer wheelbase than earlier models. They were about 600 pounds heavier than the first Mustangs offered in '64. 1971 was also the year that more stringent emissions controls took effect, which spelled death for performance engines. The BOSS 302 was dropped that year in favor of the BOSS 351. Since the cars were heavier, their engines required more torque, thus more cubic inches, for equivalent performance.

The BOSS 351 was a special-edition 351 Cleveland with 11:1 compression. The new engine was more tractable than the peaky 302, but was equally durable, if not more so, since it developed power in a more usable rev range. The car also received an excellent handling package—the "competition"

suspension—as standard equipment. This consisted of a BOSS 302-type suspension up front, staggered shocks at the rear to control axle wind-up, and both front and rear anti-sway bars—all to continue in the road-handling BOSS 302 tradition.

The deck height of the 351C block was higher than the 302, and cylinders were longer by 0.50 inch to accommodate a longer stroke—4.00 bore X 3.50 stroke. Longer pistons were used to keep the rings square in the bore for low oil consumption and extended durability, even for a performance engine certain to take a beating.

The potential of any engine rests with its ability to get the air/fuel mixture in and exhaust out, and to provide complete combustion. The 351C 4V heads were a master stroke of performance design, with huge oval intake ports leading through equally huge valves: 2.195-inch diameter intakes and 1.715-inch exhausts. Valve actuation was by solid lifters through high-strength pushrods and rocker arms. The BOSS 351 remains unique among the 351C engines in that it came factory equipped with screw-in studs and pushrod guide plates as did the earlier BOSS 302 heads.

Sound like racing stuff? You bet! The BOSS 351 engineers drew heavily on Ford's winning tradition in designing this engine.

Other components in the BOSS 351 engine received special handling—the rods, for instance. They were similar to the forged steel used in the base 351C, but were Magna-fluxed and shotpeened for increased quality and strength. However, the BOSS 351 rods received high-strength rod

Boss 429 engine was a tight squeeze in the '69—70 Mustang. Shock-tower clearancing and other mods were necessary to shoehorn the big mill in. Photo by Roger Huntington.

Ford's biggest gun ever, the 375-HP Boss 429, was dropped into a select number of '69 and '70 Mustangs to legalize the engine for NASCAR use in Grand National Torninos. Photo couresy of Ford Motor Company.

bolts and nuts. Similar to all small-block Ford engines from the 221 to the 351W plus the 351C, 351M and 400, bore spacing was 4.380 inches.

Both camshaft and crankshaft were made of selected nodular cast iron, so all you die-hard forged-steel-crankshaft fans take note. Iron cranks in balanced assemblies are very effective and less costly. Although the crank in the BOSS 351 was of the same design as used in other Clevelands, they were higher quality and a special hardness. BOSS blocks had four-bolt mains for bottom-end strength.

The BOSS 351 engine was fitted with a cast-iron intake manifold, but the carb was positioned slightly to the rear so the primaries were more centered on the engine. This provided better fuel distribution and, because optimum runner design was achieved by eliminating the water outlet and thermostat at the front of the casting, performance was improved further. It's the little things that added up to improved performance, and Ford engineers were after all they could get.

The BOSS 351 received a 750 cfm spread-bore carburetor with 1.56-inch primary throttle bores and 1.96-inch secondaries. Throttle response was excellent and economy wasn't shabby, either. Overall, the BOSS 351 was one of Ford's all-time best.

7
MID ENGINES

The New Age

In 1964, Ford's new Mustang was an appropriate pace car for the Indy 500, here trailed by the front row of cars, which included pole-sitter Jimmy Clark, slightly out of photo on right.

LOTUS FORDS

European Fords began to receive respect as healthy racing engines when the rise of interest in racing on the British Isles took off in the mid- to late-50s. It was during that time that four events took place to shape the future of Ford-Dearborn in racing.

First, Italian racing promoters were distraught that there were no top Italian drivers for their cars, Ferrari in particular, that were winning all sorts of races. They, then, established the *Formula Junior* class of open-wheel racers and got it sanctioned on an international level. Engines were based on production four-cylinders. The Fiat 1100cc was considered a natural, so the Italian cars looked good at first. That was in 1959.

Second, Ford-Britain engineers produced a new in-line 4-cylinder Anglia engine for the "blah" sort of ordinary cars being built at the time. Known as the *Kent* engine, it was a 997cc over-square design weighing 217 pounds that produced 39 HP at 5000 rpm. It was so under-powered that it required a 4-speed transmission. However, this engine turned out to have so much designed-in potential that it soon pushed British Formula Junior racing into dominating the class in spite of all Italian efforts.

Third, A. C. B. Chapman, soon to become known as *Colin*, ventured into designing cars for the Junior class. His marque became known as *Lotus*, and Lotus-Fords were the cars that

dashed the Italian plan. Later, Lotus changed the course of both the Indianapolis 500 and international Formula-1 racing, again with Ford power.

Fourth, a young and dashing Scotsman, Jimmy Clark, was honing his skills as a driver in Formula racing. His record driving remains unmatched to this day.

The plain Anglia Ford engine was improved by Chapman for racing, with the application of a double overhead-cam (DOHC) head. With that engine, British small-bore racing reigned supreme. In 1960, Lotus-Fords won 13 of the 19 major Formula Junior races—six by Clark and four by Trevor Taylor. Of the remaining six races, Cooper-BMCs won four. That left only two races, both held in Italy and both won by Italian cars when no top-rank British cars were entered.

Clark went on to Formula-1 racing, soon to be followed by an F-1 Lotus-Ford car. During the '61 Junior season, Lotus-Ford team cars won seven of the major nine international races. Chapman also built a variety of sports cars with all-enclosing bodies for his DOHC Ford engine. The tiny but sleek Lotus-23 sports car is one that proved to be another winner. This car led to the first official association of Ford-Britain with Lotus. When the new Cortina was released in the Fall of '62, a hot DOHC Lotus version improved output from the original 60 HP to upwards of 180 HP in full-bore racing preparation. With these cars, Ford-Britain won the RAC World Manufacturers' Rally Cup in '63, and the British

Dan Gurney was the man behind Ford and Lotus getting together to create the Lotus-Ford for the 1963 Indy 500. Teammate Jimmy Clark nearly won, but settled for second rather than chance spinning on oil leaking from Parnelli Jones' winning car. The next year, Jimmy Clark qualified fastest and set a new record, 158.828 mph, and Roger Ward netted another second with the Ford V8. That year, it was with the new small-block-based double overhead cam (DOHC) Ford V8. Courtesy Indianapolis Motor Speedway.

Saloon (sedan) car championship, which rapidly became an all-Ford affair.

On the F-Junior scene, the difference between Formula-1 and Formula-Junior racing was largely in name because the Juniors were capable of lap times of about 4 seconds off the pace of the more powerful F-1 cars and ran lap average speeds within 3—4 mph of them on the same courses. Thus, F-Junior was extremely competitive; Ford won 17 of 17 events, finishing 16 of them 1-2-3 to totally dominate the series. Although rules changed somewhat for the '64 season, Ford-powered F-Juniors repeated the performance of the year before.

With the record earned by the Juniors, the Lotus sports cars of 1962 and the Cortinas, Ford-Dearborn had taken notice of Chapman's achievements. And with the influence of the beginning of Total Performance, Iacocca and friends saw a Ford in the future for Indianapolis, America's most prestigious race. That largely came about because of the prevailing pro-racing climate at Ford Motor Co., and was probably inevitable in the grand scheme of things involving Ford racing.

Jack Brabham, two-time World Drivers Champion, changed the course of Indy racing in 1961 when his tiny DOHC 4-cylinder, mid-engine Cooper-Climax stunned the opposition by finishing 9th overall with an engine running only 225 HP—despite a lengthy pit stop. It was just this type

of car that idea man Dan Gurney was convinced could win the Indy 500. Chapman wasn't interested in Gurney's plans at first, but with the acclaim to be received, Chapman saw the effort as beneficial. Thus, for the Indy 500 of 1963, Dan Gurney teamed with Clark as drivers for Chapman's Lotus-Ford entry of two cars, both with engines behind the driver—the new-age machine.

Chapman's Lotus 25 Formula-1 Grand Prix car construction was carried over into the Indy Lotus-Ford. Its lightweight, one-piece *monocoque* structure of stressed-aluminum sheet riveted to bulkheads provided strong mounting points for an all-independent suspension and enclosed two fuel cells totaling 50 gallons. Up front, unequal-length wishbones were used, and cantilever upper arms operated inboard coil-over shocks. The chassis was offset to the left, as was the practice with all Indy Cars at the time. Front brakes were 10.5-inch Girlings.

The rear suspension was also an unequal-length A-arm design, but used upper and lower radius rods for controlling thrust loads. At each corner, an outboard coil-over shock was installed between the rear bulkhead at the upper point and hub carrier at the lower. The front-mounted radiator provided cooling water to the engine with tubes running to the left of the driver. The outer skin of the narrow torpedo-shaped body enclosed the car and gave the Lotus-Ford a very simple, almost kiddie-car look compared to the bigger,

Jimmy Clark, winner of the 1965 Indy 500. Clark qualified with a new record, 160.729 mph, but it stood only a few minutes until A.J. Foyt beat it with a pole winning 161.958 mph. Clark cruised to a $166,000 victory, averaging 150.686 mph. The domination of Fords at Indy began. Courtesy Indianapolis Motor Speedway.

brutish front-engine Indy *roadsters* of the time. Wheels were 15-inch diameter, pin-drive Dunlops with 6- and 8-inch widths front and rear, respectively, but were changed to wider Ford-fabricated wheels at the last moment. Steering was 2-1/2 turns lock-to-lock.

Ford Motor Co. did the engine development and furnished all-aluminum pushrod V8s derived from the new Fairlane line of small-block V8s. These were 260s reduced to 255 cid and fitted with 58mm downdraft Weber carburetors that produced a reliable 350 HP on gasoline. The decision had been made at Ford to run production-type equipment such as carburetors and gasoline. When development brought the engine up to 365 HP, things were looking good.

By race day, power of the modified production engine, dubbed the *AX230-2*, reached 376 HP at 7,200 rpm on 103-octane gasoline. A five-hour dyno test had proven the reliability of the engine, and when Gurney cracked the magic 150-mph mark in testing at Indy—running 3.477:1 final-drive ratio—the old guard began to crumble. He had run 457 miles at racing speeds with little or no difficulty. And Ford Motor Co. was no longer particularly welcome at the Speedway. And neither was Clark's ε92 Lotus-Ford in its British racing green and yellow trim. Green had, for years, been considered bad luck in American oval-track racing. Gurney's white with blue stripes ε93 Lotus-Ford was not so condemned. But when he hit the wall at over 152 mph, it looked like half of the threat to Indy's tradition was through. Then the *mule* car was rolled out and, when readied, Gurney was back at it doing 150-mph laps.

The cars were quite low—30.5-inches high—and rode on a 56-inch track with a ground clearance of just 3.75 inches. Weighing under 1,300 pounds, the Lotus-Fords were the vanguard of revolution in Indy Car racing. The old guard still spoke highly of the 407-HP Offenhauser. Its higher power and reliability were relied upon by many teams. The advantages of the Lotus-Fords were less weight, better aerodynamics and more laps on a tank of fuel.

Chapman's racing strategy called for only one pit stop because the 355-pound engine produced its 150-mph + lap speeds at around 7.5 mpg rather than under 6 mpg as was common for most other cars. Up-swept straight exhaust pipes gave away the fact that a V8 was in the car, but the overall package was so tight and the body so narrow that it didn't seem one could be fitted to the chassis.

Despite what had been bantered around as a high-dollar Ford effort, the Indy 500 racing of 1963 was done on a shoestring with little or no backup equipment and personnel—two drivers and three cars. The reliability of the Lotus car and Ford engine seemed to be the right combination, but nobody had thought of a pit crew! At the last minute, Bill Stroppe's Mercury crew was flown into Indianapolis, but they had never even seen a Lotus-Ford, much less worked on one.

Soon, the race was on. After pit stops made by thirstier cars, Clark and Gurney were 1-2. Dan's car showed excessive tire wear, though, and an early pit stop put him out of contention. Clark's Lotus-Ford was hampered only by lack of experienced pit crewmen. Luck favored Parnelli

1965 DOHC Ford Indy Car engine developed 440 HP at 8400 rpm on 103-octane gasoline, 505 HP on methanol. Courtesy Ford Motor Co.

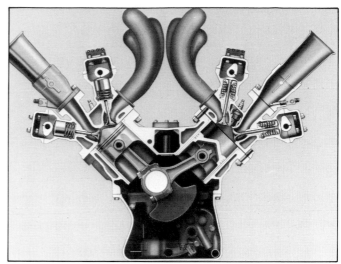

Front section of '64 Ford Indy engine illustrates unique intake- and exhaust-port layout. Engine was race-only item, from chain-driven double-overhead cams (DOHC) and oil and water pump to cast-magnesium oil pan and front cover and aluminum block.

Jones, who had won the pole, and caution flags at the right time kept him in the lead with Clark running 2nd for many laps. After Jones' second pit stop, Clark began to close on Parnelli's lead, showing that he had been holding back. It was beginning to look as if Clark's British entry could win. But, Jones' luck held as a leaking oil tank should have sidelined him according to the rules, but no one wanted a Britisher in a British car to win the Indy 500. The officials vacillated about black flagging Jones for so long that he won. Clark rolled into 2nd and Gurney, who wasn't supposed to have a chance, finished 7th.

FORD WINS INDY

Ford Motor Co. had added a new dimension to the Indy 500. After years of little change in the technology surrounding the event, which was more of a big-time social affair rather than real-world class racing, the Lotus-Fords had added excitement and revolutionized the design of Indy Cars. V8 power put the old Offy on notice and every Indy win after 1964 was won by cars with engines behind the driver.

Excitement was Iacocca's favorite word. The Lotus-Fords had indeed given Ford a great deal of acclaim while generating a lot of enthusiasm for racing inside the corporation. After the '63 event, Ford engineering set to designing a new engine. It was scheduled for testing in February, 1964! Ford intended to dominate the 500 and offer complete, race-ready engines to anyone.

Design criteria called for at least 425 HP from 255 cubic inches. The only way to get that much power from so little displacement without supercharging was to rev the engine higher. At least 8,000 rpm was needed, and to achieve that required better breathing and an all new cylinder-head design. After testing all sorts of new configurations—carburetion versus fuel injection, various shapes of ports and runner designs, single and dual spark plugs and much more—Ford engineers settled on a single spark plug per cylinder, DOHC design with a pent-roof combustion chamber allowed by intake and exhaust valves separated by 70°. Induction was by fuel injection between the cams through a single-ram stack per cylinder, and tuned exhaust headers moved from exiting the usual outboard side of the heads to the inboard side atop the engine.

Headers had been headers before the new Ford Indy engine came along, but this engine brought the pipes into new recognition. Those "bundle of snakes" exhaust tubes were the most visible aspect of the engine and received a lot of ink. The engine with twin-cam heads and unique exhaust system looked exotic; it was exotic, the most sophisticated engine Ford had ever produced.

Final output figures were even better than expected, 440 HP at 8,400 rpm on 103-octane gasoline, and as much as 545 HP at 8,200 rpm on a mixture of alcohol plus 20% nitromethane.

Clearly, the Ford Indy engine had huge potential. On race day 1964, there were four teams running the new engine in addition to the Lotus-Fords. Jimmy Clark and Dan Gurney were back in the British entries, and Clark wound up win-

Wood brothers apply their pitting skills from NASCAR circuit to Jimmy Clark's Lotus Ford at the Indianapolis Motor Speedway.

Mario Andretti winning '69 Indy 500 with a turbocharged DOHC Ford, averaging 156.867 mph. Courtesy Ford Motor Co.

ning the pole by breaking all previous records when he qualified at 158.83 mph. Qualifying was done on straight alcohol for its additional power—495 HP at 8,400 rpm—and with a final-drive ratio of 4.05:1. Gasoline was used for the race.

Tires were getting better. Both Firestone and Goodyear offered wider, lower-profile, softer-compound tires that improved adhesion. Combined with more power, better tires allowed the new-generation Indy Car to go faster than ever before. And the old Offy powered roadsters went faster, too.

The Ford engine had brought a great deal of excitement and anticipation to the Indy 500 because now there was real competition—old-style front-engine roadsters against new mid-engine cars. But questions lingered. Was the Ford engine really better than the venerable Offy? Would the British team humble the Americans? Would Clark or Gurney win?

Clark could no longer be chastised as a "rookie" by Indy promoters, even though he was clearly *the* top Grand Prix driver in the world. From the start it was clear that he was *the* driver of the Indy 500. Three mid-engine Fords were on the front row, and at the flag, Clark ran away from the field as if he were running a race by himself.

But he got only a lap before the red flag came out. Rookie Dave MacDonald of Cobra racing fame had spun and crashed into a wall. His full load of fuel went up as a giant column of flame and black smoke just as veteran Eddie Sachs crashed into the conflagration. Both drivers died; it was a sad day at Indy.

At the restart almost two hours later, Clark pulled away again, but Bobby Marshman made it a race for Clark when his white Lotus-Ford went by and steadily pulled away. Clark and Marshman put on a race for 37 laps until the white Lotus scraped off an oil plug on an infield excursion and was

out. Then, just as Gurney had experienced, Clark's Dunlop tires began to come apart, and he was sidelined when a tread came off and damaged the suspension. Ironically, A.J. Foyt sailed across the line to win in an old-style Offy roadster. Ford would have to wait another year.

The waiting paid off with more engine development that also found a place in Grand Prix racing. By the following year, 1965, only four roadsters could qualify. The remainder of the field was made up of mid-engine cars, almost all of which were DOHC Ford powered. This was Clark's year. His Lotus-Ford led all but 10 laps to win the Indy 500 by over two laps ahead of the 2nd-place car, Parnelli Jones' Lotus-Ford.

Although Ford had done in the Offy, they contracted with Meyer & Drake—as in *Meyer & Drake* Offy—to handle and distribute DOHC Ford Indy engines rather than through Ford outlets. Louis and Sonny Meyer split off to set up business in Indianapolis; Dale Drake stayed in Los Angeles with the Offy business. In 1966, the Meyer firm distributed about 20 Indy Ford engines at $23,000 retail each. Ford engineers steadily improved the engines. And when the reliable old Offy was first turbocharged in 1965, resulting in 600 HP and a win at the '68 Indy 500, Ford responded with turbos. The turbocharged DOHC Ford produced 650 HP at 9,000 rpm and was capable of propelling a test car up to 214 mph on the straights and on to more wins.

FORMULA FORDS

It was clear that the DOHC Ford had a lot of potential and it soon invaded Formula-1 racing with tremendous success. First attempts at using a Ford V8—the DOHC-powered McLarens of 1966—were not successful. But when Mike

Rick Mears, 1984 Indy 500 winner, won with a Cosworth-Ford V8, the seventh straight Indy win for the engine—another string of wins by Ford. Courtesy Indianapolis Motor Speedway.

Legendary Cosworth-Ford won more Grand Prix victories (155 as of 1986) than any other engine in history. In DFX trim (shown), it dominated Indy Car racing in a similar manner.

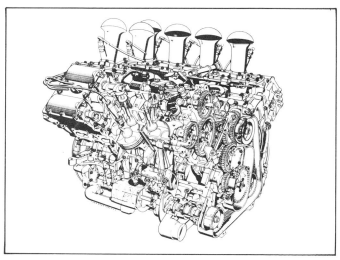

Cosworth-Ford DFV F-1 engine was turbocharged and brought into compliance with Indy car rules and re-christened DFX. Dominance of engine finally put four-cylinder Offenhauser "to bed" for good. Courtesy Ford of England.

Costin and Keith Duckworth came up with a new DOHC V8 under contract for about $300,000, Ford got a winner.

When F-1 and F-2, formally Formula Junior, rules changed for 1966 and '67, Ford-Britain found itself in an enviable position of having great prospects in both classes. New F-2 rules specified that engine capacity could be up to 1.6-liters with six or fewer pistons, rather than limited to 1-liter maximum, but still had to be based on production engines where

500 or more were built. The F-1 rules now specified that non-supercharged engines up to 3-liters were permitted against the established 1.5-liter supercharged engines. Almost all teams went the larger-engine route.

The change surprised Coventry-Climax, who was the primary engine builder for British teams for several years. That firm announced they would not build engines for the new formula.

A.J. Foyt, '67 Indy 500 winner, drove one of 23 Ford powered entries that year. He averaged 151.207 mph. Courtesy Ford Motor Co.

Phil Hill, America's only World Driving Champion, and GT-40 Ford at LeMans, France, 1964: Cars were sensational and highly admired. Hill and Bruce McLaren first raced car at the Nurburgring the same year. Courtesy Ford Motor Co.

Thus, Ford-Britain was ready with its well-developed F-2 class engine. And technology from this engine could be applied to a new V8 for the F-1 class. Commitments were made as early as June of 1965, and Cosworth Engineering—formed in 1958 by Costin and Duckworth—was given the task of developing both engines. The V8 was assigned to Lotus because of Chapman's well-developed chassis.

Cosworth began design of the F-1 engine in November, 1966. By the following April, Chapman had the first engine. Development had gone amazingly fast because the similar in-line-4 Cosworth Formula-2 engine had proven out the basics. The new Lotus-Fords made their debut in the Dutch Grand Prix of June 4, and drivers Jimmy Clark and Graham Hill let it be known that Ford had a serious contender in Formula-1 racing.

Hill won the pole with a record qualifying time of over five seconds faster than the previous mark. Clark's Lotus had wheel-bearing problems from attempting to run 15-inch-wide tires; the normal 13-inch tires were used for the race. He had little time to get acquainted with the car, but was able to qualify on the third row.

At the start, Hill jumped to the lead, but went out only 11 laps later when a timing gear broke. Clark had been moving up through the pack as he became more familiar with his car. By lap 16 he was leading and stayed there, winning comfortably.

For a new car to win its first Grand Prix was an astounding achievement. It had been 14 years since Mercedes-Benz had done the same with the legendary W-196. Chapman's Lotus-Ford had earned a similar honor that very few marques have been able to achieve.

In final form for 1967—the DFV—the Lotus-Ford weighed 1,170 pounds and produced upwards of 420 HP. That was just the beginning for Ford in international Formula-1 racing. Over the next 17 years, the engine was to earn 155 Grand Prix victories to become the winningest GP engine ever produced.

It was also to become the power for Indy style CART and USAC cars that dominated that form of racing for several years. The turboed Cosworth in American racing today—the DFX—produces about 720 HP at 10,750 rpm, a considerable evolution from the original Cosworth-Ford V8.

Ford's return to Formula-1 and Indy style racing today has brought about a new Ford engine, another Cosworth product. So far, the completely re-designed V6 has not emerged a winner, but it is showing signs of good progress. Powering Lola open-wheel cars, the Cosworth-Ford V6 made its first finish in the hands of Patrick Tambay in Montreal, Canada (1986), when he qualified 13th and finished 10th. Short-stroke versions of the Cosworth-Ford DFX V8 are still around, though, and still win. Thus, Ford is still on top—plans are to stay there.

GT-40, THE ULTIMATE FORD

In the world of super exotics, Ford has been king. Unlike some cars whose promoters claim great things, the GT-40 Fords need no claims, no promoters. They are the fastest and most durable racing Fords ever built.

Low, sleek and fast, Ford GT-40 was the premier sports racing car of the late '60s.

Carroll Shelby's Cobra 289 was well proven in his roadsters and found a new home in Mk I GT-40 Ford. Cars won at least 32 major endurance races, including two 24-Hours of LeMans—1968 and '69.

Office of champions, Ford GT-40: Most drivers of note aspired to drive one of these. The 200-mph speedometer was for real, but out of the way of useful gauges.

Although more at home on high-speed tracks with long straights, Mk II gave up only a little handling to the lighter Mk I and its small-block engine.

Facts: GT-40 Fords won the 1966 World Prototype Trophy and the 1966 World Sports Car Championship. They won the 1967 World Sports Car Championship and the 1968 World Manufacturers' Championship. GT-40s and Mk IV prototypes won the greatest race of them all, the 24-Hours of LeMans, four years straight, 1966 to '69. One of the GT-40s won LeMans back-to-back in '68 and '69, the only time that has been done. And they did it against the best Ferraris and best Porsches.

Starting in 1965, GT-40s won at least 33 of the world's toughest races. They were, quite simply—and no hype—the best racing cars in the world at the time. That is the legacy of the GT-40 Ford. As racing cars, they were virtually unbeat-

able in their day and won about everything worth winning. What makes that even more spectacular is the fact that, like the 289 Cobra, it was the small-block-powered GT-40 that was the big winner rather than those with the 427 big blocks, although they did a good bit of winning, too.

Most winning was done with GT-40s powered by production-based cast-iron 289 and 302 small-block Fords, not some sort of racing exotic. These are the cars that beat Ferrari's exotic V12 and Porsche's equally exotic flat-8 and flat-12.

In the final count, there were 11 versions of GT-40s, beginning with the first car finished in March, 1964. It was powered by the four-cam, 4.2-liter Indy engine driving

Mk I chassis was redesigned by Kar Kraft to accommodate big-block Ford. "Bundle of snakes" exhaust primaries join at collectors above transaxle.

Still in action today in vintage racing, '60s Ford GTs are once again very popular.

through a Colotti gearbox. It was the first car to exceed 200 mph on the Mulsanne Straight at LeMans.

The GT-40's driveline was changed later. Driving through 5-speed ZF transmissions, most were powered by 289s fitted with four downdraft Weber 48IDA carburetors. Mk I GT-40s weighed about 2400 pounds and reached an honest top-end of over 200 mph in race trim. Street versions were powered by 289s with cast-iron heads to give a 10.0:1 compression ratio. Four 48IDA Webers were installed. An output of 325 HP at 5750 rpm pushed these cars to a maximum of 165 mph. At the high end of the small-block scale, the Gulf GT-40 race car was powered by a 302-cid small-block sporting Gurney-Weslake heads to give a 10.2—11.1:1 compression ratio. Again, four 48IDA Weber carburetors were used and max-

imum output was 425 HP at 6250 rpm. This setup gave a top speed of about 205 mph.

The first GT-40s were built by Ford Advanced Vehicles (FAV) in England through 1966, then by J.W. Automotive Engineering afterwards when Ford sold their works to John Wyer, the director of FAV. GT-40s are still being built, a modern classic in the old design.

In 1965, the Mk II started out as an experimental Mk I fitted with Ford's NASCAR 427 side-oiler engine, another of its illustrious applications. At over 475 HP on a single 4-bbl Holley, the Mk IIs began their rise as endurance-racing champions when Ken Miles qualified for the Daytona 24-Hour Continental of 1966 with a Prototype class-record lap time of 1:57.8 minutes over the 3.81-mile road course and

Carroll Shelby and his main man, Ken Miles—one of the best sports racing drivers ever—share victor's glory. Courtesy Ford Motor Co.

Mk II GT-40 Ford received Ford's legendary side-oiler 427 for 1966. With single Holley 4-bbl, these 210-mph Fords won Daytona Continental, Sebring 12-Hour and 24-Hours of LeMans. And then went on to take the International Championship for Sports-Prototypes that year. Ken Miles shared car and victory with Lloyd Ruby at Daytona for the second year in a row. Courtesy Ford Motor Co.

Ford's famous trio, the first Ford win in all of LeMans history, 1966. Bruce McLaren and Chris Amon set new records as the first over-3000-mile LeMans—3009.350 miles at 125.389-mph average. Courtesy Ford Motor Co.

high banks. Average speed was 116.434 mph. A GT-40 in the hands of Dick Thompson qualified fastest in Sports Car class with a 2:04.0-second lap at an average of 110.612 mph.

At the end of the race, Mk II Fords held every one of the 20 race marker records for prototype cars and all but four of the sports-car records. Dan Gurney came away with the fastest race lap at 1:57.7 minutes, averaging 116.510 mph. Miles and Lloyd Ruby won the race in a Shelby team Mk II, leading a 1-2-3 sweep. They also won the Daytona 2000Km the previous year, the GT-40's first victory at a record speed of 107.633 mph.

Fords, led by the Mk II, took another 1-2-3 sweep at Sebring, and Miles and Ruby led the charge, setting another record race after completing 228 laps and 1,185.6 miles, averaging 98.8 mph.

Ford was big on 1-2-3 victories in 1966. At LeMans for the 24-Hours that year, Miles and Denny Hulme lead most of the race and were in a winning position when Ford management wanted a three-car photo-finish. Miles dropped back to conform to the order, and that cost him the race. It would have been the first time in history that a driver had won the big three—Daytona, Sebring and LeMans—but at the finish, it was Bruce McLaren and Chris Amon taking the flag and victory.

Dan Gurney set another race-lap record in his Mk II at an average of 142.979 mph, considerably faster than the previous Ferrari record of 131.375 mph. This was America's first LeMans victory, and an overwhelming win for Ford. And the Europeans didn't like that finish at all. With the third Mk II sweep, Ford locked up the 1966 World Prototype Championship. GT-40s took the World Sports Car Championship to boot.

In 1967, Ford was back to defend its honor with Mk II GT-40s and all-new Mk IV Fords—Dearborn's own designed, built and developed—running the same type engine, except that these cars ran two conventional Holley 4-bbl carbs on the 427 side-oiler.

At Daytona, the Gurney/Foyt Mk II set the qualifying record of 1:55.10 minutes and 119.165 mph. Dick Thompson, teaming with sensational newcomer Jackie Ickx, set the Sports Car fast lap in a Mk I GT-40 at 2:01.10 minutes and 114.300 mph. However, as the race developed, the new Ferrari 330 P4 proved to be the race leader and finished 1-2-3, although 12 laps off the pace set by the Fords the year before. It was not a good race for the Ford teams: The highest Ford finisher was the Thompson/Ickx team sponsored by Gulf Oil and built by John Wyer's J.W. Automotive Engineering. They actually finished ahead of the McLaren/Lucien Bianchi Mk II.

At Sebring, the Fords were back on track. Mario Andretti and McLaren took the race with a new record, going 10 laps more than the year before, or 238 total laps. The new record stood at 1237.6 miles at 103.13 mph, a Mk IV milestone and another Shelby American team win that led the 2nd-place Ford driven by Foyt and Ruby.

After the sensational LeMans victory of '66, Ford was back in '67 with cars sure to shut out the Europeans again. Ferrari's P4s were the only real challengers and the race unfolded as the clash of the titans: Ford versus Ferrari. The automotive world had taken notice when Ford made a bid to buy out Ferrari before the GT-40 program had begun in 1963. Enzo shut the door on such a proposal after letting it be known that he was interested, but wanted to control all of Ford's racing at the expense of Carroll Shelby in particular. That obviously was not going to happen, and the Ford men walked away even more determined to beat the Italian.

Pure function in long-distance endurance racing, the Mk II GT-40 was the top prototype sports/racing car in the world in 1966. Only 13 Mk IIs were built.

Although never intended to be more than fully functional endurance racers, the Mk II (shown) GT-40 Fords were of an aggressive, yet pleasing style.

Had Ford officials left the winning of LeMans to the drivers, the No. 1 car (right) driven by Ken Miles and Denny Hulme would have won rather than taking second spot. If that had happened, Miles would have been the first driver in history to have won the triple crown of racing— Daytona, Sebring and LeMans—all in Mk II Fords. Courtesy Ford Motor Co.

When program director Roy Lunn went to England to talk with distant relative and world champion, John Cooper, Cooper advised him to visit Eric Broadley, who had already designed and produced a mid-engine Ford powered GT coupe. All the basics were in place and, when Ford Advanced Vehicles was established in Slough, England, near Broadley's Lola Cars, it aroused considerable interest in the automotive world. Clearly, Ford was taking on Italy's master of endurance racing. And even though John Wyer was Britain's master of the art, it was not at all clear that they could produce a winner. But they did.

The '67 24-Hours of LeMans was a classic shoot-out. Ford

Dearborn was there with four Mk IVs and they were backed up by three Mk IIB cars, all 7-liter-powered machines. An additional set of three Mk I GT-40s lined up for an impressive Ford showing. John Wyer fielded two of his modified GT-40 coupes designed by Len Bailey, lightened and slightly restyled cars entered under the *Mirage* name. Nine Ferraris lined up against them. And two of Jim Hall's Chevrolet powered Chaparrals were spoiling for victory.

The Fords and Chaparrals gave the first hours of the race a decidedly all-American cast, but a Ferrari P4 slowly worked its way up through the field. After a few hours, the race settled into a Ford, Ferrari, Chaparral, Ferrari duel in that

Mario Andretti (right) and Bruce McLaren at Sebring 1967 with the new all-American designed-and-built Mk IV Ford. At its debut and record setting Sebring win, car traveled 1237.6 miles at an average of 103.13 mph—52 miles more and 4.33 mph faster than the Mk II win the year before. Courtesy Ford Motor Co.

Mk IV Ford's second and last race, the 24-Hours of LeMans, was completely dominated by car driven by Dan Gurney and A.J. Foyt, who set distance and average speed records not broken until 1971— 3251.567 miles, 135.482 mph. Note "Gurney bubble" over driver's head. Roof was bubbled locally to provide headroom for Dan Gurney. Courtesy Ford Motor Co.

order. The Fords were running so far out in front that LeMans officials tried to stop the cars on a technical issue when it was clear that no other cars could run with them. Then, a crash at night in the Esses took out three of the factory Mk IVs. And after the Chaparral challenge was sidelined, the Ferrari contingent looked as if they would move into the winner's circle.

But the Italians were shut out as Gurney and Foyt drove their Shelby team Mk IV through record lap after record lap in a flawless race that showed the Mk IV was clearly the superior car. At the finish, the all-American Gurney/Foyt/ Mk IV Ford won LeMans, setting new speed and distance records of 135.48 mph for 3241.57 miles, records that were not broken until 1971. This was, in large part, due to the addition of the Chicane Corner—a first-gear corner— immediately before the pit entrance following the '67 race.

They couldn't beat Ford, so the international racing rules committee promptly banned 7-liter (427-cid) engines. With new rules and no 7-liter engines allowed in 1968, the Europeans thought Ford's 215-mph racers were finished.

But then came John Wyer's team of 5-liter sports-car-class Mk I GT-40s and special Mirage cars sponsored by Gulf Oil Corporation. These light blue and orange cars won the majority of international championship races in 1968, including victory at LeMans, the third straight for Ford.

The Europeans were shaking their heads in disbelief. A conventional American V8 just wasn't supposed to do that. They had been beaten again with a car basically designed in 1964 and still powered by the Ford stock-block V8. GT-40 Fords remained the best racing cars in the world, and Wyer's team won the World Manufacturers' Championship.

For 1969, both Ferrari and Porsche brought out new cars powered by new 12-cylinder engines displacing just under 5 liters. The Gulf-Fords didn't fair well at Daytona, and the Broadley-designed Chevy-powered Lola won the marque's only major race, finishing 1-2 when all the competition broke.

Then, the Ickx/Jackie Oliver Gulf-Ford GT-40 won the Sebring 12-Hour with a new race record of 239 laps and 1,242.8 miles, averaging 103.57 mph. And, back to LeMans for the all-time classic running of the 24-Hours: A combined total of 20 Porsches and Ferraris against 2 GT-40s could not stand the pace. Wyer's Gulf-Ford, chassis number 1075, won LeMans again! It was the same car that had won in '68. And Ford had won LeMans four years in a row! But this time it wasn't against Ferrari. It was against Porsche—the marque that soon rose to become the dominate racing marque of modern times—that lost in a fender-to-fender duel with a Ford.

A total of 94 small-block GT-40s were built. These were the

Mk IV Ford, the fastest, most durable racing prototype in LeMans history through 1970. Aerodynamics as only Ford could do it in the mid-60s; the Mk IV was designed for 250-mph speeds.

Ford's side-oiler 427 is hidden in there somewhere. Dual Holley 4-bbl carbs—enclosed in clear-plastic air box—rather than single Holley was major engine change in Mk IV from Mk II.

big winners with at least 33 major racing victories. Thirteen Mk IIs were built; they won four races. Twelve Mk IVs were built; they were entered in two races and won both. Each type Ford GT won LeMans once while the Mk I was victorious twice.

Mixed in with the racing cars was a production run of seven Mk III GT-40s sold for street use. These are, no doubt, the most refined and most exotic high-performance Fords ever offered to the public. For about $17,000, one could have been yours in 1967. With just 306 HP, a Mk III could hurtle you through the 1/4-mile in 13.8 seconds at 104.8 mph, while still in 2nd gear! Top speed was modestly stated to be 140 mph, but both 4th and 5th were overdriven, making the car capable of higher speeds.

GT-40s were small two-seaters with room for not much more than thrilling driving. Getting in the car took practice.

Mk IV Ford.

John Wyer's Mk I Gulf-Ford GT-40s dominated endurance racing in 1968 to win Ford's fourth world championship in three years of international racing.

Len Bailey updated the GT-40 concept with a lighter, more aerodynamic car dubbed Mirage by Wyer. This is the last of three built, winner of four major international races.

They were very low—the source of their name—only 40 inches high. But once inside, you never wanted to leave. They felt good, tight, solid, and you itched to go fast.

A little twist of the key and the Ford V8 behind your left ear barks to life. Tap the pedal a few times to clear the cylinders. The tach needle bounces upwards of 6000 rpm as the tuned "bundle of snakes" exhaust blasts an unusual-sounding tone. That's American horsepower, alive and well.

Pointed down pit lane, and onto Road Atlanta's road course, 1st gear kicks you in the back like a rocket. The engine sharply reports your gear change to 2nd. A right hander uphill, across the top to the left and down into twisty bits with a right, a left, another right, another left is all taken like you're on rails. This is "handling." This is thrilling!

Through turn five and up another hill to the left, the engine howls to 6500 rpm over a short straight, then back off and into 2nd gear for another right hander with hard braking through turn six. A short straight, then turn seven. It comes up so fast you think you are going over the edge, but those massive brakes slow the GT-40 to 35 mph with ease. Downshift 2nd to 1st and brake hard as G-forces try to tear you out of the car. Take the line from the outside, kiss the inside and stand on it as you come out the other side.

Up a little hill to the left, then a long straight. Now you're making those Webers really work: 1st gear to 75, 2nd to 110 with a smooth-as-silk shift. And 3rd takes you to 150 as the 5-liter about 12 inches behind your head sings its song: Ford horsepower! 4th stretches toward 180 as the world becomes a blur. There's no room for 5th, the universe the GT-40 was designed for.

There you are, screaming down the back straight. It's a sound like no other racing car, a wail all its own, the sound of a GT-40 Ford!

PANTERA, MID-ENGINE CLEVELAND

Carroll Shelby's Cobra works was the foremost builder of high-performance sports cars of the time. He challenged the "Modena wizard" and won. Then along came another builder from Ferrari's stomping grounds, who leaned over into the engine bay of one of Shelby's 427 Cobras and surmised that, being Italian, he could do a much better job of putting together performance in a more civil package. The result was Alessandro de Tomaso's svelte mid-engine Mangusta—the Italian name for Mongoose, the quick Cobra-killer of the animal kingdom.

The Mangusta was indeed a quick and stylish coupe, but its high-performance 302, ZF 5-speed, disc brakes and independent suspension all around just didn't quite reach the acclaim it could have because it didn't have quite the refinement it needed to be convincing.

With Ford power and all the good stuff that made up the Mangusta, it was clear that de Tomaso was onto a good thing. He just needed the right kind of help to market it better. Along about 1969, Lee Iacocca, then the big gun at Ford, got together with de Tomaso to work out a plan for a mid-engine answer to the Corvette. With the demise of Shelby's Cobra works in 1967, no more of those sensational bombers were being made for Ford to advertise as the "fastest car in the world," a barb directed at GM's plastic car.

Results of their venture materialized in 1970 when Ford and de Tomaso jointly announced the arrival of another sleek animal into Ford showrooms, the Pantera—Italian for Panther. How the name came about no doubt followed Ford's image of exciting things from the wilder side of life,

JOHN WYER

After the 1959 racing season when Britain's Aston Martin factory team won the World Sports Car Championship, John Wyer had accomplished the primary objective of a nine year goal. He became Aston Martin racing manager in 1950, a one-year assignment that grew into a 13-year association with the marque. He rose to Racing Engineer, then Technical Manager, and finally General Manager in 1957. He remained at that post until joining Ford in 1963.

It took nearly a decade of racing, but Wyer's Aston Martin team won the 24-Hours of LeMans in 1959 with team drivers Roy Salvadori and Carroll Shelby, whose DBR1 averaged 112.569 mph for 2,701.654 miles in an Aston Martin 1-2 finish. Three previous 2nd overall finishes had been recorded by DB3S Astons in 1955, '56 and '58. By 1959, Wyer was recognized as the premier manager in all aspects of sports-car design, development and racing.

Because of his wide acclaim, Ford attracted Wyer to head up its Ford Advanced Vehicles in September, 1963. The GT-40 program was gearing up, and Wyer was the man who put the works in motion.

Aston Martin retired from racing after the 1959 world championship. Although several other factory cars were built and raced, the firm led a much more reclusive existence related to racing. That was in part the reason Wyer went to Ford.

"It was a difficult transition," relates Wyer, "because the methods were entirely different than I had been used to. For 13 years I had been working for David Brown, a benevolent dictator who knew what he wanted and didn't have to ask anyone else. Nothing was decided by committee. If David decided he had confidence in you and you were the man for the job, he gave you a great deal of latitude. You could make your own mistakes as long as you had successes to go along with them.

"At Ford, everything was decided by committee, or rather, not decided by committee. Frequently, what would happen was that I was coming over here once or twice a month for meetings in Detroit, where we would sit down and solemnly reach a lot of conclusions. Then I would go happily back to England and start working, trying to put those things into effect. Then I would get a telephone call from someone in Detroit and, when telling them what I was doing, they would say, Haven't you heard? That's all changed now. We're not going 'north,' we're going 'south!'

"Nobody had even thought to pick up a phone and tell me about it. That's the way things happened. There were so many different schools of thought. So, I would say it was a difficult period of adjustment for me because I had been in the habit of having things clearly defined, and when decisions had been made, everybody went away to carry on with them. At Ford, if you didn't agree with a decision, you went off somewhere by yourself and started working another way. Ford justified the system by saying, 'That's all right. It may be wasteful to have people working in so many different directions, but out of it we may get a winner, a winner we might lose if we kept things too narrow. If we get a winner, that justifies the whole system.'

"It's a question, I suppose, of how much money you have to throw at it. At Aston Martin, we worked along fairly narrow lines because we didn't have enough budget to do anything else. With Ford, money wasn't really considered at all. You had a budget, but everybody knew it would be exceeded, and nobody got upset about it except the financial controller, and no one took much notice of him.

"Winning LeMans '68 with the GT-40 was, for me, very satisfactory at the moment because we were sharply divided at Ford between the big-engine and small-engine schools. I was always a small-engine man, and when we won the race in '68 and followed again by winning in '69 with the same car, with the small engine, it was vindication of everything I had tried to say throughout my period with Ford.

"I never believed the 427-cubic inch engine was necessary. I always thought the job could be done with the small engine. Powerful people at Ford said, 'Why do it with a small engine when you can do it with a big one?' The Ford philosophy was to use the biggest engine you can.

"I said, no, I didn't agree. You don't race with engines, you race with complete cars. When you start with a big engine, you finish up with a big car. So now, everything has to do more work—brakes, wheels, running gear and so on. So you've magnified those problems with a heavier car. You should go to the smallest, lightest engine you can.

"Personally, it was very satisfying to win LeMans and the World Championship with the small engine in the GT-40s, and '69 just confirmed '68, one of the outstanding moments in my motor-racing career. It was very satisfactory to do it again. By that time, particularly the GT-40 was really getting a bit ancient, but it was vindication of the small-engine philosophy, although it was far from a popular point of view at Ford."

John Wyer remains the only manager whose teams have won the FIA World Championship with three different marques: Aston Martin (1959), Ford (1968) and Porsche (1970 and '71). As director of Ford Advanced Vehicles, and later as owner of J.W. Automotive, his direction produced the most successful sports car of the time—the GT-40, the car that dominated international road racing and wrote an illustrious chapter in Ford's quest for Total Performance.

Cobra, Mustang, etc. Somehow, Ford power had become so associated. Tiger, Mangusta and Cougar are other examples, but GT-40 was a notable exception.

De Tomaso was not new to spine-tingling performance. His association with Carroll Shelby's works went back to at least 1964 when Pete Brock designed the body for a mid-engine Ford-powered racing car for him. Brock was the Shelby engineer responsible for the design of the Cobra Daytona Coupe body and the following unfinished 427 Super Coupe. His race car for de Tomaso appeared in 1966 with plans for Italian bodyman Fantuzzi to build 10. Famed designers, Ghia, provided financial support for racing, and the car thus became the *Ghia-de Tomaso*. Weighing 1,450 pounds, these 400 HP cars with 289 Ford power promised to be "tall" racing machines, but their subsequent record is obscure.

Mangusta production was set at one a day. Its magnificent

Pantera, marketed through Lincoln-Mercury, was the most sports car for the money of the early '70s. Built in Italy and powered by 351 Cleveland, a Pantera was the equal of Ferrari and Maserati GT cars at less than half the price. Squire Gabbard Photo.

Styling in Italian tradition, performance in Ford tradition were main features of the Pantera. Squire Gabbard Photo.

styling was the work of Ghia, a design firm controlled by de Tomaso and, subsequently, purchased by Ford Motor Co. in the mid '70s. The Mangusta set the stage for later Ford associations with performance uncommon for the price. Just 15 minutes down the road from Maranello where Enzo turned out his high-dollar Ferraris, de Tomaso built his Mangusta stock with a 230-HP 302 or with 306 HP Shelby power, or up to a super-wild 506-HP fuel-injected engine that could beat most any Ferrari at about half the price, or $11,150 base. That made the Mangusta a lot of car for the money.

At 3,050 pounds, the lower-powered Mangusta was not all that fast: 0-60 in 7 seconds, top speed well over 125. What it did was give de Tomaso cars a bad name for a lot of irritating quirks: "tricky handling, mediocre brakes and a terrible shift linkage," along with "uncomfortable seating" said *Road & Track*. On the other side, it was a sensational Italian sports car of high-quality construction that people wanted to be seen in.

About this time, 1968, FoMoCo bought into Ghia, de Tomaso and Vignale, another noted Italian designer. A four-seat car was planned. Fortunately, two seats became the target and the resulting wedge-shaped Italiano express, the Pantera, was a fabulous and instant success.

In May, 1971, Panteras began showing up in Lincoln-Mercury showrooms. Not since the E-Type Jaguar had so much car been offered for the price—$9800 complete. These were immensely tempting coupes that produced eye strain in everyone looking at it.

In this Ghia coupe, the 351 Cleveland in the back prom-

351 Cleveland and ZF 5-speed transaxle were combined in the Pantera's mid-engine layout. Squire Gabbard Photo.

ised sizzling performance in Ford's reliable form, and styling was comparable to anything from Ferrari. The lines were simply ultra-svelte in the Italian tradition—but a comparable Ferrari cost $24,700 and a Maserati nearly $20,000. Thus, the price of a Pantera was bargain basement for what you got—a real Italian sports car for less than a Lincoln.

Test reports of the car noted some deficiencies such as seating comfort and interior noise. But if a sports-car buff wanted over-stuffed comfort and pure stereo sound, there were all sorts of living-room combinations to buy. If the same buff were placed blind-folded in a contemporary Ferrari or Maserati, he would most likely not be able to tell which car he was in, except for the beat of a big V8.

The prevailing Ferrari philosophy has always been one that said you endured anything to be considered a *Ferraristi.* For the Cobra owner, driving meant another brutal, but thrilling encounter that bordered on the need for a kidney belt. For the Pantera driver, his car was about everything one could want in an Italian coupe, the closest thing to a GT-40 you'll ever find, and one that came at a remarkably low price. All that added up to the Pantera being selected as *Road Test* magazine's car of the year in 1973.

At 3205 pounds, the Pantera with its 310-HP Cleveland was a smooth performer for the road, every bit of a Ferrari without all the frustration and expense associated with temperamental engines.

Mandatory air conditioning on the Pantera meant the car was intended for GT motoring. Attention to styling detail produced a very impressive car with beautiful styling throughout. Pantera driving pleasures were enhanced as the cars were steadily improved. In some earlier cars, recalls accounted for some problems, including lack of proper splash shields and drainage in the body that caused premature rusting in key areas. Ford became so distraught with the cars that they made de Tomaso a deal that took him out of the picture and began concentrating on improving the cars. The most serious problem was the lack of sufficient structure at the rear, which resulted in rear-suspension deflection and severe oversteer during hard cornering. Bill Stroppe in the west and Holman & Moody in the east were contracted by Ford Motor Co. to correct the problem on cars in service.

Production lagged way behind schedule. Instead of 10,000 cars a year, only about 5000 had been built by mid-1973. And only around 2000 were imported to the U.S. by then. Ford Motor Co. says the last assigned serial number was 7380, with the first being 1001. The first imported into the U.S. was number 1286. The Pantera International Club says that 5400 were ultimately imported.

As things went, federal regulations kept getting in the way, and the Pantera continued to leave a bad taste in Ford's corporate mouth. They were high-effort cars that made demands on the driver—stiff steering and stiff clutch, corrected in later cars by a change in the pedal linkage—that took some getting used to. Then there were complaints about interior noise which was, after all, the nature of mid-engine cars.

Gulf-Mirage was mid-70s version of the GT-40. Mid-engine, extremely low and highly aerodynamic, GR8/801 is shown being driven by Jackie Ickx (Derek Bell co-drove) to last Ford victory at LeMans, 1975. Photo courtesy John Horsman.

De Tomaso backed a LeMans racing effort in 1972 that prepared GT4 Panteras for long-distance endurance racing. Not since 1969 had Ford been racing, and that was with cars of a rather similar name, GT-40. Comparison of the two cars shows the Pantera with almost identical aerodynamics and a layout that was inspired by the GT-40, ZF 5-speed and all. Bud Moore of Trans-Am BOSS 302 and circle-track fame developed the engines to the tune of 500 HP at 7,000 rpm, enough to send the car down the long Mulsanne Straight at LeMans at 205 mph.

Alessandro de Tomaso had LeMans experience by winning the Index of Performance in 1958 with a 46 cubic inch, 4-cylinder OSCA and finishing 11th overall. His four Pantera entries in 1972 in the GTS category were against five Corvettes, seven Porsches and nine Ferraris. Unfortunately, the cars didn't place. Other versions of the Pantera continued to be built, but Lincoln-Mercury stopped importing the car, mostly because of difficulties in meeting constantly changing federal standards.

Panteras that were imported offered Ford power in a very exotic package, and one that could achieve upwards of 150 mph on its 200-mph speedometer. Then there's the GTS model—for $11,488 when new—that reportedly posted a maximum speed of 174 mph. Panteras were still being built in 1987 and imported into the U.S. for a price of about $55,000. At the same time, nicely restored older Panteras, still the most exotic Ford powered machine for the money, sold for about $20,000,

FORDS IN EUROPE

Little news about European racing seemed to reach the U.S. So little is known about Ford-Europe's exotic racing efforts. However, if you are a Ford buff, you probably would like to know more about these efforts. Let's start with the Gulf-Mirage. The *Gulf* part comes from sponsorship by Gulf Oil Corp.; the *Mirage* name from the line of cars built by John Wyer of J.W. Automotive, in Slough, England, once known as *Ford Advanced Vehicles*.

Wyer was the man behind the sensational Ford GT-40s of the '60s. After the factory Ford Mk IVs were retired in 1967, Wyer's team of GT-40 Mk I cars went on to win the World Championship in 1968 and won the 24-Hours of LeMans, the world's most renowned race, in both 1968 and '69. The '69 win has become recognized as the classic of classics among LeMans races, a race that was close-fought to the finish. The brilliant young driver Jackie Ickx drove his Gulf-Ford in Sports Car class to beat the veteran, Hans Herrmann, in a new prototype 908LH Porsche.

The first Mirage, the M1, was a successful upgrade of the GT-40, but the M2, a replacement for the GT-40-based M1, proved to be fraught with problems, mostly because of its BRM engine. Porsche solved this in a round-about way. They intervened with an offer to run their Type 917 program in 1970 and '71. Wyer accepted, and he won two more World Championships with those Gulf-Porsches.

Then, after that two-year effort, Wyer semi-retired in Jan. 1972. Gulf Research Racing Company, Inc. was then formed and John Horsman, Wyer's able ex-assistant, was named Managing Director, reporting to Grady Davis of Gulf Oil in Pittsburgh. The first car, dubbed the M6—meaning *Mirage 6*—was designed by Len Bailey and constructed under the direction of John Horsman. Cars carrying serial numbers 601, 602, 603, 604 and 605 were built.

The *GR7*—designation is explained later—shown here is the 1974 car. "This car was constructed in 1972 as an M6 by Gulf Research Racing Company, Inc.," says John Horsman. "It was allocated serial-number 603 when built and was the test chassis for the Weslake V12, 3-liter engine. The car was completed in August, 1972, and was first tested at Goodwood race circuit in England by Derek Bell on August 9, 1972. Considerable testing continued into '73, including at Daytona prior to the '73 24-Hour race. The Weslake engine was finally abandoned in March '73. Chassis 603 was converted to accept the DFV Cosworth."

Like any new car, the M6 had teething problems, but was a good test bed of ideas. One was to get rid of the Weslake V12 in favor of a Ford-Cosworth DFV V8. In this form and with many updates, the car was re-serialized as GR7/703, but was not run again until 1974. It ran four races that year, and performed excellently in the Monza 1000Km in Italy, finishing 4th overall and setting the fastest lap.

The cars were raced as M6s in 1972 and '73. All Gulf-Mirage cars received open-cockpit bodies except for one—see photos. This setup was abandoned in favor of the open body. In open-cockpit form, they were capable of major wins.

With the return of the Mirage name to LeMans racing in 1973, two cars were entered against a host of Ferrari, Porsche

Only closed-body Gulf-Mirage car built: Due to teething problems, team returned to successful open-body configuration.

Jean-Paul Jaussaud in GR8/801 pausing for photo during shakedown tests at Silverstone prior to '75 Le Mans. Photo courtesy John Horsman.

Cosworth-Ford DOHC 3-liter proved to be an endurance champion in a variety of cars, including this Gulf-Mirage.

and Matra competitors. Even so, the Mirage of the Hailwood/Watson/Schuppan driving team ran as high as 3rd before being sidelined by a crash.

In 1974, Gulf Oil dropped the name *Mirage* and, for identification purposes, renamed the cars *Gulf GR7s* for Gulf Racing. The original M6s were upgraded and renumbered GR-701, 702, 703, 704 and 705. The Bell/Hailwood team finished 4th overall at the 1974 24-Hours of LeMans and the GR7s finished second to Matra in the 1974 World Championship points standings.

The finish of the '74 season signaled even better things to come. In 1975, the Gulf-Ford team was back again and raced in the Sports over 2-liter class. Of 55 starters, no less than 27 were Porsches. Two of Grady's Gulf-Fords were entered against four other cars running the Cosworth DFV 3-liter (183-cid) engine—two British Lolas and two Ligiers from France.

For the 1975 fuel-consumption-limited LeMans, the Gulf GR8 was created. Conceived by Horsman and Wyer, it had a 6.1-inch longer wheelbase and new bodywork, which greatly improved aerodynamics. The driving duo of Derek Bell and Jackie Ickx put their GR8 into the lead at the start of the race and never gave it up. After 24 hours of intense driving, day and night, rain and shine, they posted victory by traveling 2855.6 miles at more than a 118-mph average. The second Gulf-Ford finished 3rd, and the 2nd-place car, a

Line-up of Fords of all sorts shows range of Ford power—champions in every way.

Ligier powered by a Ford-Cosworth engine, gave the DOHC V8 engine a 1-2-3 sweep.

Top speed was 193.87 mph down the famed Mulsanne Straight, but overall lap times were lower than previous years because of the fuel-consumption limitation imposed that year. However, average lap speeds approached 130 mph over the 8.3 miles of sharp curves, hills, dips and straights.

LeMans '75 was the first British win since 1959—Aston Martin DBR1 driven by Roy Salvadori and Carroll Shelby—and the last victory for Ford, either American or European. It was, however, an outstanding triumph for John Wyer and, in particular, John Horsman, who had assumed the position of Gulf Research Racing Company's director and team manager. The 1959 Aston Martin win was under his direction, the Ford GT-40 wins of 1968 and '69 were his team, and the Gulf-Ford DFV Cosworth victory of '75 made it four wins.

In 1976, Harley Cluxton of Phoenix, Arizona, purchased the entire ex-GRRC team. The cars were prepared by John Horsman in England for running LeMans without fuel-consumption limits. They finished 2nd and 5th that year before the age of Porsche domination set in. The Gulf-Ford *Mirage*—renamed so—with its DFV Cosworth V8 actually exceeded the statistics of the previous year due to the removal of fuel-consumption limitations of 1975. Lafosse and Migault ran 2871.218 mph averaging 119.634 mph in '76 for a 2nd behind Ickx in a Porsche.

With the rebirth of interest in international racing, Ford, Jaguar and other classic marques are once again eyeing LeMans. Who knows, there may be another Ford effort around the corner.

8

RETURN IN THE '80s

Racing & Performance Rediscovered

Fifth major redesign of Mustang was for '79 model year. Ford's 5-liter—new designation for the 302—engine came back to life in production with 133 HP at 3600 rpm. Ford racing was also a new beginning in the form of the Bill Scott Racing "Team Miller" Mustang. Klaus Ludwig won the car's first IMSA GTO race on June 14, 1981, at Brainerd, Minnesota. Courtesy Ford Motor Co.

Everywhere racing goes on, you'll find Ford. Like the '60s, Ford Motor Company's return to competition in the '80s has been like the phoenix of legend that rose from ashes to fly again. For about 10 years following the early '70s, Ford performance was noticeably absent; remembering the glorious '60s was to recall the good times. The good times came back in the '80s, giving Ford fans a lot to cheer about.

NASCAR Stock-car racing, a product of the Southeast, has grown into a nationwide program with feature races in many locations. These races draw fans who cheer Bill Elliott—the most popular driver on the NASCAR circuit in the '80s—and his Coors-Melling Thunderbird, Ricky Rudd and his Motorcraft T-Bird, Kyle Petty's 7-Eleven 'Bird and Davey Allison's Havoline 'Bird.

Drag racing is once again drawing large crowds of spectators who see a few Fords, mostly driven by Bob Glidden and Rickie Smith, taking on all sorts of ProStockers and putting them down. Kenny Bernstein's Super Team gave Ford drag racing a tremendous amount of acclaim through 1986, when he switched to Buick. And his Budweiser King Ford Tempo Top Fuel Funny Car of that year set records unmatched today. It is still the strongest-running full-bodied car in the world.

SCCA Trans-Am and IMSA GTO racing has seen the Ford-versus-Chevrolet feud continue with Ford Mustangs, Mercury Capris and Merkurs finding their way into winner's circles and record books. Tom Gloy's Capris, and Jack Roush Mustangs and Merkurs have made it tough on other makes.

IMSA GTP (Prototype) racing now leads in the technology of racing cars and, although Porsche dominates, Ford's first GTP Mustang of a few years ago and the new Ford Probe are Dearborn's leading edge attack against the German cars, GM prototypes, Jaguars and others who race the series.

In showroom-stock racing where fans can see for them-

SVO

Michael Kranefuss, director of SVO, announced in 1981 the beginning of Ford's entry into performance by saying, "The basic idea is not just to do one car, but to create an organization like Special Vehicle Operations that can respond to rapidly changing demands in the performance market. When Mr. Petersen (Ford Motor Co. president) announced the formation of the Special Vehicle Operations in late 1980, the idea was to do something that would indicate excitement coming out of Ford Motor Co., which eventually would be seen in the products. One of SVO's objectives is the engineering and production of specialty products that you can widely describe as high-performance vehicles which means, as far as the product content is concerned, applying race-derived technology.

"SVO has 32 people. It's a three-pronged kind of approach: engineering of specialty production cars; conducting motors-orts programs; and initiating and establishing a high-performance-parts program. By far the largest department in SVO is Engineering. We've got chassis people, body people and engine people. And they're all established people out of Ford's engineering community."

In May 1981, Dennis Mecham debuted his specially prepared Mustang in the season-opening 100-mile SCCA Trans-Am race at the Charlotte Motor Speedway. And plans were laid to compete in the entire 10-race Trans-Am schedule that year.

"Our association with Dennis Mecham's Mustang is a continuation of our reinvolvement with motorsport in the United States," said Kranefuss. "While Mecham will be working toward the overall points championship, Ford engineers will be using his race car as a test bed to evaluate and develop future Mustang technology. We are counting on motorsports to help reinforce our fun-to-drive small-car image and to draw attention to the good performance of our cars."

As of May 1981, two other teams were associated with Ford: Klaus Ludwig raced his turbocharged Mustang to 2nd overall at Road Atlanta in an IMSA race, and Lyn St. James finished 4th in her Mercury Capri in the first IMSA American Challenge race of the season at Lime Rock.

Lyn, owner of an auto-parts retail outlet, Autodyne, later qualified her bright red Motorcraft sponsored Capri 7th, then finished 4th overall at Road Atlanta. Ludwig's Team Miller Mustang won its first IMSA GTO event at Brainerd International Raceway on June 14. Ludwig beat John Paul's Jr.'s Lola T-600 and John Fitzpatrick's Porsche 935 with a race average of 109.987 mph. This was the first win for a Ford-backed product in a major American road race in nearly a decade. It was particularly satisfying because the mile-long straight at Brainerd did not favor the 4-cylinder engine in the Mustang.

On June 17, 1981, Ford announced that a second Team Miller Mustang had been built and an invitation was accepted for John Paul Jr. to drive in a road race at the Nonoring, West Germany, on June 28. That date marked the return of Ford Dearborn to international competition.

But before that happened, Ludwig passed leader Brian Redman on the last lap at Sears Point in Sonoma, California, to take the second consecutive Team Miller Ford Mustang win in IMSA racing. Ludwig qualified 2nd and led most of the race, then tapped Redman's Lola T-600 from behind on the next to last lap in a braking duel. Redman spun and Ludwig squeaked by to win and set a race average record speed of 92.931 mph.

SVO Mustang was an impressive showcase for Ford and gave high-tech performance. Turbo-4 of 1985 produced 205 HP at 5000 rpm from 140 cubic inches. Torque of 248 lb-ft at 3000 rpm propelled car length of quarter mile in 15.5 seconds. Top speed was 135 mph. Courtesy Ford Motor Co.

On the SCCA Trans-Am trail, the Dennis Mecham Mustang sponsored by Coors and Polyglycoat took the first factory Ford Trans-Am win in over a decade when Tom Gloy won the final national championship race of the '81 season at Sears Point on October 28th. Gloy set a class record by beating the Corvettes of 1981 champion Eppie Wietzes and Greg Pickett, George Follmer's Camaro and Bob Tullius' Jaguar XJS.

SVO was growing, and when Ford Motor Co. announced that 351-cid engine blocks of an improved design were to be remanufactured and aluminum cylinder heads were to be made available, it was the beginning of Ford's return to NASCAR racing. Kranefuss said, "This is the next logical step in our widening motorsport involvement. There has been a strong demand for the Company's return to NASCAR...one of the most popular racing series in the world. It is a major-league sport, uniquely American, that commands the loyalty of hundreds of thousands of potential car buyers every year. I think the parts program will ensure a continuing Ford presence in NASCAR racing."

And it wasn't long afterwards that the molds for the BOSS 429 engine were dusted off and Ford was back into drag racing.

"The Company's contingency award program for 1982 has been expanded to cover 173 events in eight championship series sanctioned by six different organizations," he confirmed. "The dollar amount of those awards has been increased to $312,000."

By that announcement, Ford's Special Vehicle Operations was firmly entrenched and determined to put Ford performance in front of American motorsports fans in a winning way. The rest is history.

Roush Racing IMSA GTO Mustang shared by Scott Pruett and Bruce Jenner at Charlotte in '86: Jenner finished IMSA GTO season 2nd in driving this Mustang to Pruett's winning Motorcraft Mustang. The 2700-lb car was powered by Roush prepared 358-cid SVO engine. Car won 1986 IMSA GTO Manufacturers' Championship.

better than ever. And Ford products lead the American automotive industry in styling, quality and performance. They are a major force around the world, a fitting tribute to Henry Ford's ideas of 1903 that led to the founding of the Ford Motor Co.

Ford trucks have emerged as very popular in recent years, with Motorcraft parts along with Ford's Special Vehicle Operations (SVO). Although cars are the main subject here, Fords in any motorsport are hard to beat.

PONYCAR WARS II

The "rejuvenated" Mustang was introduced in 1979 as a heavily redesigned model. It came in a variety of spirited styles from hardtop coupe to hatchback. Power in top form came from the 5-liter (302-cid) Windsor, Ford's mainstay engine of modern times. Unfortunately, performance was only name deep. The "Cobra" option had commercial value with the legendary name, and tempted buyers with the promise of performance, but it came up short. Turbocharging was coming into vogue in smaller engine models, but they, too, were really econo-Fords used for improving the government-mandated corporate average fuel economy (CAFE). As for being performance cars, these early attempts were not successful.

In the midst of it all, Ford racing was stirring. In a few years, the Mustang of old was replaced by modern Mustangs with "teeth." Although the '70s were a definite low in interesting cars, the period did produce considerable advances in chassis and tire technology that made cars ride and handle better. Improved still further in the '80s, top performing cars became better than ever, and aerodynamics became state of the art with modern aero-aids. Engine technology improved as well. By 1982, the 5.0-liter High Output had

selves what Fords can do in road racing, a new force is building. And Ford engines now receive considerable attention to performance. Roller-tappet cams, tube headers and other power-producing hardware are factory original equipment.

Cars have indeed come a long way. Regardless of where your interests lie, whether the '50s or '60s, racing or street, it takes only a brief look at modern cars to see that they are

1987 Mustang GT with potent 5-liter V8 is a top performer. Its styling with spoiler, skirts, air dam and detailing resulted in the most dramatic and boldest Mustang since the G.T.350.

come on line in production Mustangs. Power output steadily rose from 157 HP at 4200 rpm that year to 175 HP in '83, then 210 HP in '85 to arrive at 225 horses with Ford's Multi-Port fuel injection in the top pony in '86. *Road & Track* tested an '87 HO, achieving 0-60 in 6.7 seconds and a top speed of over 148 mph!

Ford's 302 V8 has the same huge potential of years past. And with SVO equipment came true Ford performance, once again in the form of factory heavy-duty parts. Even though the big-blocks are gone from production, SVO revived a huge catalog of parts to suit almost any racer running Ford big-blocks of old, along with extensive equipment for the new technology 4-bangers and mainstay small-blocks.

An example of Mustang build-up from SVO parts is SVO's Driveline and Chassis engineer, Don Walsh, who installed Ford Motorsport parts on his daily driver to produce a car that turns the quarter in 13.70 seconds at 100.55 mph. Compare that to the BOSS 429 and BOSS 351 Mustangs seen earlier. The new-generation Mustang can compete heads up with the old guard, then out-handle them by a wide margin.

As an example of big cubes at work today, Walsh built another Mustang with a 514-cid "mountain mill" that puts down serious quarters, or 10.84 seconds at 130.4 mph. The engine is a 429 Super Cobra Jet with a single 4-bbl that cranks out 650 HP at 6,000 rpm!

Probably the real beginning of Ford's return to modern racing began with the "tire wars" of the early '80s when Firestone returned to racing and sponsored a specially built McLaren Mustang, the type M-81. In their first showing, Tom Klausler and John Morton drove the "Firestone HPR" car to win the GTP class of the 24-Hours of Daytona in 1981 and showed a lot of Ford fans that a Henry could still race

and win. In this case, it was on Firestone's regular-production street tires, the new-at-the-time High Performance Radial. The 2150-pound Mustang ran a Cosworth 4-cylinder engine and was partially sponsored by Motorcraft. The car, with Klausler and Morton driving, also finished the 12-Hours of Sebring that year. Ford's announced return to motorsports after being inactive for 11 years was looking good.

For 1982, a pair of Mustangs were entered by Firestone and Motorcraft in the IMSA GTO category. That signaled the significant entry of Ford's Special Vehicle Operations, headed by Michael Kranefuss, into racing. These 5-liter V8 cars were created by SVO's Bob Riley and built by Roush/Protofab in Livonia, Michigan. Long-time Ford man, Bud Moore, built the engines. When fitted with 4-speed over-drive manual transmissions, these Mustang GTs were front-rank cars capable of winning endurance racing over cars like the BMW M-1, Porsche 924 and Datsun 280ZX.

During that year, Ford's motorsports program expanded on a limited basis to also include NASCAR, drag racing, off-road and pro-rally racing. The primary program was Indy stars Rick Mears and Kevin Cogan driving a space-frame Mustang with a turbocharged 1.7-liter Fiesta engine in selected IMSA GT races. Lyn St. James of Ft. Lauderdale, Florida, drove another Motorcraft car, a Mercury Capri, in the IMSA Kelly American Challenge series. And Tom Gloy raced a Mustang in the Trans-Am series.

No doubt the high point of the '82 season was when the Firestone-Motorcraft Mustangs were taken to Japan for the World Endurance Championship where the GTO Mustang was the only V8-powered car run. The tally: FIA Group 2 (small engine) World Championship over a Datsun 200SX

Tucked away in there is a powerful 5-liter small-block with advanced computer-controlled ignition, roller lifters, fuel injection and tube headers. Called HO for High Output, this small-block makes for the hottest Mustang.

Wally Dallenbach drove Roush/Protofab Mustang to GTO lap record of 1.11:18 seconds at Charlotte with an average of 113.804 mph. In May of '86, Pruett qualified Roush Racing Mustang at 106.982 mph after a chicane had been installed along back straight to reduce speed.

NASCAR ace Bill Elliott finished 4th overall at Road Atlanta (1986) in Folgers/Motorcraft Mustang and moved up to 4th overall in IMSA standings. At the time, he was higher in IMSA road racing than in the Winston Cup standings. Courtesy Ford Motor Co.

(2nd) and a BMW 75S (3rd) and, in GTO, another World Championship victory over a BMW M1 (2nd) and a Datsun 280ZX (3rd).

In 1983, General Motors struck back at Ford's re-entry into racing with the DeAtley Camaros that gave Gloy, St. James and other Ford racers fits. Driven by David Hobbs and Willy T. Ribbs, the Camaros were consistent winners. Fortunately, Jack Roush, one-time Ford engineer turned ProStock drag racer, then engine and car builder, stepped in with a lot of knowledge that put Ford back in front.

Jack worked with Zakspeed USA on the GTP Mustang, Ford's GTP car that year, then the Trans-Am cars of Gloy and Greg Pickett. Working with the new SVO Hi-Perf 4-bolt-main block, derived from the old BOSS 302, and with new SVO aluminum heads, Roush squeezed out 520 horses from 310 cubes, which went up to 550 HP on a single Holley 830-cfm carb when the racing began. Roush brought in Protófab—thus the name *Roush/Protófab*—to build a new car that was designed by SVO chassis man Bob Riley. Ford Motor Co. selected Lincoln-Mercury's Division to compete with GM in the Trans-Am series. Thus, the finished products were Mercury Capris, not Mustangs. After extensive aerodynamic testing and overall development, the first car was delivered to Tom Gloy in northern California. The second went to Greg Pickett, where the new Ford challenge debuted at Road Atlanta. Unfortunately, Pickett was side-

lined by a minor shunt. He came back at Summit Point to dominate the race, only to be bumped off the track by a slow *back-marker* late in the race. Pickett then went on to win at Sears Point and Portland, showing that Ford was definitely back.

Willy T. Ribbs came over to join Pickett on the Roush/ Protofab team. At Detroit at the Trans-Am race preceding the Detroit Grand Prix, Gloy led the Roush cars across the finish line for a 1-2-3 sweep. Ribbs then won at Daytona and again at Brainerd. The cars were so dominant that SCCA slapped a 125-pound penalty on them in an effort to give the GM cars a chance. The Capris' major competition was a pair of Corvettes that couldn't make a go of it. Ah! The Trans-Am wars of old were back, and the Ford-versus-Chevy feud came alive on road-racing tracks all over again.

IMSA's GTP class of racing, the Camel GT, began attracting top cars and teams from around the world and soon became the premier form of sports-car racing. Unfortunately, it was dominated by imports. SVO's Kranefuss jumped into the fray with a new Ford. Designed again by Bob Riley, this was the first really exotic Ford racing car since the Mk IV of 1967. Known as the *Zakspeed Mustang GTP*, it weighed 1770 pounds and was capable of 210 mph on a 600-HP (at 9,000 rpm) DOHC in-line 4. The engine, which was in front of the driver, was intercooled, turbocharged, fuel-injected and mostly made of aluminum, displaced

1,745cc (106.5 cid) and delivered its power through a Hewland 5-speed transaxle.

The car's ultra-modern carbon-fiber monocoque chassis bonded by adhesives was a high-tech showcase for Ford's Aerospace division. It weighed just 100 pounds, about 250 pounds less than an equally strong aluminum tub. More American materials technology was shown in DuPont Nomex, Kevlar and Nextal synthetics used elsewhere. The original fiberglass outer body panels were phased out in favor of lighter, stronger carbon-fiber composites. The GTP suspension of unequal length A-arms throughout was all-independent—another computer-designed masterpiece—and 13-inch diameter ventilated 4-piston disc brakes with sticky Goodyear Eagles on BBS wheels provided excellent braking and handling. Overall aerodynamics received considerable input from Ford's Probe design studies of ultra-smooth cars that showed a best drag coefficient (C_d) of just 0.15. The Mustang GTP's C_d of just over 0.5, much higher due to its wing and ground effects, was less than most contemporary race cars with similar equipment, or usually more than 0.6. Thus, the Mustang GTP had the aerodynamic edge on other cars. In fact, the entire concept was a Ford high-tech showcase.

The overall package looked to be a significant GTP challenger, and in the car's first outing at Road America, the cars finished 1st and 3rd. This was a magnificent debut among the Porsches, Lolas and Jaguars that provoked a vocal outpouring of nationalism as spectators broke into a "Ford! Ford! Ford!" chant when the number 06 Mustang GTP surged into the lead on the 7th lap and went on to win. Unfortunately, for the duration of 1983 and all of '84, the cars didn't score another victory.

In SCCA Trans-Am racing, Tom Gloy's 7-Eleven sponsored Mercury Capri won the 1984 Championship by finishing in the top five in 14 of the scheduled 16 races. Three of those were wins and six were seconds for the best overall record of the season. It turned out that the toughest competition was not from GM, but from the Roush/Protofab Capris of Pickett and Ribbs, whose Motorcraft sponsored cars won eight races—four by each driver—but couldn't match Gloy's reliability. Altogether, the Fords overwhelmed Trans-Am racing with 11 victories. The main difference between the Gloy and Roush/Protofab cars—they were all built by Roush/Protofab—was Gloy's 305-inch engines by Jennings Racing of Santa Ana, California, that turned out 550 HP at 8200 rpm on a single 4-bbl and propelled the car to 11.8 second quarters at 125 mph and a top speed in excess of 180. The car weighed 2380 pounds, but carried enough ballast to make the required 2600-pound minimum. The ballast could be placed so the "ideal" 50/50 front-to-rear weight distribution could be achieved.

Ford Motor Co. recognized the marketing advantages of road racing over other motorsports, and funneled a lot more contingency money into the Trans-Am series for 1985: 1st got $30,000, 2nd $20,000 and 3rd $10,000. Ford was serious about road racing.

The Roush/Protofab Mustang entered IMSA GTO racing by winning the 1984 season finale. The next year, Roush/

Roush Racing Merkurs replaced Capris in '86 Trans-Am racing after Capris had won 24 of 32 races run in '84 and '85. Cars were so dominant that they led 1217 of 1492 Trans-Am miles raced, and led 538 of 662 total laps. Merkurs' turbocharged 2.3 liter inline-4 produced 530 HP at 7600 rpm as first raced. A 5-speed manual transmission gave the 2350-lb car a top of 190 mph, more than enough to beat Chevy V8s that ended up with little more than a third the total points earned by Capris. Lincoln-Mercury won again in '86. Courtesy Ford Motor Co.

Protofab cars were overwhelming, winning the Trans-Am series with 13 wins in 16 races and posted a 1-2-5 final standing with drivers Wally Dallenbach, Jr., Ribbs and Chris Kneifel in Mercury Capris. Roush/Protofab Mustangs driven by Dallenbach and Canadian John Jones took the IMSA GTO title with a season finish of 1-3-5 in the points standings: Jones (7 wins), Dallenbach (5 wins) and Lyn St. James (3 wins). Second overall for the season was Thunderbird (surprised?) with driver Darin Brassfield getting five wins and 115 points to Jones' whopping 216 points.

Fords won all but three of the 26 IMSA races in '85. Roush/Protofab cars won 17. In those two seasons, Roush/Protofab prepared cars won 32 of 49 races entered, an astounding record that dumped GM as planned—Corvettes, Camaros and Firebirds included. Jones, just 19 years old at the time, was the youngest driver to ever win a major American racing series. Ford (Mustang) won the IMSA Manufacturers' Championship, and Lincoln-Mercury Division Capris locked up the Trans-Am Championship.

Ford Division entries in 1985 captured the GTO Manufacturers' Championship after only 12 of the 17 scheduled races. Ten wins in the first 12 races, along with track records in four of those, made Ford racing overpowering. In addition to winning short, fast races, Jones and Dallenbach combined to win GTO in both of America's top long-distance endurance races: the 24-Hours of Daytona and 12-Hours of Sebring. Not only were the Roush/Protofab Capris and Mustangs fast, they were durable.

1985 Rookie of the Year, Chris Kneifel, was first official Merkur driver, but Pete Halsmer was first to race car in its shakedown debut at Riverside in May, '86. Halsmer qualified 6th and finished 2nd for a Mercury 1-2-3 sweep: 1st, Scott Pruett—Capri; 2nd, Halsmer—Merkur; 3rd, Kneifel—Capri. Pruett, in his first Trans-Am race, set fastest race lap of 109.079 mph. Courtesy Ford Motor Co.

1986 was a tougher year. A major reason for this was the defection of Protofab—the vehicle-build side of Roush/Protofab—to head up Chevrolet's Trans-Am effort, taking Wally Dallenbach and Jim Miller along in the deal. They also added Greg Pickett to drive in selected races. Regardless, 1986 was still a very good year. It was tougher, though, as the Ford team of three Mustangs, driven by Scott Pruett, Bruce Jenner and Bill Elliott, went into the season finale at Daytona six points down in the Manufacturers' Championship. Ford needed a win from the Roush team. Pruett and Elliott were headed for a 1-2 until Elliott's Coors Mustang retired with a broken rocker-arm stud on lap 49. Jenner's 7-Eleven Mustang moved up, and Pruett in the Motorcraft Mustang held off the field from flag-to-flag to win the race and Drivers' Championship. Jenner finished 3rd to nail down 2nd in the drivers' race, giving the Roush team drivers a 1-2 for the season.

Pruett's season included seven wins, nine pole positions and a new IMSA record of seven Norelco Drivers' Cups for outstanding driving. It was also the second consecutive GTO Drivers' title for Roush Racing. Pruett (196 points) and Jenner (175 points) shut out the nearest Camaro, Jack Baldwin's 3rd place with 159 points.

Add to that Pruett's Camel GT Endurance Championship victory. Five long-distance races during the year counted toward the title, and the driver earning the most points was named the endurance champion. Pruett finished 4th overall at Road America on August 25, and his GTO pole position and new track record in the Roush Motorcraft Mustang gave him a total of 203 points to lead Jenner's total of 201. Al Holbert, GTP Porsche hot shoe, finished 3rd with 190 points, beaten by two Mustangs!

"We did it!" said Pruett after Daytona. "We got the three championships we wanted all year." He led from flag-to-flag. "Bruce and I had said all year we wanted to bring home the Camel GT Endurance Championship, the GTO Drivers' Championship and the GTO Manufacturers' Championship. I don't think anyone outside our team thought it was possible, but we pulled it off, and that is a credit to our Roush Racing team, our sponsors and Ford.

"It was like living on nails the last few weeks. There was a lot of tension because the drivers' championship wasn't settled and we were trailing in the manufacturers' points.

"I know Bruce and the crew felt a lot of pressure, too, and we all knew we needed to put together one great team performance at Daytona. Well, we got it and it makes the season all that much more special."

Jenner related that, "We've been a close team all year—really, a family of sorts—and I don't think any of us will forget the good times and the difficult times we all went through to get where we were at the end. I'm just happy to have been a part of this and to have helped us win the three championships."

Both Pruett and Jenner gave a lot of credit to team owner Jack Roush and GTO team manager Alan Ladyman.

"Jack, Alan and the crew made my job easier because I knew my car would be competitive," continued Pruett. "Championships are won on strong, consistent performances. And my Mustang was not only strong, it was consistent over the long haul."

Jenner confirmed the reliability of the Roush Mustangs, saying, "My 7-Eleven Mustang ran all 17 races this year and probably has as many miles as any car in IMSA. That says a lot for the Mustang, but also a lot for the crew who prepared it every week."

Jenner's first full season of auto racing netted two wins, 14 top-six finishes in 17 races and one Norelco Drivers' Cup for outstanding driving.

Roush Team SCCA Trans-Am drivers Chris Kneifel and Pete Halsmer in Merkurs, trailed arch-rival Camaro driver Wally Dallenbach Jr. late in the season. With only two races to go, four points separated Lincoln-Mercury and Chevrolet in the makes race. Unfortunately, Halsmer had to sit out the next to last race, and Dallenbach lengthened his point lead to take the Trans-Am Championship, a narrow win for the 5-liter, Protofab Camaro with its V8 engine over the turbocharged 2.5-liter, 4-cylinder Roush Merkur, soon to be known as the *giant killer*.

It all began at the SCCA Bendix Trans-Am season opener at California's Riverside International Raceway on May 18. The Merkurs had not even turned a wheel on a race track two weeks before the race, and Merkur team manager Lee White observed that the team was "faced with the situation of having to hit a home run first time up!"

The 2.5-liter, 4-cylinder turboed engine looked good on the dyno. And, when one was tested to its limits, the 4-banger proved to be quite durable. "The engine so far has been bullet-proof," said White.

Pete Halsmer ran Riverside at a conservative boost pressure, and qualified sixth, then drove an excellent race to finish 2nd—perhaps not a home run, but at least a stand-up triple. It might have been a grand slam were it not for Scott Pruett's cross-country hop after finishing 3rd at Charlotte in a Mustang the day before, then to jump into a Roush Capri in his first-ever Trans-Am race at Riverside. He was gridded 31st, then charged through the field to lead a Mercury 1-2-3 sweep with the Merkurs of Halsmer and Kneifel. That is Ford Power!

White commented about the Merkur after Riverside: "It showed good power and ran without a hitch." Later on, he noted, "I guess you might say the engine has been almost too durable. It has proven to be a very solid foundation. We're encouraged that it's durable, now we have to get on the dyno and explore closer to the limits of rpm and turbo-boost level.

"We've been holding the rpm down; consequently, in the turns—especially at Sears Point—we were doing a lot of part throttle where we were down in the range where we had no boost response, and it hurt our times drastically. Higher revs and more boost should also make the car easier to drive. Another thing we've found is we haven't even begun to use the brakes on the Merkur, and that will certainly be a plus."

The Merkurs crank out 530 HP at 7600 rpm and, with an overall weight of just 2350 pounds, they are capable of 190 mph. At the Motor City 100 in Detroit, a street race consisting mostly of 10 short drag races where drivers blast down a straight, stand on the brakes, rotate and blast off again, the Merkur's exceptional brakes proved to be a great advantage. The point was proven by Pete Halsmer who started 22nd

Roush Racing Mustangs for '87 were forces to be reckoned with in IMSA GTO racing. These powerful Fords set the pace for several years that other makes could not match. Squire Gabbard photo.

and finished 2nd in front of the corporate Chevrolet crowd who saw the Mercury blast their best. And the Merkur pole winner Klaus Ludwig did so with a time of 2:05 minutes over the 2.5-mile course to average 74.058 mph.

Against the quick response of V8 engines, Halsmer says turbo-4 drivers have to modify their style. "The difference

In pits at Sebring '87, Tom Gloy and Bruce Jenner observe preparations for another long-distance race. Squire Gabbard photo.

Revival of 351C as a pure racing engine available through Ford's SVO organization is at home in Roush Racing Mustang. Its 358 cubic inches drawing through a single 4-bbl and SVO intake produce over 600 HP. Squire Gabbard photo.

Scott Pruett, Ford's top IMSA GTO driver, fires up his Roush Mustang. Interior has nothing but barest essentials. Squire Gabbard photo.

with a turbocharger is that once you are on the gas and starting to accelerate through a turn, you can't back out much. You can come off a little, but if the turbocharger slows down, once you get back on it again, it will take a moment or two before it starts to make horsepower. You have to commit to a straighter line because you don't want to ever have to lift off the gas."

Chris Kneifel wheeled his Motorcraft MAC Tools Merkur XR4Ti through the wet to his first victory in the Trans-Am at Road Atlanta on Oct. 12. That closed the manufacturers' points race four points: 69 to 73 points behind arch-rival Chevrolet.

"Winning your first race is always sweet," he said afterwards, "and this is especially sweet. I've been after my first Trans-Am win for almost two years now. I'm glad to contribute to Lincoln-Mercury-Merkur's manufacturers' points, and I think we're going to be there at the end."

The Roush Mercury Trans-Am cars closed out the '86 season with another championship, third in a row, and opened the '87 season with a blast—a blast that blew GM out of the water. Losing consistently to Ford turbocharged 4-bangers against the ancient, and supposedly mighty, Chevy small-block V8s was too much. So much so that GM retired from factory participation in the Trans-Am series.

Putting the needle to arch-rival Chevrolet was a sweet victory for Ford fans to savor, but without the Detroit bowtie boys to play with, who will be Ford's competition? Perhaps some of the new and highly competitive Japanese machines will continue to make the series exciting, but without factory Chevrolets, it just isn't the same. The Trans-Am has produced some of the most exciting racing seen on America's race tracks, both in the '60s and '80s, but when the factory

teams pulled out in '70, except for American Motors, popularity in the series went away. Are we seeing the beginning of the same thing in the '80s?

Perhaps, but there are interesting things happening! In the first round of the '87 series, who but Scott Pruett driving a Roush Merkur was leading the Bendix Trans-Am points race after the first round of 14 races. Second in points was Tom Kendall's Capri. In third position was Jenner in a—what? Porsche! Oh well, driving and winning in Fords has produced a lot of talent over the years.

Ex-Trans-Am wizard Tom Gloy made the switch to IMSA GTO and, along with teammates St. James, Jenner, Bobby Akin, Jr., Pruett and Halsmer, the Roush Mustangs opened the '87 season against a new foe. Dan Gurney's All American Racers Toyota Celica turbos came off the '86 development year with two victories and several top three finishes to launch into the '87 season aimed squarely at putting the reigning GTO champ Mustangs aside at season's end. Drivers Willy T. Ribbs and Chris Cord did indeed provide the stiffest competition Roush Racing had seen in years. After six of 18 races, Cord's victories had built up a sizable point margin on second place Gloy, 99 to 72. Jack Baldwin's Camaro was running a close third at 64 points. Thus, the "traditional" American V8s were being put to the test and, like the Trans-Am, it is from another turbo 4-cylinder.

Over the years, the V8 has been declared dead from time to time, only to rise with more spirit than ever before. However, in both forms of road racing, Trans-Am and IMSA GTO, the dominance of the V8 is wanning as the new high-tech turbocharged 4-bangers in smaller cars that are both lighter and more aerodynamic than Americas V8 powered cars emerged as the combination to beat.

"Awesome Bill from Dawsonille," Georgia, in most famous Thunderbird of all time. Car went so fast to so many wins that GM had to "trick" up the Monte Carlo to make it competitive.

THUNDERING 'BIRDS

In October, 1982, Ford Motor Co. made a bold move by introducing an up-dated 351 Cleveland engine through Special Vehicle Operations. The block was a cross between the 351W and 351C. With that engine, Ford was back into stock-car racing, and thundering Thunderbirds began to take to the high banks. It was a beginning and Ford was yet to show its stuff.

Stock-car racing soon took on a new look—the shape of the smooth Thunderbird—and the number-9 Coors-Melling 'Bird of Bill Elliott became a favorite. He became the winningest car and driver team in NASCAR history.

Ford was back, and many parallels can be drawn from the early '60s when Ford was NASCAR's underdog, yet emerged as the make to beat. It was done with an aerodynamic fastback top and 427-cid engine back then—say, 1965—when Ford took 48 Grand National wins. When introduced in '83, the Thunderbird was the most aerodynamic production car of its type built in America. And being slippery at high speeds gave the 'Birds an edge that produced Ford wins just like 20 years before.

High banks, high speeds and incredibly close finishes are the norm for stock-car racing, and the slightest advantage is often what makes a winner. All that is what gives the sport its huge excitement, its spectator appeal and its millions of television viewers. In this sport of swarming stockers roaring around thunderdomes, it is common to have several cars within seconds of each other, even after running 500 miles. That's just how competitive stock-car racing is.

The reason is, no doubt, that NASCAR entered the '80s as the richest and most competitive motorsport in history and grew from there. Ten years of association with the R.J.Reynolds Tobacco Co., which sponsored a healthy portion of the sport with the Winston Cup points ladder, had built the NASCAR season purse to $6.1 million divided among 31 races in 1980. Over 1.5 million spectators made the NASCAR Winston Cup series the most popular form of motorsport in America, and fans saw the top money winner take home $588,926.

Winnings for '81 reached $7.1 million, and attendance topped 1.6 million fans. Clearly, Ford was losing a lot of free advertising from nationwide TV coverage of stock-car racing, and the combination of the 351-cid engine, SVO and the aerodynamic Thunderbird seemed like a good match. First came the desire to win, then came the engines, cars and drivers to do it.

NASCAR and Winston officials continued to expand stock-car racing. In 1984, all point funds were sizably increased with the added incentive that R.J.Reynolds offered $1,000,000 to the driver who won three of the big four: Daytona 500, Winston 500, World 600 and Southern 500.

1985, will forever be remembered as the year of Bill Elliott and his Thunderbird. He won three of the big four—Daytona 500, Winston 500 and Southern 500—to collect the first "Winston Million."

After setting a record of 11 superspeedway wins and tying the record of four in a row, Elliott's driving at Talladega set an international 500-mile closed-course race speed record of

Ricky Rudd's Bud Moore Engineering Motorcraft Thunderbird on the starting grid at Charlotte. Rudd finished 5th in 1986 Winston Cup standings, 6th in '85.

Bill's million-dollar ride, the winningest Ford in the history of racing, has consistently set fastest closed-course racing-speed record at Talladega since Coors-Melling Thunderbird came on the scene— 212.229 mph in 1986, '87 car raised record to 212.809 mph.

186.288 mph. His four straight superspeedway wins tied Bobby Allison, who did it twice in 1971, and Richard Petty and David Pearson, who set their records between 1971 and '73.

"Awesome Bill" holds the record for the most consecutive poles won—seven—to surpass the legendary Glenn "Fireball" Roberts, whose mark of five was set in 1960—61. Because "Fireball's" record stood for a quarter-century, it is unlikely that Elliott's record will be broken, ever!

The new Thunderbirds set the pace that year. Elliott turned better than 209 mph at Talladega to become the fastest stocker in history. Then, early in '86, he won the pole position at Daytona with a 205.039 and followed that in May with a sensational Talladega track record and pole position of 212.229 mph! That was his 4th consecutive pole win at the 2.66-mile Alabama speedway. And he did it again for the 1987 running of the Winston 500 with another record, 212.809 mph.

What Elliott and all other stockers were after was a piece of the $12.5-million Winston pie, and "Awesome Bill from Dawsonville" carved out the biggest piece to bring his total winnings in 1985 to $2,433,187.

There was a beginning, though, and it wasn't stuffed with dollars. Born in 1955, Elliott began racing at 20. At Charlotte in February, 1976, he started 34th and finished 33rd to take home $640. 117 races later, he became the 17th driver in NASCAR history to earn a career total of $1 million.

Just 38 races after that, he became the 12th driver to earn $2 million. Then, after winning the Southern 500 at Darlington in September 1985 just 11 races later, he became the 5th driver to earn $3 million. It took only eight more races to become the 5th driver to earn $4 million—that happened at Riverside in November when he finished 31st!

The season points race was decided going into the final round at Riverside. Elliott's Coors/Melling Thunderbird was in a two-car race against Junior Johnson's Chevrolet with Darrell Waltrip at the wheel.

"All the things we've done this year merely have put us in the position where now we have a one-race season," commented Elliott. "It doesn't matter about all the wins, the Winston Million, the records… Now it's down to one. Whoever has the best day and the best luck on the winding road course is going to be the champion. We'll make every effort—try as hard as we can. It boils down to a run in the California desert for both of us."

Ernie Elliott, Bill's older brother and team crew chief, wasn't concerned about the championship. Riverside was just another race he wanted to win. "I really don't care if we win this points race or not," he said. "This has been a remarkable year for us already. I said before the season started that I expected us to win seven races, and we've done better than that. If Darrell wins, I'll be the first to congratulate him."

Younger brother Dan Elliott disagreed. "We need this

NASCAR Fords at their best: Bill Elliott and Cale Yarborough at speed.

SVO 351 enlarged to 358 cid produces about 625 HP, enough to send 3,700-lb Elliott prepared Coors-Melling 'Bird to hours of over 200 mph on the highbanks.

Bill Elliott's office.

one, it's as simple as that. Ernie says he doesn't care about the points championship, but I do. To do all we've done this year and then fall short would leave me with a bad feeling. But whatever happens at Riverside, we've learned an awful lot this year. We've learned how high the highs can be and how low the lows can be. We've learned how to relax and be ourselves."

The final showdown for '85 took place over Riverside's nine turns and long back straight where stockers reached 170 mph before braking for turn 9. Average lap speeds during the race reach in the neighborhood of 110 mph, and drivers shift gears about 10 times per lap.

"The Esses are important," Bill explained, "because that's where you can gain or lose a lot of speed, and exit has to be precise because it sets you up for the uphill turn six. It's a blind, cresting turn you enter and commit to before you can see what's waiting for you on the other side.

"Turn 9 is the last turn on the track, and it's critical to lap

Cale Yarborough and Hardee's Thunderbird.

speeds because it's the longest turn on the track. The car has to handle in this turn or all your efforts all the rest of the way around the track are wasted. It's banked a little, but you have to be perfect there if you're going to keep the good lap time you've worked for the rest of the way around."

Best laid plans sometimes run afoul for the smallest of failures, and the Elliott team lost a chance at the championship and $250,000 in the NASCAR Winner's Circle program because of an $8 transmission pin. The piece broke in the first 20 laps of the 119-lap feature. And although the team frantically tried repairs, it ended the season with Elliott in 31st spot trailing Waltrip 4191 points to 4292.

For Ford fans, though, the race was a tight one as Ricky Rudd wheeled his Bud Moore Motorcraft Thunderbird to his first victory of the season, worth $37,875. Rudd outran Terry Labonte to the finish line by two car lengths in a sensational finish that had the record crowd of over 50,000 on its feet.

"We took it easy on the car early in the race, trying to make sure it would last," said Rudd, who moved into the lead for good on the 96th lap.

"The decision to go with new tires on the last pit stop was the key to the win. Bud and the crew did a great job today. That last pit stop was only 11.72 seconds for tires and fuel, and we got out just ahead of Labonte."

When Bill Elliott was a $640 winner, nobody saw his name in print or even cared that a north Georgia boy was starting out in the big leagues. But the wins of '85 changed things, what with the record books stuffed with his name, and Ford

Motor Co. back on top of stock-car racing. Although racing out front for only three years, Elliott rose to rank 5th in the Winston Cup Series all-time standings, and his red and white Thunderbird is now among the most recognized cars in America. Bill Elliott is a new American hero among fans and has twice been voted NASCAR's Most Popular Driver—for 1984 and '85.

He's a top driver with a car that reflects his team's efforts. He couldn't win without a good crew. Harry Melling owns the team and has been in racing for 30 years. Bill's father, George, oversees the total operation; brother Ernie is crew chief. Along with engine man, brother Dan, the Coors-Melling Thunderbird is a family team with racing roots dating back to the mid '70s.

Compared to the Pettys, the Wood brothers, Bud Moore and Junior Johnson, the Elliotts are relative new-comers to the sport. But what they brought to the speedway has eclipsed all the old guard who must hustle with factory optional aero-tricks to get in the running with Bill's Thunderbird. GM offered a special series of "fastback" Chevys and Pontiacs just to get back in the race with Ford's Thunderbird.

The T-Bird caused Cale Yarborough (Hardee's), Ricky Rudd (Motorcraft) and Kyle Petty (7-Eleven) to switch. In addition to these drivers, several other Thunderbird teams are running the NASCAR circuit, and Ford is definitely back.

What it takes today is a lot different than the stockers of 20 years ago. Back then, the cars were gutted and reinforced production cars with little more than hot engines and sus-

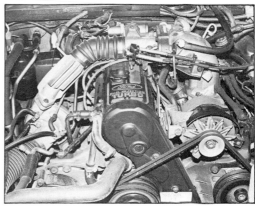

1985 Turbo 2.3-liter OHC 4-banger produced 170 HP—1.2 HP per cubic inch.

T-Bird Turbo Coupe, one of Ford's new generation 4-bangers, offered buyers high-tech performance in a very stylish and aerodynamic package when introduced in 1983; '85 model is shown. An innovative car in the beginning, 'Bird is once again the leader in its field, and destined to be another classic.

pensions modified for banked left-handers. The cars ran as-manufactured steel bodies with basic engines and transmissions available through dealers as production models.

Today, the cars race on the same tracks, but are very different than showroom models. And none of their equipment is available in production cars. The typical modern NASCAR stocker is a tube-frame racer covered with steel exterior body panels designed and built specifically for stock-car racing. Although the overall body shape must maintain production lines, little else resembles a production car.

Bill Elliott's '83 T-Bird was such a car. Its wheelbase measured 110 inches, and it tipped the scales at 3700 pounds. Unlike most other T-Bird teams, he stuck with the old-style 351C block, rather than experimenting with the new SVO 351 block. It was increased to 358 cubic inches, then received SVO heads and intake, and a single Holley 4-bbl carb. Tweaking brought the engine to around 625 HP at 7900 rpm. This made the number-9 'Bird the fastest stock car for 1985, '86 and '87. Bills Thundering 'Birds proved to be the fastest stockers in history.

And, once again, they were Fords.

The rivalry between Ford and Chevrolet exploded into a personal rivalry in '87, as one-time friends Elliott and Dale Earnhardt clashed, literally, both at high speed—and with words. Earnhardt's NASCAR season opened with a succession of wins that set the stage for another championship year, but this time the bashing, blocking and bullying tactics launched him into infamy among fellow drivers and fans who gifted him with more thumbs-down boos than any driver of modern times.

In fairness, though, today's turn toward bitter rivalries between drivers is fueled by the huge sums of prize money.

Comfort, class, style and performance: the mark of Thunderbird Turbo Coupe.

Earnhardt didn't change his style of driving; he just moved into the front where TV camera viewers could see him in action. He became the "bad boy" of NASCAR for doing so. Dale joins a succession of drivers of the past who used similar tactics, Curtis Turner for one. But in those days, bashing and bouncing cars into the wall was an exciting part of the sport. Today's level of sophisticated professional driving and high speeds has supposedly left that behind.

Ford's Turbo 2.3-liter with intercooler was rated at 190 HP at 4600 rpm for '87.

1987 Turbo Coupe 'Bird is a true performance car in the most modern ways: turbocharged/intercooled 4-banger, computer-controlled shock-absorber valving and slick aerodynamics.

However, over the years, rivalries have been the "spice" that fired the interest of fans and contributed to making NAS-CAR racing the most-watched sport in history. Stirring up a little trouble gets a lot of coverage.

Fortunately, no drivers or fans have been injured so far, but sudden changes of course at today's speeds are considerably more serious than they were 25 years ago. For instance, the aerodynamics of modern stockers is such that they can be "launched," literally airborn, at around 190 mph if air gets under the car. Testimony of that effect was shown when Bobby Allison's Buick, averaging 208 mph, ran over something, lost the air in the right rear tire, then got sideways, lifted off and soared toward the packed grandstand near the start/finish line during the '87 Talladega 500. A new safety fence with two 2-inch-diameter steel cables added for more strength prevented what could have been the worst carnage in auto-racing history. In an instant, the course of stock-car racing, and racing in general, would have changed.

Elliott led off the season with a convincing win in the Busch Clash at Daytona, then followed up with a record pace in the Daytona 511, a blistering new record of 210.364 mph around the legendary 2.5-mile tri-oval where over 37 drivers qualified at over 200 mph. One big surprise of the day was rookie Davey Allison, the second fastest qualifier in the Havoline Thunderbird, followed by Ken Schrader in the Red Baron Pizza Thunderbird.

Later, in the Coca Cola World 600 at Charlotte, GM used the event to spotlight its Oldsmobiles, but the race was an all-Thunderbird show. Elliott led off with an astounding pace, but left the race near the 3/4 mark only to be replaced by Davey Allison's Havoline Star 'Bird. At that point, both Elliott and Allison were contesting the Winston Million, but with Elliott sidelined, Allison looked to be heading for his second win of the big four, Daytona, Talladega, Charlotte

and Darlington. He didn't make it though, and the million had to wait, but another 'Bird moved up, Kyle Petty's Citgo 7-Eleven sponsored Thunderbird. Kyle and father, "King" Richard in a Pontiac, toured the final laps around the Charlotte Motor Speedway in tandem. When Kyle won, it had been a Ford showcase, another dominating victory, just like Daytona and Talladega.

4-BANGERS...AGAIN

Ford Motor Co. built millions of cars with 4-cylinder engines in the early days of the company. And like racers of those days, all sorts of aftermarket equipment are being offered today to hotrod the modern-day descendants of those engines. Interest in in-line 4-cylinder engines has revived the Pinto 2.3-liter engine, just to name one of Ford's modern 4-cylinders, from its original intentions as an economy engine to one powering production SVO Mustangs and Turbo Coupe Thunderbirds. Although the SVO Mustang was short-lived, the 2.3 has come a long way to become the heart of the Turbo Coupe 'Bird, Ford's high-style four-place highway handler in the tradition of the BOSS 302 Mustang of 1969 and '70. The engine also has a lot of designed-in potential as a pure racer, street sleeper or quick drag racer.

Success with the 4-banger has no doubt been highlighted by the mid-engine IMSA GTP—under 2.5-liter—Ford Probe. The Probe was an out-growth of the earlier Mustang GTP that incorporated the latest technology throughout.

The major change from the earlier car was the location of the engine—behind the driver instead of in front—and that required an all-new overall shape because of the cockpit being moved forward. The state-of-the-art monocoque chassis consisted of carbon-fiber composites and aluminum honeycomb forming a very rigid structure. The carbon fiber/Nomex composite body was secured to the chassis. When a

Davey Allison and Bill Elliott pace start of '87 Daytona 500 in their 'Birds. It was another classic Elliott win seen by millions of TV race fans. Later, Allison took a sensational victory at Talladega with a final pace no one could match. Kyle Petty followed up with an equally strong win at Charlotte. Courtesy NASCAR.

The beginning, front-engine Mustang GTP of 1985 was SVO Ford's entry into the toughest road-racing series in existence: IMSA GTP. Weighing in at 1770 pounds with composite structure by Ford Aerospace and powered by Zakspeed 600+ HP DOHC, fuel-injected turbo-4, car was capable of 210 mph. Ultimate Fords such as GT-40 of old were once powered by production-based V8s. New ultimate Fords were intended to be powered by 4-bangers such as this. But, as of 1987, Ford prototypes are back to using V8s. Courtesy Ford Motor Co.

210 mph from this? You bet, and only 129 cubic inches! Electronic engine controls manage ignition and multi-port fuel injection. With turbo blowing through intercooler, double overhead cams, and SVO-Ford high-tech, engine produces 650 HP at 8800 rpm, 351 lb-ft of torque at 8800 rpm.

Zakspeed USA, SVO and Ford Motor Co. combined to produce Mustang Probe shown here at the Miami GP of February, 1986. Two cars were entered. Klaus Ludwig and Tom Gloy were running strong in this car until debris from track stuck throttle open. A pit stop later, car was out of contention, but finished 5th overall anyway. Courtesy Ford Motor Co.

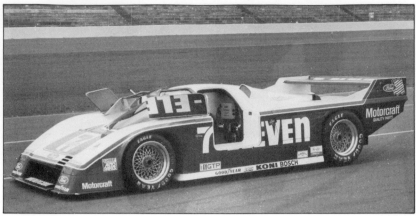

On starting grid at Charlotte for the IMSA Camel GT, Mustang Probe looks the part of a space-age vehicle. Klaus Ludwig scored Probe's first victory at Riverside in Stroh's 300-kilometer Camel Grand Prix. He took the pole with a record 120.652-mph lap, then led entire 98-lap race to win by almost 37 seconds over a V12 Jaguar. It was the Probe's 13th race, almost a year after car made its debut at Leguna Seca.

three-car crash at around 170 mph caught Lyn St. James in a pinch in turn 1 at Riverside in early 1986, the structure of the Probe proved to be so durable that Lyn crawled out of the cockpit shaken, but unhurt. The driver's capsule was designed by Ford Aerospace and proved that the Ford engineered design could take the punishment of her heavily damaged Ford.

The all-aluminum, twin-cam in-line 4 developed 650 HP and 351 lb-ft of torque at 8,800 rpm in a four valves-per-cylinder configuration. The turboed 2.1-liter (129 cid) engine derived from the 2.3-liter Pinto block produced 309.5 HP per liter in the Probe.

Compared to the '67 LeMans winning Mk IV Ford—427 cid and 500 HP—of just 71.4 HP per liter, that should illustrate the advances Ford has made with engine technology in the years since the iron-block 427. The Mk IV's top speed of around 215 mph on the Mulsanne Straight at LeMans would likely be exceeded by the Probe. Wind-tunnel tests show that the Probe is capable of 230 mph.

While the Mk IV was a heavy but durable racing car at 2650 pounds, the Probe came in at only 1980 pounds. But the car didn't prove to be the master of durability the Mk IV was. However, in its initial races, the Probe finished in the top five each time. With Klaus Ludwig and Doc Bundy driving, the team started 3rd and finished 2nd at the IMSA Camel Continental GTP race at Watkins Glen. They finished on the same lap as the winner after running a conservative race in the beginning, then matched the winner's lap times later in the race.

The 2.3-liter 4 has proven to be a Trans-Am threat in the Jack Roush built MAC Tools-Motorcraft Mercury Merkur XR4Tis. Running SVO blocks of just 2.5 liters, these electronic fuel injection, turbocharged/intercooled pure racers devel-

op 530 HP at 7,600 rpm and 420 lb-ft of torque at 6,000. Weighing in at 2350 pounds, these giant killers have shown themselves to be both quicker and faster against 5-liter V8-powered cars. Capable of around 190 mph, the Roush Merkurs are building another chapter in the legacy of fast Fords.

On the drag strips, one-time Ford Motor Co. 2.3-liter engine engineer Tom Reider has built up a 2.3-liter-powered, fully equipped, 3100-pound '83 Thunderbird for bracket racing that puts down consistent 12.21-second quarter-miles at 112 mph. Few over-400-cid muscle cars of the '60s were capable of those figures. And Reider thinks 11-second runs are within the capability of the 2.3-liter engine. He established Reider Racing to further the cause of proving the engine can produce such performances. The engine is capable of 200 HP in street tune with the right equipment that is supplied from several sources. Reider's know-how is proven by his two NHRA Stock Eliminator championships in 2.3-liter Pintos: 1976 Gatornationals, 15.63 seconds at 83.87 mph, and '76 U.S. Nationals, 15.62 at 84.26. His more recent Thunderbird runs would put down almost all stock musclecars of the '60s.

SVO, along with suppliers of Ford performance equipment, provides extensive technical assistance and parts for Ford racers, not limited to just the 2.3-liter engine, but all Ford engines. And *Hot Rod magazine* has published extensive annual Ford performance information and sources along with up-dated SVO catalogs for several years. See their *Ford High Performance* annuals for a wealth of information.

Ford's new corporate motto, "Racing into the Future," is more than a motto. Like "Total Performance" of the '60s, it is a serious commitment to be the best. To prove it, Ford unveiled plans to market the new Mustang Probe as a factory-built racing car for IMSA Camel GT events. The new

Debut of SVO's GTP car, 2.1-liter twin-turbocharged DOHC Ford DFP V8, was September 21, '86 at Watkins Glen for an IMSA 500-km race with Scott Pruett driving. Gear linkage broke in early stages, resulting in a DNF. Like V8 GT-40, car is capable of winning 24-Hours of LeMans. Courtesy Ford Motor Co.

GTP racer was designed with a modular chassis for quick and easy repairs in the event that a section should need to be replaced.

If you missed your chance at a GT-40 in the '60s, now you have a shot at Ford's most modern racing machine. SVO's prototype racer is designed specifically for sale to private teams.

And like the GT-40 of old, the new Mustang Probe is V8 powered. After several years of developing the most sophisticated turbocharged 4s seen in modern racing cars, the move to a V8 is a step up in Ford's move to beat Porsche. Ford Motor Co. made its move against Ferrari, the dominant marque of the early '60s and beat the Italian cars at their best game. Whether or not Ford can oust Porsche has yet to be proven, but the future looks exciting to say the least.

Klaus Ludwig, German national racing champion in 1979 and '81, joined Ford at the beginning of the Probe program; 1986 was his sixth year with Ford. He is a three-time winner of the 24-Hours of LeMans, the world's most acclaimed race. In the Probe's first season in 1985, he drove to four top-five finishes in the final six races in the IMSA series. He also raced in GTO and compared the cars saying, "I really love driving the GTP cars and I love driving the Probe. With the Probe, we have the best handling car in the world right now. It's also the safest. We are in good shape for power; the only advantage the GTP Porsche has is torque—the bigger engine. In GTO, we have enough torque because it's a larger engine and tremendously powerful all through the rev range. It's nice to drive, but compared to GTP cars, everything seems in slow motion—braking, cornering speed. . . . GTO cars compare well coming out of turns because the engines have tremendous torque and power."

The new Mustang Probe doesn't look much different, but what makes it go is an outgrowth of the most successful Formula-1 and Indy 500 engine ever built. The 3.0-liter Cosworth-Ford V8, the *DFV*—meaning *Double Four Valves*—won 155 races over an illustrious Formula-1 racing career spanning 17 years. And its derivative, the 2.6-liter *DFX,* has powered every Indy 500 winner since 1978.

The '86 Mustang Probe is powered by a de-stroked version of the DFX to become the *DFP.* The DFP displaces 2.1 liters (128 cubic inches), and twin turbos have replaced the single turbo of the DFX. Instead of alcohol, the DFP is set up to run on gasoline. At the start of the '86 season, it looked to be a healthy challenger of Porsche's supremacy in world-class endurance racing, but that threat, once again, did not mature.

However, this just might be the car to win another 24-Hours of LeMans for Ford, another World Manufacturers' Championship, another dominating Ford—the only American make that has been there. But it might not be a Ford Motor Co. factory team like the 1967 Mk IV win. The reason? SVO is now offering customer cars.

"We've planned all along to do a customer version of the Probe, for sale to independent teams," says Kranefuss, SVO chief. "And the DFX derivative is something we've been thinking about for some time. The reason we chose to adapt the DFX was that, to a large extent, it's already thoroughly engineered, and it's well proven and accepted by the racing community as a viable endurance package."

Continuing interest in the car from teams competing in the IMSA Camel GTP series led to SVO embarking on "Phase 2" of the Mustang Probe GTP project: the customer car. Zakspeed USA in Livonia, Michigan, adapted the new DFP engine to the Probe's transaxle and cooling system. First tests looked good, but the proof is yet to be seen.

And Ford is back into Formula-1 racing with a new engine, a 91-cid turbo V6 producing 750 HP. Ford is taking on the world, and with the new corporate commitment, "Racing into the Future" is becoming another set of glory years of Ford racing.

"Formula-1 racing is highly competitive, and the most technologically advanced racing series in the world," says Kranefuss. "Ford involvement makes perfect sense because F-1 demands the best in efficiency and power from small-displacement engines—the same demands being faced by Ford and all automakers in the mass-production market.

"For this reason, the F-1 program makes sense from a marketing standpoint because it draws worldwide attention to Ford's leading position in the development of small, fuel-efficient, but high-performance engines.

"The reach is global, too. We took a survey of our Ford affiliates to get a consensus on the best form of motorsport for Ford to be involved with on an international level, and the answer was Formula-1—even from countries that probably will never have a Grand Prix race. On a worldwide basis, it's the most extensively publicized automotive sport."

Patrick Tambay and Alan Jones raced F-1 Fords in 1986. Tambay says, "It's a very young engine, but at this stage in its development, it is more advanced than any other new

Bob Glidden's crew in '86 kept his Thunderbird in the running for an ultra-strong season finish that netted 12,834 points to win the NHRA ProStock championship over Warren Johnson who finished 1842 points behind in his Oldsmobile. At mid-season '86, Glidden was 5th in ProStock points race, but in the final seven events of the season he drove to a spectacular finish: six wins and three national e.t. records. With the bigger IHRA engine, he posted the fastest ProStock speed of 193.13 mph—200 mph can't be far away for the Whiteland, Indiana, team.

engine I've ever been associated with."

Jones, the 1980 World Driving Champion, confirmed first impressions of the F-1 engine after real racing experiences in Europe by saying, "I could sum up my feelings by saying I could take it to LeMans with confidence."

QUARTER-MILE FORDS

At the end of the 1969 drag racing season, a group of drivers who had factory support banded together and petitioned the drag-racing sanctioning bodies for a class of their own. It just wasn't fair to race against the low-dollar guys who financed their own racing and rarely won against the factory cars. And, it wasn't fair for amateurs to have to compete against pros. The result was the formation of the ProStock class for heads-up racing like the sport had been before brackets were imposed. The professional drivers liked it, the crowds loved it and ProStock drag racing has been with us ever since.

It took about a year for the class to fully develop. By 1971, the fastest cars were usually the Hemi-powered Dodges and Plymouths. Low time that year was set by Don Carlton in the famous *Motown Missile* Dodge Challenger at 9.48 seconds and 146.10 mph. The '71 NHRA world champ was Ronnie Sox in his Sox and Martin Plymouth 'Cuda.

Things have changed!

Unlike the early '70s when Ford and Chevy gave very little support to drivers and drag racing was a MoPar playground, ProStock racing today has become America's favorite form of the sport. And Ford is back in a big way. And there's not a Chrysler product to be seen. The best Ronnie Sox has been able to do since then was 10th overall in NHRA points, over 6,500 points behind Bob Glidden's championship total in '79.

Glidden's family Thunderbird team, sponsored by Chief Auto Parts through '86 and Motorcraft in '87, finished 2,710 points ahead of runner-up Warren Johnson in 1985. 1986 looked to be another title year, but a new chassis caused some problems at first. The ProStock champ was barely able to qualify in the season-opening NHRA Winternationals at Pomona, then lost in the first round. He advanced to the finals of the NHRA Southern Nationals, then took a wild ride that all but destroyed his new T-Bird.

"We did seven somersaults, but the roll cage held together; the seat belts didn't show any stress and my helmet didn't have a mark on it," he says. "However, the engine was ruined and all the fiberglass and sheet metal on the car was torn up. Things couldn't have looked much worse in terms of defending our championship. It did shake me up, but the whole family simply made the commitment to do whatever it took to get ourselves back on top."

"On top" had a lot of people shaking their heads that it couldn't be done. For wife and crew chief, Etta, sons Billy and Rusty, and all the fans following Glidden's Thunderbird, what happened next is a tremendous success story. When another 'Bird was ready, Glidden came back to qualify 1st at eight NHRA events and won six of seven to pull out another championship! He set NHRA national elapsed-time records of 7.493 seconds at the Summernationals in Englishtown (July 13, 1986), then broke that record with a sensational 7.377-second pass at the U.S. Nationals at Indianapolis (August 31, 1986). Where does it go from there?

"I don't think there are any limits on how high speeds will go. ProStock racers are some of the most innovative people in all of motorsports. We've already gone 195 mph in 7.2 seconds in IHRA. Next year, I expect that we'll be running 200 in IHRA."

The difference between NHRA and IHRA ProStockers is that NHRA limits engine displacement to 500 cubic inches; IHRA cars are unlimited. Glidden's 660-cid—around 1170 HP—Jerry Haas built T-Bird electrified the crowd at the IHRA Gateway Nationals in St. Louis when he turned a fantastic 7.324 at 193.13 mph to set the fastest pass ever recorded in the class at the time. What the crowd got was a look at Ford total domination as the fastest ProStocker in the world rolled to the line for the finals against Roy Hill's Tempo—the man and car that had held the previous record. It was another win for Glidden, and another Ford 1-2 in national competition. Glidden ran *seven* consecutive passes under 7.40 seconds, and came up against eventual IHRA ProStock World Champion, Rickie Smith, in the semi-finals to put him away before facing Hill.

Bob Glidden raced Ford EXP in 1982 in one of his few off years of ProStock drag racing. Finishing 4th overall in NHRA season finals is not bad by any standard. Glidden won Springnationals round, 7.928/170.77 and was runner up in three other nationals. Courtesy Ford Motor Co.

Glidden went on to set e.t. records at the Mile High Nationals in Denver, Keystone Nationals in Reading, Pennsylvania, and the Winston World Finals at Pomona. Mr. "ProStock" was rolling.

Bob Glidden gets wheels up in his Motorcraft ProStock Thunderbird at IHRA Winter Nationals at Darlington. Glidden blasted quickest time and fastest run ever in ProStock—7.197 seconds at 199.11 mph—in a round preceding eliminations. . . . then came Rickie Smith. Squire Gabbard Photo.

Smith's Sonny Leonard built 665-cid engine cranked out over 1200 HP with carburetors and pump gas. Custom-built tube-frame ProStockers are in no way similar to production cars, but fans like the fierce competition between makes. Lightweight components, such as sheet-metal valve covers and intake manifold are custom-made items.

IHRA ProStock champ Rickie Smith and crew "push" the world's fastest Mustang— 192.30 mph at Bristol in May '86. Roy Hill's Budget Rent-A-Car Tempo set a sizzling low e.t. of 7.233 seconds at Darlington. During the season, Hill, Smith and Glidden were running the three fastest ProStockers, all Fords.

Over the years since his runner-up in the Supernationals of 1972, Glidden has built a tremendous win record. He leads all NHRA categories with national event wins, totaling 52 at the end of the '86 season. The nearest any other Pro-Stocker has gotten is Lee Shepard, more than a dozen wins down. Nobody seems to be getting any closer. Thus, Ford and Bob Glidden Racing are the premier team in NHRA ProStock racing.

Glidden's main objective has been NHRA racing while Rickie Smith has been Ford's main man in IHRA. Both 1983 and '84 were Thunderbird years for Smith, who finished as runner-up both seasons. He won four IHRA rounds in '83— the ProAm, World Nationals, Spring Nationals and U.S. Open—but just missed the season championship. The next year, Smith ended the season by matching Roy Hill's speed record of 189.07. Smith's T-Bird and Hill's Mercury Topaz were the fastest ProStockers in the world that season.

By then, Smith was a two-time IHRA World Champion: "We dominated IHRA Super Modified with 16 top wins in 18 major events in 1976, and I was named the Winston Sportsman Driver of the Year. Jack Roush and Wayne Gapp completely built the car, a Maverick running a 351 Cleveland engine. And we came back the next year to dominate again. Country music promoter Keith Fowler sponsored the car and the name on the side was 'Country Shindig.' We won the championship, along with the Driver of the Year award again. And because we had about run off all the competition, IHRA did away with the class!

"We wanted to do the same type of racing and moved up to ProStock with a Don Hardy built Mustang late in '78, then took off on the circuit in '79 and finished 10th in points our first year. In '80 and '81, we moved into 2nd place both years with a '79 model Mustang while everyone else was updating to newer cars. Toward the end of '81, the car blew a tire on the back and I wrecked it—just about a total loss. With my earnings and a loan from a bank along with backing from nightclub owner Wayne Wilson, I bought the engine and transmission out of the wreck and went back to Don Hardy and bought a new car, an '82 Mustang. The nightclub's name was SRO (Standing Room Only) and that's what we put on the car. We ended up winning the IHRA ProStock championship that year—as independents!"

Not only did he win, Smith became the first ProStocker to ever exceed 180 mph—181.08 in 7.82 seconds set at the IHRA World Nationals in Norwalk, Connecticut.

Ford introduced the new aero Thunderbird in 1983 and wanted Smith to campaign one that year. That was his first backing from Ford and it resulted in two more IHRA runner-up spots—'83 and '84. Smith also finished 7th in NHRA standings in '83—Glidden was 3rd that year—but being from the South (King, North Carolina), he concentrated on IHRA racing. His consistent high finishes showed great things, and 1985 was another good year with a 3rd overall in the point standings. Smith's Don Hardy built Motorcraft Thunderbird posted 0.10-second quicker times at the beginning of the season, and was very competitive.

"In '86, we went back to a Mustang because I thought a short wheelbase car would hook up better. Rules allowed a 2% increase in wheelbase so we stretched the wheelbase to 102.5 inches and left the engine in the stock location, which put it closer to the rear end housing. The Thunderbird wheelbase puts the engine 4 inches farther away, so that's

Rickie Smith's ProStock crew from King, North Carolina, performs pit chores during IHRA Spring Nationals at Bristol's Thunder Valley. Out of 11 IHRA races, Fords won seven. Smith was in finals of five of those, winning two. His consistency during the season earned 7706 points for his Mustang to beat Darrell Alderman's 6981 in a Camaro.

the reason for going to the Mustang: better weight transfer and to stay hooked up better down the track. It wasn't as aerodynamic, but we ended up winning the IHRA World Championship anyway and didn't finish worse than 4th all season!"

Like NIIRA ProStock drag racing, 1986 was definitely a Ford year on the IHRA ProStock circuit, as eight of 11 events on the calendar went to Fords. Five of those were all-Ford finals. Smith's *Boss Hoss* Mustang finished no worse than the semi-finals in every event, proving he was Ford's main man. The Don Hardy built car with its all-aluminum Sonny Leonard built 665-cid engine, derived from the BOSS 429, qualified as the second quickest ProStocker in the world with a 7.321-second pass at the season opener at Darlington.

Sonny's Automotive in Lynchburg, Virginia, does Smith's engines. The aluminum block evolved from the BOSS 429 introduced in 1969, but the heads are re-designed with full hemispherical combustion chambers. The block design came through Ford's Holman-Moody connection of that decade, and was thoroughly beefed up for modern drag racing applications by Alan Root. A 5-inch stroke and 4.600-inch bore gives a displacement of 665 cubic inches; over 700 is possible! The crank is steel from Crankshaft Specialists in Memphis. Bill Miller aluminum rods and Venolia 14.6:1 pistons combine to produce more than 1160 HP. Qualifying and national racing was done on another engine that showed over 1200 HP on the dyno.

The cast-aluminum heads were much improved over the old BOSS 429, with redesigned and more efficient runners.

Rickie Smith on his way to another win in '86. Tom Swabe Photo.

The canted valves were retained for full hemispherical combustion chambers.

Sonny's own fabricated sheet-metal tunnel-ram intake manifold saved weight, along with fabricated valve covers. Twin 1150-cfm Holley Dominators fed the engine. The carbs

Ford's BOSS 429 is back! SVO aluminum block can be increased to 670 cubic inches.

Canted valves of BOSS 429 allow a near hemispherical—crescent-shaped—combustion chamber. When new in 1969, it was not the dominating drag-racing engine that it became in the mid-80s.

were split, allowing one barrel per runner and a straighter shot to the combustion chamber.

A Hays clutch and—almost unbreakable according to Smith—Lenco 4-speed transmission delivered power to a 9-inch Ford rear end housing. Strange-Engineering supplied gears and axles are contained in that durable piece of Ford's golden days from the '60s, the 9-inch rear-axle housing. About everybody these days, Chevy guys included, uses them.

Smith's consistency during the entire '86 season is proof of his ideas. Five times he was in the final rounds of nationals competition; he won two of those. The season came together at the U.S. Open Nationals in Rockingham, where he faced off against Roy Hill's Budget Rent-A-Car Tempo in another sizzling all Ford final round. Smith won a close one: 7.430/187.89 to Hill's 7.455/188.67.

Those numbers showed the incredible competitiveness of ProStock racing. With that win, Smith had to only qualify in the top five at the IHRA Fall Nationals to win the championship. His qualifying time of 7.408 seconds was 3rd for Smith's fourth World Championship.

ProStock car bodies must retain stock appearance, but can use ultra-light body panels. Underneath, the chassis is constructed of tubular steel. You couldn't buy a ProStocker from

a dealer if you tried. But you can build one.

1986 IHRA rules said the cars must be 1980 or later and engines must be 1966 or later, like those installed in assembly-line American cars or trucks. There is no displacement limit, but big-block cars must run with a minimum of 2350 pounds; small-block cars must meet a 2100-pound minimum.

Of the top four cars in the Winston/IHRA final points standings, three were Fords. The spread between Smith's Motorcraft Mustang and 2nd-place Darrell Alderman's Camaro was a whopping 725 points. Alderman was just 60 points ahead of Roy Hill and 270 in front of Glidden.

In all of drag racing, Fords are noticeably few in number. Most classes are overwhelmingly stuffed with the "General's" cars, so racing a Ford means facing off against a lot of competition. But those few have continually made it tough for anything but a Ford to win. Being "First On Race Day" has given a lot of other racers ulcers because few off-brands can run with Ford ProStocks. When the '87 IHRA season opened, it was even better if you were a Ford fan; worse if you weren't. Glidden and Smith were at their drag-racing best.

At the All Pro Winter Nationals at Darlington, the opening round of the IHRA season, Glidden smashed both ends of the ProStock record with a sensational 7.197/199.11 blast in the Hurst ProStock Shootout preceding eliminations. As the final unfolded, though, it was Smith's Motorcraft Thunderbird that came away with the win, made history again with the all-time quickest ProStock pass ever recorded. Smith laid down a perfect run against, who else but Roy Hill's Thunderbird, and lowered the world ProStock record to 7.172 seconds, surpassing Hill's 1986 record at Darlington (7.233).

Crowder Racing Team, running the Roses Stores banner, captured IHRA 1/8-mile world record two years in a row, running 700-HP SVO 351 built by Sonny Leonard.

In A/Modified Production, Crowder posted a 6.002 at 117.18 mph to set 1/8-mile record. Under 9.20 seconds and over 145 mph in 1/4-mile is about what it takes to set that record.

Smith's fabulous Jerry Bickel built Thunderbird began a rampage through the masses of off-brands and grabbed a runner-up finish in the IHRA Pro-Am Nationals at Rockingham, where his thundering 'Bird lost traction in the final round.

That loss was avenged in the Spring Nationals, though, and Bristol's "Thunder Valley" echoed with the sounds of Thunderbird as Smith laid all other ProStockers aside for his 15th national event win, second only to Glidden's 16 victories. The '87 season developed into another year of Thunderbird domination in ProStock drag racing, and of only two Motorcraft Thunderbirds racing against all those off-brands,

Rickie Smith's initial ride for '87 was a Don Hardy-built Thunderbird powered by a Sonny Leonard "mountain mill." Later, he set an all-time quickest ProStock e.t. in a Jerry Bickel-built 'Bird at Darlington. Both cars are capable of exceeding 200 mph.

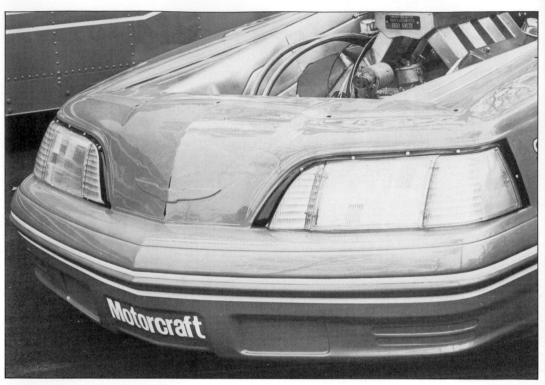

Smooth look of aero 'Bird in drag racing is illustrated by Rickie Smith's Motorcraft Thunderbird.

Split Dominators for a straighter shot into combustion chambers is said to be worth 30 HP on Ford ProStock engine.

both have proven to be quicker than all the rest.

Quarter-mile Fords cleaned house in both NHRA and IHRA ProStock racing in 1986, to make it another great Ford year, one the history books will show forever. But that wasn't all that Ford fans can boast about. One of the most popular drivers on the NHRA circuit, Kenny Bernstein, wheeled his magnificent Top Fuel Funny Car into another championship with an overwhelming point total in 1985 of 12,652 points to lead 2nd place by over 5,000 points.

Bernstein's Budweiser King/Motorcraft Ford Tempo of '86 wrapped up the NHRA Funny Car season with a record-smashing charge and his second straight Winston World Funny Car Championship. He won the final three nationals—his 15th, 16th and 17th career victories in NHRA Nationals—by setting a new elapsed-time world record to become the first Funny Car driver in history to run under 5.5 seconds.

The Budweiser King/Motorcraft Tempo qualified number-1 at the inaugural Chief Auto Parts Nationals at Billy Meyer's Texas Motorplex. His 5.425-second pass was Bernstein's eighth top qualifying time of the year, and he went on to lock up his third national of the season. Two weeks later at Firebird Raceway in Phoenix, he faced Jim Head in the final round and clocked a 5.590 to win and set another new track record!

That victory brought Kenny the NHRA Funny Car crown, but there was another round, the Winston World Finals at Pomona, in October. The pressure was off, but Bernstein didn't let up. He qualified 2nd to make it 19 straight events in which he qualified either 1st or 2nd. In the finals, it was another all Ford show: Bernstein's Tempo against Billy Meyer's Chief Auto Parts Mustang. It was another close one, with the red and white Budweiser King taking the win at 5.569 versus 5.695 seconds. That made it Bernstein's fifth national win of the season, his tenth in the past two years

Quickest ProStocker in the history of drag racing, Rickie Smith at wheel of his Jerry Bickel built Motorcraft Thunderbird. In IHRA ProStock racing, engine displacement is unlimited, and Smith's Sonny Leonard built 665-cid BOSS 429-based engine cranked out an awesome 7.172-second winning round against Roy Hill's Penny's Thunderbird, another all Ford final. Squire Gabbard photo.

and his second consecutive World Funny Car Championship. Bernstein has become known as *the king* for having taken three Winston World Funny Car Championships and scored 38 winning rounds in one season to establish another NHRA record.

Crew chief Dale Armstrong, an innovative drag racer with an illustrious racing career of his own, received a lot of credit from Bernstein for making the car work. And Billy Meyer, another top competitor who was NHRA 2nd-place finisher in 1984, '82 and '81 along with several 3rd-place finishes in earlier years, made the going tough for Bernstein.

"We get about six runs out of our Goodyear slicks, and from 3000 HP on nitromethane, that's not bad." commented Bernstein. "The car goes from 0-100 mph in 1.2 seconds. Our recorders show acceleration of 5g, and on every run we use about 10 gallons of nitromethane. At $30 a gallon, our economy isn't very good, either. We go 265+ mph in 5.5 seconds on $300 worth of fuel!

"The body, an aerodynamic carbon-fiber in the Ford Tempo style, is stronger and holds its shape better than fiberglass. Dale Armstrong and my excellent crew, Geoff Scarp on engines, completely assemble the engine from parts we buy from other sources. Peak power is produced around 8000 rpm. And that means each cylinder of our 500-cubic inch engine puts out 375 HP."

In typical funny-car fashion these days, the King's mill is positioned up front and a titanium-encased transmission connects to the rear end.

For a long time now, the crew has carefully covered the section of the car's tubular frame just behind the right front wheel to prevent anyone from getting a look at what's there. The "Mystery Towel" has become legendary these days. Kenny isn't saying what it hides.

What's under the towel?

"I won't tell you," says Kenny, "but it's definitely a functional thing under there that we don't want people to know about."

A little intrigue never hurt any good story, and the Budweiser King/Motorcraft Tempo is without doubt the best and most sophisticated full-bodied machine in drag racing today. Kenny is the technological leader of modern funny-car racing. He was the first to test his machine in a wind tunnel, the first to use a carbon-fiber body, and the first to employ electronics to better understand the nearly infinite combinations of power-transfer adjustments available to the funny-car racer. "Gut feelings" are steadily being replaced by microchips, and the king uses an electronics package to record engine rpm, drive-shaft speed, blower pressure, fuel pressure and lots of other data to improve the car's performance and consistency. Consistent 5.5-second blasts are the result.

After providing a tremendous showcase for Ford with his

Legendary Budweiser King, Kenny Bernstein's Motorcraft Top Fuel Funny Car, was the fastest, most consistent NHRA funny car of '86. Out of 14 races, Fords won five with nine top qualifiers. Kenny collected 12,786 points to lead Mark Oswald's Pontiac by 2276 points. He set quickest funny-car time ever of 5.42 seconds.

"Super Team," Kenny went to Buick for 1987 sponsorship. The Motorcraft name then went to Mark Oswald's Candies & Hughes Pro Funny Car, a radical version of the Thunderbird shape.

During the 1986 season, car owner Paul Candies and Leonard Hughes, and driver Oswald came off the most spectacular record setting Pro Funny Car season in IHRA history. The "Big Red Machine" Candies & Hughes Trans-Am won *five* Pro Funny Car National victories. That was enough to bag the fourth World Championship for the C&H team and Oswald's third World Championship as a driver.

Just four seasons before, then 27-year-old Mark Oswald strapped himself into the seat of the C&H Top Fuel Dragster for his first season of Pro competition. There were doubts that he could do the job that World Champion Richard Tharp had done. But after two NHRA Funny Car titles that year, skeptics stepped aside. Oswald then became one of the golden boys of professional drag racing.

A year after that, in his very first year of funny-car competition, Oswald drove the Candies & Hughes stripper to an astounding IHRA World Championship *and* finished the season in 2nd place in the NHRA Winston World Championship series.

Then, in 1984, Oswald and the Candies & Hughes team accomplished the near impossible, the never-before achieved feat of winning both IHRA and NHRA Pro Funny Car World. No longer was Oswald a golden boy, he had

become king, and the Candies & Hughes machine promised drag-racing fans the best; they got it.

The following season the team "tried too many things that didn't work," says Oswald, but he still won two National titles on his way to a 3rd-place finish overall in IHRA, while notching his fifth straight title at Norwalk, Ohio. That set a 19-0 win record on that track, the longest win streak at one location in IHRA history.

For 1986, Oswald brought the Candies & Hughes Funny Car to seven consecutive IHRA final rounds winning five and the season championship with a total of 7366 points, over 2000 more than 2nd place, and 2715 more than Tom "The Mongoose" McEwen in 3rd place, and 3616 more than Bernstein's 5th place overall. Along the way, he also scored three NHRA National titles and several high finishes to grab runner-up to Bernstein's Budweiser King Tempo, the most aerodynamic Pro Funny Car in drag racing at the time.

Thus, Oswald and Bernstein have been and remain top competitors among a growing field of over 3000-HP ground rockets that produce 5g acceleration every pass. Imagine sitting straddle that kind of power, Goodyear gumballs at your elbows and another missile just 15 feet to your side. Then accelerate from a standstill to 265 mph in 5.5 seconds!

When Bernstein switched to Buick, Candies & Hughes left the Trans-Am behind and moved into Motorcraft sponsorship for the '87 season with a super-slick Thunderbird, a new "Big Red Machine."

Oswald came into the '87 season as the nitro funny car top-speed record holder at over 268.09 mph, then squeezed out a 5.52-second, 268.65-mph pass in the 'Bird during the first round of the NHRA season, the Winternationals at Pomona. He then backed that up during the NHRA Motorcraft Gatornationals in Florida with a 268.696-mph run on his way to consistent over-270-mph blasts.

Oswald says the Motorcraft Thunderbird is an "aerodynamic masterpiece," but during the IHRA season with his new machine at the IHRA Winter Nationals at Darlington, he fell victim to an exploding supercharger just out of the hole that blew off the body, sent shrapnel into the driver's compartment and broke a finger.

The next IHRA round, the Pro-Am Nationals at Rockingham, Oswald qualified 3rd in spite of his injuries behind Bernstein in number-1 spot. That was a prophetic placing as Oswald made it to the semi-finals while Bernstein took the title.

It took a while to get the Motorcraft 'Bird on track after Darlington's explosion, and it looked like Oswald was back on top when he posted the top qualifying spot with a 5.644/263.15 blast in the Spring Nationals at Bristol, IHRA headquarters. In the first round Oswald shut down Scott Kalitta's Olds Firenza with an easy 5.807/252.80. The semi-finals brought up Tom Hoover's Trans-Am which was dispatched by the Motorcraft 'Bird with a 5.775/260.11. Then Mike Dunn's Firenza put down a win against Oswald's tire blistering shut down that cost him the victory.

During the Motorcraft/Keystone/Key Auto Parts Summer Nationals at Atco, New Jersey, Oswald returned to his winning form among a tough field where Tom McEwen just made 2nd alternate. Trying some more tricks resulted in Oswald having to settle for 4th qualifier with a 5.758/263.92. In the first round, he blasted past a broken competitor to make the semi-finals, a face off against "Doc" Halladay's Dodge Daytona. Oswald pulled out all the stops as he gunned down Halladay on a thundering 5.575-second/263.92-mph win to make the finals.

"The car ran real well and everything went pretty smooth," said Oswald. "It's getting better every week. We're real close to getting everything perfect. We felt real good going into the championship round. I felt confident that we could take it."

But it wasn't going to be easy because Ed McCulloch's first round in the Miller American Oldsmobile set a new single pass IHRA Pro Funny Car e.t. record of 5.516 seconds.

Without a backup time close enough, McCoulloch missed the official record that required a another run within 1% to become official. McCulloch's next pass of 5.584 did erase Bernstein's earlier record of 5.585, but Oswald was hammering the record books, too. His semi-final 5.575-second pass against Halladay was backed up in the winning final against McCulloch when he squeezed by with just 0.18 second to spare to post victory with a 5.606 at 265.48 mph!

Thus the Pro Funny Car record was broken twice during the eliminations, a spectacle of raw power that saw the Motorcraft Thunderbird running within 0.1 second of Dan Pastorini's top-qualifying Pro Nitro Dragster.

The Motorcraft team scored in Pro Stock when Bob Glidden and Roy Hill faced off in another all-Thunderbird Pro Stock final at Atco. Leading the 16-car Pro Stock qualifiers was Glidden's in the number-one spot at 7.205 followed by Hill's 7.210 and Rickie Smith's 7.217, a Thunderbird 1-2-3.

NEW AGE OF FORD RACING

A lot of people look back at the '60s as the golden age of Ford racing. But with Ford's return in the '80s, the golden age is back. Just count up the Trans-Am championships, 1984, '85 and '86. Add the IMSA GTO championships of 1985 and '86. Then roll in the domination of ProStock drag racing by the Glidden and Smith Fords, and look at the record years of Bernstein's Ford team. Consider NASCAR racing with the Thunderbirds of Bill, Cale, Davey, Ricky and Kyle out in front so often that stock-car-racing fans expect a Ford to be there. And don't forget the 20-year reign of the Ford-Cosworth V8 as *THE* winningest Formula 1 engine of all time. That adds up to a lot of excitement! All that's left is Ford's return to the winner's circle at LeMans for history to repeat.

If you want to go Ford racing with a highly competitive car, you might follow the path of Tom Gross, Ford transmission development engineer, who began with an Alston Pro-Stock kit and built a 106-inch-wheelbase Thunderbird. The engine in the Tom Gross Super Gas T-Bird is a single Holley Dominator 4-bbl 1970 429 SCJ. Built by Total Performance of Mt. Clemens, Michigan, it was increased to 514 cubic inches. Being built by a transmission man, Tom's 'Bird uses an automatic with "secret" internals. But with a 5.43:1 final drive, it runs through the quarter-mile in 9.5 seconds at 139 mph. Tom won "Best Appearing Car" at the NHRA Springnationals.

Not bad for something old, something new in a Fast Ford.

HIGHLITES

Fast Fords Heritage

1901
• Henry Ford wins "The World's Championship and first bit race in the West."

1904
• Henry Ford sets a new World Land Speed Record of 91.37 mph in the "999" on the ice of Lake St. Clair.

1909
• Drivers Scott and Smith win Transcontinental Race in Model-T Fords.

1923
• L. L. "Slim" Coram finishes fifth at Indianapolis 500 in his "Fronty Ford."

1933
• Fred Frame wins Elgin Road Races in a V8 Ford leading a Ford seven-car sweep.

1935
• Ford Motor Co. returns to Indianapolis 500 with team of factory cars with V8 engines.

1950
• Ford Motor Co. wins its first NASCAR Grand National Race. Mercury wins two, Lincoln wins two.

1952
• Lincolns sweep top three places in touring car category of Carrera Panamerica in Mexico.

1955
• Ford wins 2nd & 3rd NASCAR Grand National Race.

1956
• Curtis Turner wins NASCAR's Showcase, the Southern 500 at Darlington. Ford wins 14 Grand Nationals, Mercury wins five.

1957
• Glen "Fireball" Roberts is Ford's top driver with eight NASCAR Grand National wins of Ford's 27 victories to lead all makes.

1958
• Junior Johnson is Ford's top driver with six NASCAR Grand National wins of Ford's 16 victories.

1959
• Junior Johnson again leads Ford's NASCAR Grand National wins with five of 15 victories.

1960
• Joe Weatherley wins the Southern 500.
• Ned Jarrett is leading Ford driver with five of Ford's 15 Grand National wins to lead all makes.

1965
• Nelson Stacey wins Southern 500.

1962
• Larry Frank wins the Southern 500, his only Grand National win.
• Nelson Stacey wins World 600.

1963
• Fords sweep top four places at Daytona 500.
• Ford-powered 289 Cobras win U.S. Road Racing championship.
• Ford-powered 289 Cobras win SCCA's A/Production National Championship.
• Ford-powered 289 Cobras win NHRA Stock Eliminator.

1964
• Ford-powered 289 Daytona Coupe Cobra finishes 1st in GT at 24-Hours of LeMans.
• 289 Cobras win U.S. Road Racing Championship.
• 289 Cobras win SCCA's A/Production National Championship.
• 289 Cobras win NHRA Stock Eliminator.

1965
• Jimmy Clark wins Indianapolis 500 in a Ford-powered Lotus 49.
• GT-40s place 1st and 3rd in 2000 Km Daytona Continental.
• Shelby American wins World Manufacturers' Championship for sports cars.
• Ford wins Daytona 500 with Fred Lorenzen driving. Lorenzen also wins World 600.
• Ned Jarret wins Southern 500.
• Connie Kalitta's Ford AA/FD sets a new quarter-mile record of 206.42 mph.
• Shelby GT-350 wins SCCA's B/Production National Championship (repeated in 1966 and '67).
• 427 Cobra wins SCCA's A/Production National Championship (repeated in 1966, '67, '68 and '73).
• Ford wins 87% of NASCAR races.

1966
• Ford GT-40 Mk IIs sweep top three places at 24-Hours of Daytona Continental, Sebring 12-Hour and LeMans 24-Hour.
• Ford wins World Manufacturers' Championship for prototype sports cars.
• Mustang wins Trans-Am Championship.
• Darel Dieringer's Mercury wins Southern 500.

1967
- Ford Mk IV wins Sebring 12-Hour in its racing debut.
- Ford Mk IV dominated the LeMans 24-Hour, winning at a race speed record of 135.48 mph and distance record of 3,251.567 miles.
- Jimmy Clark scores first victory for Cosworth-Ford DFV Grand Prix engine at Dutch Grand Prix.
- Pete Robinson sets a new quarter-mile record with an elapsed time of 6.97 seconds in his Ford AA/FD.
- Ford wins Daytona 500 with Mario Andretti driving.
- Mustang wins Trans-Am Championship.

1968
- Ford GT-40 wins its third straight LeMans 24-Hour.
- Graham Hill, driving a Lotus 49B, wins first World Championship for Ford DFV engine.
- 289 Cobra wins SCCA's B/Production National Championship.
- Ford GT-40 wins World Manufacturers' Championship.
- Cale Yarborough's Mercury wins Southern 500 and Daytona 500.

1969
- Ford GT-40 wins Sebring 12-Hour.
- Ford GT-40 wins LeMans 24-Hour.
- BOSS 302 Mustang places 2nd in Trans-Am.
- Jackie Stewart wins his first World Championship in a Matra-Ford.
- Ford wins NASCAR championship.
- LeeRoy Yarborough wins Daytona 500 and Southern 500 and World 600 in a Mercury.

1970
- BOSS 302 Mustangs dominate and win Trans-Am championship.
- Dennis Allison wins World 600 in a '69 Mercury.

1971
- Jackie Stewart captures his second World Championship, this time in a Tyrrell-Ford.
- Bobby Allison wins Southern 500, World 600 & Talladega 500 in '69 Mercury.

1972
- James Hylton wins Talladega 500 in '71 Mercury.
- A.J. Foyt wins Daytona in '71 Mercury.

1973
- Jackie Stewart wins his third World Championship with Ford power.

1974
- Bob Glidden wins his first NHRA ProStock World Championship in a Pinto.
- David Pearson wins World 600 in '73 Mercury.

1975
- Cosworth-Ford powered Mirage wins LeMans 24-Hour.
- Bob Glidden wins his second NHRA ProStock World Championship in a Pinto.
- Buddy Baker's Ford wins Talladega 500.

1976
- David Pearson's Mercury wins World 600 and Southern 500 and Daytona 500.
- Bob Glidden wins IHRA ProStock World Championship.

1977
- Jody Scheckter wins 100th Ford DFV Grand Prix engine victory at Grand Prix of Monaco.
- David Pearson's Mercury wins Southern 500.
- Rickie Smith wins IHRA Super Modified World Championship in a Maverick.

1978
- Al Unser scores his first victory at Indianapolis 500 with Cosworth Ford DFX engine.
- Bob Glidden wins his third NHRA ProStock World Championship in a Fairmont Futura.
- Courier wins SCORE Class 7 Championship for off-road racing.
- Bobby Allison's Ford wins Daytona 500.
- Rickie Smith wins 2nd IHRA Super Modified World Championship in a Maverick.

1979
- Danny Moore in BOSS 302 Mustang wins A/SCCA Trans-Am finals at Road Atlanta.

1980
- Ford powered Rondeau wins LeMans 24-Hour.
- Bob Glidden wins his fifth NHRA ProStock World Championship.
- Neil Bonnett wins Talladega 500 with a Mercury.

1981
- Turbocharged Mustang GT wins its first IMSA races at Brainerd, Minnesota, and Sears Point, California.
- Mustang wins SCCA's Showroom Stock "A" National Championship.
- Courier wins SCORE Class 7 Championship for off-road racing.
- Neil Bonnett wins Southern 500 with a Ford.

1982
- Elio DeAngelis wins 150th victory for Cosworth-Ford DFV Grand Prix engine at Austrian Grand Prix.
- John Watson wins inaugural Detroit Grand Prix in a McLaren-Ford.
- Turbocharged Mustang wins IMSA race at Sears Point, California.
- Mustang 5-liter V8 wins World Endurance Championship in Japan.
- Ranger wins SCORE Class 7 Championship for off-road racing.
- Rickie Smith wins his first IHRA ProStock World Championship and became first ProStocker to exceed 180 mph, 181.08/7.82 and was 1st ProStocker to run under 8 seconds.
- Neil Bonnett's Ford wins World 600.

1983
- Dale Earnhardt's Ford wins Talladega 500.
- Rickie Smith is IHRA ProStock runner-up.
- Michele Alboreto wins Detroit Grand Prix in a Tyrrell-Ford, 155th win for Cosworth-Ford DFV engine.
- Buddy Baker scores first NASCAR win for 1983 Thunderbird in Daytona Firecracker 400.
- Ranger wins "triple crown" of off-road racing (Mint 400, Frontier 500, Baja 1000).
- Mustang GTP wins IMSA Camel GT at Road America in its debut race.
- Donnie Moore wins IHRA Super Stock World Championship in '68 428 Cobra Jet Fastback Mustang.

1984
- Rickie Smith is IHRA ProStock runner-up.
- Danny Sullivan scores 100th victory for Cosworth-Ford DFX engine at Cleveland GT (CART).
- Kenny Bernstein becomes first funny-car driver to exceed 260 mph in his Budweiser King Ford Tempo.
- Bob Glidden sets a new ProStock ET national record of 7.61 seconds in a Thunderbird.
- Tom Gloy Capri wins Trans-Am championship.

1985
- Cade Yarborough wins Talladega 500.
- Bill Elliott becomes highest money winner in NASCAR history with his Coors/Melling Thunderbird.

- Bill Elliott sets NASCAR record of 11 super speedway wins in his Coors/Melling Thunderbird and wins Southern 500 and Daytona 500.
- Bill Elliott wins first "Winston Million" in his Coors/Melling Thunderbird.
- Bob Glidden wins his sixth NHRA ProStock World Championship.
- John Jones wins IMSA GTO Championship in Roush/Protofab Mustang.
- Wally Dallenbach, Jr. wins Trans-Am championship in Roush/Protofab Capri.
- Kenny Bernstein wins NHRA Top Fuel Funny Car World Championship in a Tempo.

1986
- Cale Yarborough wins Talladega 500.
- Rickie Smith wins his second IHRA ProStock World Championship in a Mustang.
- Bob Glidden wins his seventh NHRA ProStock World Championship in a Thunderbird.
- Bill Elliott sets NASCAR speed record at Talladega, 212.229 mph, in his Coors/Melling Thunderbird, and wins Southern 500.
- Bill Elliott sets 500-mile speed record of 186.288 mph in his Coors/Melling Thunderbird.
- Kenny Bernstein wins NHRA Top Fuel Funny Car World Championship in a "Tempo".
- Scott Pruett wins IMSA GTO Championship in a Roush/Racing Mustang.
- Scott Pruett wins IMSA Endurance Championship in a Roush/Racing Mustang.
- Vinny Barone wins NHRA Competition World Championship in his Ford.

1987
- Bill Elliott sets speed record of 212.809 mph at Talladega, in Coors/Melling Thunderbird.
- Bill Elliott wins Daytona 500.
- Davey Allison wins Talladega 500.
- Kyle Petty wins NASCAR's longest race, the Coca Cola World 600 at Charlotte.
- Bob Glidden sets IHRA ProStock top speed record of 199.11 in his Motorcraft Thunderbird.
- Rickie Smith sets IHRA ProStock low elapsed-time record of 7.172 seconds to win Winter Nationals. Later wins Spring Nationals.

Acknowledgements

Following are the organizations and people who help make this book complete, correct and possible. They provided information, opened their files, supplied photography, or provided their cars for photography by the author. It is with great satisfaction that I have been able to compile this book, and I extend many thanks to all those who have contributed in one way or another. I hope I haven't overlooked anyone. Should any errors be found, however, the responsibility is mine alone.

Alex Gabbard
Lenoir City, Tennessee

Ford Motor Company: Tom Land, Bill Buffa
Special Vehicle Operations: Michael Kranefuss, Tom Hutchinson, Rodney Girolami, Hank Dertian
Henry Ford Museum: Dave Crippen, Cynthia Reid-Miller
Roush Racing: Jack Roush
Campbell & Co.
Indianapolis Motor Speedway Museum: Jack Martin,
National Hot Rod Association: Leslie Lovett, Bob Glidden, Kenny Bernstein
ProStock Owners Association
International Hot Rod Association: Butch McCall, Rickie Smith
International Motor Sport Association: John Bishop, Dic Van der Veen, Scott Pruett, Bruce Jenner
Charlotte Motor Speedway: Susan Russo
Darlington International Raceway: Tommy Britt
NASCAR: Daytona International Speedway: Bill France, Chip Williams, Bill Elliott, Ricky Rudd, Cale Yarborough
Sebring International Grand Prix of Endurance:
Bud Moore Engineering
Reider Racing: Tom Reider
Shelby American Automobile Club: Rick Kopec, Lynn Park, Chuck Gutke, Lee Mathais, Bill Bradford, George Stauffer, Pat & Dale Nichols, Dale Sale, Ed Ludtke, Gary Henkel, Mike Miles, Gordon & Derrick Stennis, Al Mclean, Susie Wilson, Connie Moore, Jeff Jensen, Sam Feinstein, Bill & Bud Jones, Fred Derring
Shelby Automobiles, Inc.: Carroll Shelby, Lew Spencer
Sportscar Vintage Racing Association: Ford & Kate Heacock, Dick Leppla, Terry Clark, Dale Sale, Hans Huwyler, Don Walker, Tony Goodchild, Bill Wonder, Don Marsh, Brian Redman
Walter Mitty Challenge: Steve Simpson, Howard Turner, John Steen
Classic Ford Association: Bob & Susan Murphy, Randy & Judy Cecucci, Junior & Charlotte Hope, Burl Cloninger, Ronnie Selvidge, Bob Patterson, Ralph Patterson, Henry Rains, Blake McCampbell, Randy Moats, Bob Fielden, Max & Willene Mason, Bud DeFord, Larry Murphy, Doug Owen
Walden Ridge Early V8 Club: Tom Hamby, J.D. Williams, Earl Duff
Car owners: Howard Murr, Jeff Murr, Butch Bunnell, Rusty Perkins, Bill Wells, George Steigerwalt, John Rathman, Ron Graves, Jim Smart, Randy Kindsfather, Kim Haynes, Mark Price, Joe Antrican

Photographers: Bob D'Olivo, Pete Pesterre, Donald Farr, Squire Gabbard, Wesley Gabbard and Ford photographers of old.

Special Thanks: John Wyer, Carroll Shelby, John Elliot, George Montgomery, John Horsman, Rickie Smith, Bob Glidden, Kenny Bernstein, Gary Kohs, Bob Bondurant, Scott Pruett, and many more Ford drivers, builders and promoters since the early 1900s.

Models: Mary Gabbard, Becky Brown, Stephanie Hope, Johnna Easter